Tituba, Reluctant Witch of Salem

The American Social Experience

SERIES

James Kirby Martin
GENERAL EDITOR

Paula S. Fass, Steven H. Mintz, Carl Prince, James W. Reed & Peter N. Stearns
EDITORS

Tituba, Reluctant Witch of Salem

Devilish Indians and Puritan Fantasies

Elaine G. Breslaw

New York University Press
New York and London

NEW YORK UNIVERSITY PRESS
New York and London

Library of Congress Cataloging-in-Publication Data
Breslaw, Elaine G., 1932–
Tituba, reluctant witch of Salem : devilish Indians and Puritan
fantasies / Elaine G. Breslaw.
p.   cm.—The Americam social experience series ; 35)
Includes bibliographical references and index.
ISBN 0-8147-1227-4 (alk. paper)
1. Tituba.   2. Arawak Indians—Biography.   3. Slaves—Barbados—
Biography.   4. Slaves—Massachusetts—Biography.   5. Salem (Mass.)—
History—Colonial period, ca. 1600–1775.   6. Witchcraft—
Massachusetts—Salem—History.   I. Title.   II. Series.
F2230.2.A7T573   1996
974.4'5—dc20   95-38417
                      CIP
New York University Press books are printed on acid-free paper,
and their binding materials are chosen for strength and durability.

Manufactured in the United States of America

10   9   8   7   6   5   4   3   2   1

In memory of
Joseph Breslaw
1957–1990

Whose courage made this book possible.

Contents

Illustrations

Acknowledgments

After six years of working on Tituba's story, I am in debt to so many people and institutions that it would be impossible to mention all by name. However, some continue to be remembered for particularly valuable contributions. I am grateful to my former students at Johns Hopkins University School of Continuing Studies who, in the early 1980s, first suggested a course on witchcraft in early America. John Krugler of Marquette University generously permitted me to pattern my syllabus for such a course on his and started me on the road to explore the nuances of witchcraft beliefs. Over the years other students continued to ask demanding questions about Tituba's role in those events, the answers to which were not available in the existing literature. Curiosity aroused, I tentatively explored the published Salem records for clues, sensing that the answers lay in Barbados.

The Council for the International Exchange of Scholars and the Fulbright program made that initial research into Barbados sources possible and I am grateful for that financial support. A sabbatical leave from Morgan State University in Baltimore gave me the 1989–90 year off from my usual teaching responsibilities to pursue that teaching/research Fulbright Grant. I subsequently received two faculty research grants from Morgan State that lightened my teaching load to permit more time for writing.

During that year in Barbados I benefited from many courtesies and help in my research from the staff of the Barbados Archives, particularly the Archivist Christine Matthews, and from Shirley Archer who rules the search room. The same thanks go to the Barbados Museum and

Historical Society, particularly the Librarian Betty Shannon; and to the
Barbados Public Library and the University of the West Indies Library
for the use of their collections. I received wholehearted support from the
history faculty at the University of the West Indies, Cave Hill branch in
Barbados. I thank the many there who listened so patiently to my early
attempts to articulate what I thought were important elements in Tituba's
background and Tony Phillips who chaired the department that year. I
am grateful to Woodville Marshall, Alvin Thompson, John Gilmore,
Peter Campbell, Ronnie Hughes, Karl Watson, Anthea Morrison, and
Alan Cobley who, in their different ways, offered support and information.

Many other librarians and archivists came to my rescue at critical
moments. Elaine Tsubota of the Morgan State University Library provided essential bibliographic assistance in tracking down information on
Indian cultures. Additionally I wish to thank the staffs of the Johns
Hopkins Library in Baltimore and the University of Tennessee Library,
especially Anne Bridges, for their many courtesies. I am grateful to an
unidentified researcher at the Salem City Archives who responded so
quickly to my queries. The staffs of the Public Record Office in Kew and
the British Museum in London were helpful in locating material during
the initial stages of research.

For permission to reproduce pictures, thanks are due to the Barbados
Archives and Edward Benjamin who photographed their material, and to
the Barbados Museum and Historical History and its Curator of Art,
Lesley Barrow-Whately. For tracking down illustrations and for permis-
sion to reproduce their photographs I am grateful to Aaron Schmidt and
Sinclair Hitchings of the Boston Public Library Print Department,
Nancy Heywood and Jane Ward of the Peabody Essex Museum, Georgia
Barnhill of the American Antiquarian Society, and J. Jan Jansen of the
Topsfield Historical Society. The map of the Spanish Main was produced with the assistance of William Fontanez and Bryan Williams of the
University of Tennessee Cartographic Laboratory. I owe a special debt
to Richard Trask at the Danvers Archival Center for advice and assistance
in preparing some of the illustrations and for providing a photo from his
own collection.

Many people read parts of this book in various stages of preparation,
making valuable suggestions and offering thoughtful, useful advice regarding sources, analyses, and treatment of the subject. They helped me
avoid some awful gaffes. Nonetheless, the conclusions are mine alone and

I take full responsibility for any errors of fact or interpretation. Among those readers, I am most grateful to Jerome Handler, Richard Godbeer, Alden Vaughan, James Kirby Martin, Michael McGiffert, Richard Price, and some unidentified referees of articles submitted to various journals. Each suggestion helped me to rethink some of my earlier assumptions and to clarify my thoughts with greater precision. My debt to the many scholars who have worked on aspects of seventeenth-century history and anthropology is inestimable. If not mentioned above by name, I hope I have given them the credit due in my notes.

I particularly want to thank my friends and colleagues who have encouraged this project over the years with their sustained and enthusiastic interest in the subject and their many leads to sources of highly specialized information, especially Virginia Barnhard, Thomas Cripps, Peter Hoffer, Milton Klein, John Krugler, Ellen Macek, Nancy Norris, Lydia Pulsipher, Bruce Wheeler, and Inge Williams. The same thanks apply to the perceptive and probing inquiries of my many correspondents and students in various universities. In attempting to answer the questions they posed I understood that their curiosity reflected that of my potential reading audience. This study then is as much the product of public interest in Tituba as it is of my own research and intellectual curiosity.

The final preparation of the manuscript was facilitated by the generous assistance of the History Department of the University of Tennessee in Knoxville where the head of the Department, Russell Buhite, made available office resources, duplicating facilities, and mailing privileges. The research assistance of a graduate student, Megan Taylor, eased the burden of that tedious last-minute checking of notes and citations and the preparation of the index. Special thanks also are due to my editor at New York University Press, Niko Pfund, whose encouragement and faith in me were essential to completing the project and whose staff provided useful technical advice on improving the style and flow of the narrative.

Finally, this book could not have been completed as quickly and comfortably without the everyday practical support and understanding of my husband, John Muldowny. I am especially grateful for his unfailing sense of humor and tolerance for the emotional ups and downs that accompany the writing process.

Elaine G. Breslaw
Knoxville, Tennessee

Introduction

The Amerindian slave woman called Tituba was among the first three persons to be accused of witchcraft in Salem, Massachusetts, in 1692. The other two—Sarah Osborne and Sarah Good—vehemently protested their innocence. But Tituba confessed and thereby gave the Salem magistrates reasons to suspect that the Devil's followers had invaded their midst. Nineteen people were subsequently hanged for witchcraft, one man was pressed to death, and close to two hundred were accused of witchcraft; over fifty of them confessed. The lives and fate of accused and accusers have captivated the American imagination.[1]

Tituba, however, in spite of her central and early role in that witch-hunt, has attracted little serious attention.[2] The Salem records provide very sparse details about her background and few scholars have turned to alternate sources for information on her life. She has no descendants who can speak for her or spark new interest in her guilt or innocence. Surprisingly, there has been minimal interest in her ethnicity or the relationship of her racial background to the accusations. Most important, the multicultural dimensions of Tituba's confession, the most significant evidence of a diabolical conspiracy in Salem, have been either misunderstood or ignored.

Tituba's roles in that tragedy, as both victim and willing participant, as both scapegoat and manipulator of Puritan fears, beg for reexamination. Tituba is here viewed in the context of the Salem events as a woman, as a slave, as an American Indian, and as an outsider in a Puritan society. This biography brings the American Indian slave woman to the forefront of events that so overwhelmed her contemporaries they almost destroyed their own society.

Tituba the storyteller prolonged her life in 1692 through an imaginative ability to weave and embellish plausible tales. In the process of confessing to fantastic experiences, she created a new idiom of resistance against abusive treatment and inadvertently led the way for other innocents accused of the terrible crime of witchcraft. Her resistance, a calculated manipulation of the Puritan fears, was intimately related to her ethnic heritages. Puritans were predisposed to believe that Indians willingly participated in Devil worship. That perception of Indians as supporters of the Devil encouraged Tituba to fuel their fantasies of a diabolical plot. As she hesitantly capitalized on Puritan assumptions regarding Satanism, Tituba drew on the memories of her past life for the wondrous details of a story so frightening in its implications that she had to be kept alive as a witness.

Interest in Tituba and her role in the 1692 events has traditionally focused on her supposed indoctrination of a group of girls into a witchcraft molded by the practice of voodoo. In the accepted wisdom, Tituba stood at the center of a circle of girls practicing sorcery derived from African folklore.[3] Her confession notwithstanding, there is no proof that Tituba ever took part in occult activities. Nor is there any proof that the girls, at her instigation, took part in occult rituals or danced in the woods or drank blood or stuck pins in dolls. But those allegations and the sensationalist nature of the trials have overwhelmed the importance of Tituba's background and her status as a symbol of Puritan fears.[4]

There is good reason for Tituba's low profile in the history books. It stems from the dearth of useful, direct information about her. Historians need reliable written, artifactual, or statistical evidence with which they can detail events or on which to base their conclusions. The absence of reliable sources often means that a particular potentially significant element has to be omitted from a study. Such has been the case for most of the underclass in history, particularly women, Africans, and American Indians, who leave few useful trails for others to follow and are, therefore, easy to ignore in the historical record.

As expected, the biographical information about Tituba in the Salem documents is very thin. Nevertheless, some important information can be extracted from these meager sources. It is clearly evident from all references in those written records that Tituba was an American Indian and *not* African as later writers have assumed, and that she and her husband, John, also an American Indian, were slaves living in the household of the Reverend Samuel Parris. There is no reference anywhere in the seventeenth-century documents to Tituba as an African or as someone of African background. Like the mythology of Tituba as a voodoo priestess, there is no indication in the extant records that either Tituba or her husband had African ancestry. None of her contemporaries saw her as an African or even someone of mixed ancestry.[5] She was never described as black or as a Negro. Nowhere in the seventeenth-century records is there so much as a hint that she was of even partial African descent.

Thus there should be no question of her ancestry. All of her contemporaries, without exception, describe Tituba as an Indian woman or as Parris's Indian servant. Her husband John's racial-ethnic background is just as clearly delineated in those records. He is always identified as Indian John or John Indian, or simply as the Indian man. The gradual metamorphosis of Tituba from an Indian to an African since the nineteenth century is an unfortunate mistake based on embellishment, imagination, and a tinge of racial bias, and has been a convenient way to fill in blanks left by the absence of more substantive information.

What is less clear from those seventeenth-century commentaries is where Tituba came from, how and when Parris acquired her, and what kind of intellectual and cultural baggage she brought with her to Massachusetts. The most reasonable theory for Tituba's origins was first put forward by Charles Upham, writing in the middle of the nineteenth century. Tituba and John "were spoken of," Upham said, "as having come from New Spain . . . that is, the Spanish West Indies, and the adjacent mainland."[6] They were then sold in Barbados as slaves and subsequently brought to Massachusetts by Samuel Parris. Upham offered no direct evidence but because a good part of his narrative was based on Samuel Drake's work, he probably made use of Drake's edition of Samuel Fowler's 1866 "Account of the Life of Samuel Parris" in which Fowler claimed that Tituba and John were "Natives of South America called New Spain."[7]

Unfortunately, Upham's likely suggestion has received some unlikely embellishments. Almost fifty years later, George Lincoln Burr asserted that Tituba and John were Carib Indians, probably from the mistaken association of all Caribbean natives with the Carib tribes.[8] But there were other tribes resident in the Caribbean area, notably the Arawak-speaking peoples. Many of the Arawak tribes had migrated to the South American coast in the wake of the early Spanish conquests and, for reasons discussed in chapter 1, "Tituba's Roots," were of particular interest to slave catchers in Barbados.[9] Nonetheless, Burr's mistaken assumption regarding Tituba's ancestry as a Carib continues to influence views of her cultural origins.

Barbados seemed to be a reasonable place to begin a search for Tituba's roots. Until 1989 no one had explored the documentary possibilities for searching out Tituba's background in West Indian colonial records or local sources on the island. Those records have finally yielded some tantalizing information that can permit a partial reconstruction of Tituba's early life. They provide evidence of Tituba's residence on the island and help to establish the most likely origins of an Amerindian slave in Barbados for that time.

The painstaking effort to look through the handwritten documents resulted in the discovery of the name "Tattuba" for a slave girl in a 1676 deed.[10] The connection between Samuel Parris and that child are sufficient to make a case for Tituba's life on a Barbados plantation some four years before Parris left the island. The arguments for that association are discussed in detail in chapter 2, "My Own Country." The existence of such a unique name, which to date has not appeared in any other seventeenth-century slave list, certainly adds substantial support for Tituba's Barbados background. I also argue in that chapter that Tituba was not born on the island but was most likely a captive from South America who was brought to Barbados to be sold as a slave. This supposition again is based on substantial circumstantial evidence regarding the small Amerindian slave trade that prevailed during the thirty years before Parris left the island to return to Massachusetts.

Chapter 3 recreates the "Strange New World" of life on a Barbados sugar plantation by examining the sociofamilial environment that American Indians experienced during the decade prior to 1680 when Parris was known to be in Barbados. Amerindian slaves by that time were becoming integrated into the larger African-dominated culture. As early as the seventeenth century, Barbados was developing a syncretic culture that included elements of English, American Indian, and multicultural African lifestyles.[11] That background lends support to the theory that Tituba was familiar with African folklore, but does not prove she was capable of practicing a witchcraft derived from African sources.

During her Barbados years Tituba lived in a society overwhelmingly African in population, one in which the African elements played a major role in shaping the development of a Creole culture. Indian culture probably had the least influence on that syncretic process, but it was not insignificant.[12] Chapter 3 examines the relative effect of these various influences on the life of an Amerindian slave and speculates on how that Creole society, derived mainly from African customs and adaption to the conditions of slavery, would have shaped Tituba's life and the mental images she brought to Massachusetts.

Part II of this study focuses on life in Massachusetts. Chapter 4 examines New England life from the perspective of an American Indian slave, summarizing what is known about working conditions, legal status, health, religious influences, and other aspects of social-cultural life imposed on Indians and slaves by the Puritans. As we will see, Tituba successfully assimilated the outward appearance of selected aspects of Puritan culture and thus hid her identity as an Indian behind a servile camouflage that provided, at least until 1692, protection against abuse.

Chapter 5, "The Devil in Massachusetts: Accusations," examines the immediate events leading up to the witchhunt that began in the spring of 1692. After a brief description of Puritan attitudes toward witchcraft and the fear of American Indians, this chapter traces the events early in 1692 that led to Tituba's arrest and subsequent confession. The Salem nightmare stripped away her servile facade, exposed her as a woman of imagination and will, and left Tituba vulnerable to persecution and possible execution.

Chapter 6, "The Reluctant Witch: Fueling Puritan Fantasies," provides a close analysis of Tituba's testimony and its multicultural dimensions and highlights its immediate effect on the community. That confession, given early in March, with its evidence of a diabolical conspiracy, initiated the legal process that led to the arrest of over one hundred fifty people and the hanging of nineteen before Governor William Phips finally called a halt to the persecutions in October of 1692. It was Tituba who supplied the framework of, and the inspiration for the belief in, a diabolical conspiracy in Massachusetts.

Chapter 7 deals with the continuing subtle, but insidious, influence of

Tituba's confession on the testimony of others and the creative use of her stories that both reinforced and reshaped traditional notions of the Devil. Confessors in particular reformulated Tituba's notion of evil to conform to their own preconception. This creative application of Indian-Creole ideas contributed to the convergence of folk and ministerial notions of witchcraft and eventually to the discrediting of witchhunts themselves.

Why did the Puritans, folk and elite alike, believe Tituba's confession? Chapter 8 explores the Puritan perception of her behavior and how she was able to convince and captivate that audience. Tituba's acculturation made her testimony believable. That credibility was reinforced ironically by the continued association of native Americans with witchcraft and a refusal to fully integrate Indians into Puritan society.

In the absence of much hard evidence, the Epilogue draws some conclusions about Tituba's fate and that of her family after 1692. It also considers the long-term effect of Tituba's confession on the Puritan community. She participated in a process of cultural exchange that merged the world of print culture with that of the folk, activating change from the bottom up. This transformation was as much the result of the details of Tituba's fantasy as it was of the Puritan need to believe her story and accommodate the unfamiliar Indian ideas to their own notions of evil.

The analysis of Tituba's testimony and the reexamination of her role in the Salem events suggest a new type of approach to an understanding of early New England life, one that emphasizes the role of non-English influences on the shaping of colonial intellectual life. It assumes that interaction of people from various cultural mixes played a significant part in forming Puritan society in America. Scholars have demonstrated some interest in the impact of Africans on that developing society, but these works have only limited usefulness and make no case for cultural transmission.[13] Studies of Indians in early America, on the other hand, stress the violent contacts between the native Americans and the English intruders, focusing on the reactive rather than the integrative aspects of cultural contact.[14] Peaceful interaction, beyond the superficial borrowing of maize-based foods and hunting techniques from Indians, has not been an important factor in Puritan-Indian studies.

Tituba's prominence in Salem and the reaction of Puritans to her fantastic story suggest that there may have been other non-English ethnic influences on early New England history and that the process of cultural borrowing—the creation of a syncretic culture—did not stop at the edge of the Caribbean. New England too came under the influence of a dynamic exchange among red, white, and black peoples in early America. The effect may have been more subtle and thus more difficult to discern in New England, but the nuances of change were just as tenacious and imaginative.

Tituba's emergence as a major protagonist in the 1692 cataclysm allows us to glimpse one moment—albeit a powerful one—in the process of change in the New England mind brought on by multicultural contact. Was it, however, unique? To what extent was the Salem incident just another episode in the regular interaction of non-English oral or popular cultures with that of the literate, print-oriented population? How often, for instance, did New Englanders consult American Indians about sickness or misfortune? To what extent did those confrontations reshape old-world notions? Were Tituba's experience and the Salem events a culmination of years of intellectual interactions, or was that incident a one-time occurrence of cultural borrowing? Only more creative and speculative evaluations of the known sources can answer those questions.

There is no doubt that the Salem witch investigation enabled the Indian woman Tituba to emerge from obscurity. She was a slave who left an indelible mark on American history and no study of the Salem events can or should ignore her ill-fated contribution. Permitted to speak of things alien to English thought, she inspired a creative adaptation of ideas derived from West Indian slave society. It was Tituba's mental images that fueled Puritan fantasies of a devilish conspiracy and, tragically, launched the most gruesome but fascinating witchscare of early American history.

Barbados

Tituba's Roots: An Arawak from Guiana

> They are spoken of as having come from New Spain, as
> it was then called,—that is, the Spanish West Indies,
> and the adjacent mainlands of Central and South
> America.
>   —Charles Upham, *Salem Witchcraft*

In July of 1674 Captain Peter Wroth, lately of Kent in England, set
sail from Barbados on his sloop *Sanoy* bound for the northeast coast
of South America.[1] His mission was to locate and kidnap American
Indians to sell as slaves in Barbados and, as an incidental part of the trip,
to trade with friendly Indians. The vessel, propelled by the easterly trade
winds, sailed generally south/southwest for three hundred miles past
Trinidad to the Orinoco River delta on the coast of South America. A
starboard turn to a more westerly course brought them up the Orinoco to
one of its tributaries, the Amacura River, their chosen destination (see
Fig. 1).

Sailing southeast on the Amacura, the crew spied canoes carrying
fourteen Indians, who were invited on board to trade. As some of the
men bargained with the Indians, Wroth decided to permit the peaceful
trade. They were, he assured his ship's master, William Price, of the
wrong tribe to kidnap. Probably Carib, they were protected by the
English King's orders to maintain friendly relations with the enemies of
the Dutch settlers. The continuing hostility between the Caribs and the
Dutch in America encouraged the English monarch to woo the Carib or
Carib-allied tribes as potential allies in a continuing Anglo-Dutch conflict.[2]

English trade rivalry with the Dutch had resulted in sporadic warfare,

3

Figure 1: Map of the West Indies and the Spanish Main in the seventeenth century.

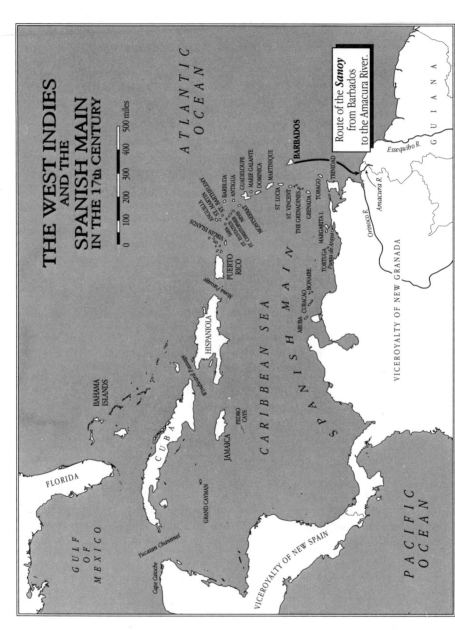

The route of the *Sanoy* in 1674 from Barbados to the Orinoco delta and Amacura River is shown. The dimensions of Barbados are enlarged for this map. (*Map courtesy of the University of Tennessee Cartographic Services Laboratory.*)

which was renewed in 1672. At the time of Wroth's kidnapping expedition, those competitors for world commerce were engaged in the third Anglo-Dutch War of the century.[3] Entrepreneurs like Wroth, encouraged by Barbados's Governor Lord Willoughby and his successor in 1673, Sir Peter Colleton, to raid and spy on the Dutch colonies, had seized the opportunity to kidnap Indian allies of the Dutch, particularly Arawak-related tribes. Wroth had erred during previous escapades when he had attempted to establish a trade in Indian slaves and had captured Caribs, who were under the protection of the English King. The entrepreneur had been ordered to desist and return the captive Caribs to the South American coast.[4] But in the summer of 1674 Wroth was determined to find tribes that lacked sufficient European support to cause diplomatic or military reprisals.

The *Sanoy* continued its upriver course on the Amacura and met another twenty-four Indians who also came aboard to trade. Again, after consultation with his crew, Wroth decided that they should not molest that group of men. Ostensibly, so far they had encountered only English allies and Wroth was not about to run afoul of the King's orders a second time. But it is also possible that from the start Wroth and his crew were intent on locating women for his intended slave trade. In the first two encounters the *Sanoy* had met only men in the visiting canoes. For reasons discussed below, the planters in Barbados favored women slaves in general and Amerindian women in particular. Wroth may well have wanted to satisfy that demand and therefore maintained peaceful contact with the male Indians he met while keeping an eye out for women traders.

On the second of August, eight women and two children approached the *Sanoy* with more trade goods. They too were welcomed aboard. Again Wroth consulted his crew. This time the men agreed they had likely captives and they devised a plan to kidnap the women and children. Some of the crew were told to guard the Indians' canoes and be prepared to pursue those who resisted. Wroth grabbed the first woman and his crew seized three more and then the children. In the confusion, four women were able to jump overboard. They frantically began to swim away. Wroth, anticipating that the women would resist and familiar with the swimming ability of the local Indians, ordered his men to paddle the canoes to catch the runaways. The women swam gracefully and swiftly with heads under the water. But they were no match for the speed of the canoes.[5] The men set off immediately, caught up with the women, and the fleeing swimmers were brought back to the sloop.

Satisfied with their successes and still on the alert, the crew waited for the tide to turn. As it ebbed, the *Sanoy* sailed down the Amacura River northward into the Orinoco and out to the Atlantic. Within a month they arrived back in Barbados with their booty of trade goods and ten captive Indians to sell into slavery. Immediately upon landing in Bridgetown, the main port in Barbados, William Price, the master of the vessel, entered his deposition on September 2, 1674, to prove that the captured Indians were not of a friendly tribe protected by any treaty.[6] Price suggested that they were Arawak Indians or from an Arawak-related tribe known to be allied with the Dutch and, therefore, vulnerable to English attack.

Wroth and Price brought their captives to Barbados to satisfy what they perceived as a potential market for American Indian household slaves. The fact that the captives were women was, therefore, no mere accident. The enterprising Peter Wroth seemed determined to supply Indian women to substitute for the declining number of English house servants arriving on Barbados's shores.

The experience of those eight women and two children goes far to explain Tituba's presence in Barbados. Charles Upham's report in the nineteenth century that, according to local legend, Tituba and her husband, John, "were spoken of as having come from New Spain . . . that is, the Spanish West Indies, and the adjacent mainland," is borne out by the record of known slave-capturing activities in South America.[7] Peter Wroth's ventures are evidence of an existing, albeit small, slave trade between the South American coast—identified at the time as the Spanish Main—and Barbados. It is there on the northeast coast of South America in present-day Venezuela that Tituba, the Indian slave woman, probably had her beginnings.

It is possible that Tituba could have been born in Barbados, the daughter of earlier captives or natives to the island. While possible, this scenario is improbable given the demographics of the Indian population on the island. At the time of English settlement in 1627, no American Indians were living in Barbados. Archeological evidence indicates they had lived there in earlier times, but the English colonists found an uninhabited island in 1627. Within a few years of the arrival of the English, a small group of Arawaks had been persuaded to move to Barbados from the

Guiana coast of South America to teach the islanders how to grow appropriate crops. Subsequently enslaved, those Arawaks were by the 1650s either dead or they and their descendants had been returned to the mainland.[8] Thereafter, until the 1660s, Indian slaves, when acquired, were usually a result of warfare with other Europeans in the West Indies. The number was never very large and, as a result, few of the Indian slaves left descendants. At no time were American Indians a significant demographic factor in Barbados or capable of sustaining an independent American Indian society there. During the course of the seventeenth century they shrank in numbers and economic importance as planters turned to other population resources.

The major source of labor in Barbados until the middle of the seventeenth century was immigrant indentured servants from the British Isles, particularly England. Their number declined during the 1660s as a result of a growing anti-emigration campaign in England supported by government programs that increased the cost of recruiting servants and growing competition for a labor force from other English colonies: Virginia, Maryland, Jamaica, and South Carolina.[9] At the same time new efforts on the part of English merchants to tap into the African slave trade brought down the price of African labor and sugar planters in Barbados shifted to black slave labor.[10]

Indian labor for field work, either slave or free, was not of particular interest to the planters of the British West Indies. The Indian death rate was so high following contact with Europeans and their passive resistance to the labor demands of the seventeenth-century invaders so profound that English colonizers gave little thought to using native labor in the sugar fields. They linked susceptibility to disease and a refusal to work under European supervision with a general physical weakness that rendered Indians unfit for agricultural labor. It is true that by the seventeenth century the worst of the epidemics that resulted from first contact between Europeans and Indians, and that had killed untold millions of native Americans, was over. The survivors of that sixteenth-century demographic disaster had begun to increase in numbers and to develop the means to resist both European diseases and European warfare.[11] Continued violent resistance coupled with a European mythology of a native population unable to cope with the demands of large-scale agriculture discouraged an interest in using Indian labor on the tobacco or sugar plantations of the West Indies.[12]

There was, however, continued low-level interest in American Indians as domestic servants in Barbados until at least 1675. The earlier Arawaks had impressed the planters with their skill at fishing and cooking.[13] Englishmen in Surinam had also employed Indians as domestic labor.[14] The continued association of native Americans with household work along the coast reinforced the earlier views of the Barbados planters. After midcentury, as fewer English immigrants were available for domestic service, planters in the island colony renewed their interest in training the few available Indians for household work. They often rejected the Irish or Africans as potential sources of domestic workers. African slaves were more valuable in the sugar fields, but were often suspected of conspiracies against the planters. The Irish they considered lazy, undependable, and even more dangerous than Africans.[15] Planters in both Bermuda and Barbados feared that Irish servants and African slaves were natural conspirators. One planter complained in 1655 that the Irish were "a profligate race who were in the habit of joining themselves to runaway slaves."[16] The mild-mannered Arawaks had no such reputation.

Most Indian resistance to enslavement tended to be passive, taking the form of mass suicide or a reluctance to perform physically demanding tasks. The native peoples appeared to submit completely to their fate once captured. The refusal to work was explained by Europeans as a sign of inherent physical weakness on the part of all Indian groups, the absence of violent reaction proof of total submission.[17] Such Indian forms of resistance were incomprehensible to Europeans, constituting an invisible barrier between the two cultures that aroused little concern or, at the worst, disparaging comment.[18] Passive resistance was not perceived as a threat to property or life.

Until the end of the century, the very small American Indian presence on the island conjured up little threat to the Barbados planters. Arawaks in particular had the reputation of being a peaceful, unaggressive people. Caribs were less attractive as slaves because of their violent resistance against European infiltration and their reputation for the unpleasant custom of cannibalism. They were, however, a rare presence in Barbados.

During the seventeenth century the intricacies of British policy vis-à-vis the Spanish, French, and Dutch had dictated which Caribbean Indians were most vulnerable to capture and enslavement. Sporadically, as hostilities among the European rivals rose and fell during the seventeenth century, Amerindian captives were brought from Jamaica, St. Vincent,

St. Lucia, and Dominica to Barbados and enslaved. Occasionally an unsuspecting Carib trading with the Barbados settlers was trapped on the island and forced into slavery.[19] In Dominica, however, the Caribs held on tenaciously defying European attempts at control. By 1670, moreover, the English found that some islands, particularly the French-controlled St. Vincent and St. Lucia, were more valuable as a source of trade in wood than as the object of warfare, so kidnapping ventures soon ended there.[20] As hostilities with the French declined, so did the capture of Indian slaves from the other islands. In addition, very few descendants of the small number of captive Caribs remained in Barbados. Those who survived the high mortality among slaves found little opportunity to form family groups.[21]

Other potential but less likely sources for an Indian slave in Barbados include the Carolinas and Massachusetts, where conflicts between the English and the Indians had led to the transport of mainland Indians to the West Indies. It has been suggested that Tituba was a Wampanoag who had been captured during King Philip's War in Massachusetts, sold to the West Indies as a slave, and subsequently brought back to Massachusetts by Samuel Parris.[22] That scenario is possible, but in light of the very bitter heritage of Puritan-Wampanoag hostility, somewhat improbable. King Philip's War of 1675–76 had led to the expulsion of most Wampanoags.[23] It seems unlikely that Parris would have brought back to Massachusetts members of the tribes that had been banished to the West Indies as punishment for the death of thousands of English settlers.

There is some indication that Indians from South Carolina may have been forcibly transported to Barbados during the last quarter of the seventeenth century. Barbadians migrating to the new colonies in the Carolinas became involved with an Indian trade that included slave captives. Some of those Indian slaves may have been sold into slavery but there is no specific evidence of such sales in Barbados, apart from comments by Indian traders that the slave trade resulted in sales to the West Indies following clashes in 1670 and 1674. Most of the Indian-white clashes in South Carolina, however, occurred after 1680 and following the prohibition in Barbados of the importation of Indians.[24] The Carolina-Barbados ties may hint at such slave-trading connections, but there is no record that they actually conducted such a trade with the island or that Tituba had roots among those Carolina tribes.

Most of the available evidence for the presence of Indian slaves in Barbados points to contact with the Circum-Caribbean area that includes the northeast coast of South America and not North America.[25] It is most likely that the small number of Indian slaves in Barbados during the 1670s were immigrants brought there as captives in war or kidnapped from other Caribbean areas including the coast of the mainland that, although called the Spanish Main, included English and Dutch colonies in Guiana.[26] As Peter Wroth's escapade in the Orinoco area indicates, a recent Arawak-Guiana background seems to be the most likely explanation for Tituba's origins.

These Dutch settlements on the mainland of South America continued to be a minor source of Indian slaves for the English from the 1660s until at least 1674. Wroth's expedition was not the first of its kind, although it may have been the last attempt to find slaves on the South American coast. The area called Guiana included a string of trading posts between the Amazon and the Orinoco where Dutch merchants had built up a good trade with the Arawaks. Sandwiched between the Dutch allies and the Spanish was the small English settlement at Surinam. At the end of the second Anglo-Dutch War in 1667, the Dutch lost their settlement along the Hudson River in North America and took over Surinam. Nevertheless, the English in Barbados, in violation of the peace treaty, continued to raid Dutch-allied Arawak villages, providing a small stream of Indian slaves from the mainland to supply the market for domestic servants. Peter Wroth had been involved in that trade beginning in 1665 at least.[27]

The outbreak of the third Anglo-Dutch War in 1672 coincided with a sudden increase in the price of Africans. In its zeal to eliminate the Dutch carrying trade from its American possessions, English imperial policy granted a monopoly of the slave trade to the Royal African Company in 1672. The inexperienced company, however, was unable to satisfy the demand for African labor and the price of slaves rose precipitously. Barbados planters protested against the loss of their energetic Dutch suppliers, but it was only after 1676 that supplies would increase, due to increasing competition from small English slave-trading promoters.[28] In the interim, the inadequate supply of African labor gave renewed impetus to raids on Indian villages in both the Essequibo and the Orinoco/Amacura River areas of South America. In 1673 Peter Wroth stepped up his activities on the South American coast.

The official English policy was to maintain friendly relations with mainland Caribs hostile to the Dutch and their Arawak allies. Carib support was valued. Lord Willoughby, for instance, as the Governor of Barbados, had sent expeditions to Guiana in 1665 to take Essequibo and Nova Zeelandia. He expected and drew on assistance from the Caribs who were at war with the Dutch and their Arawak allies.[29] Nonetheless, in the years of official peace following that second Anglo-Dutch War (1655–67), Wroth indiscriminately raided both Arawak and Carib villages on the periphery of the Dutch colonies. During the third war with Holland in 1673 he brought eleven Caribs from the Amacura River to Barbados as slaves. The King ordered him to return them to South America and to stop antagonizing the friendly Indians.[30] Arawaks received no such protection and would continue as fair game for his exploits.

The following year Peter Wroth returned to the Amacura River, possibly to return those Caribs, but also to look for more acceptable captives. During that trip he brought back another ten Indians—the eight women and two children mentioned above—presumably Arawaks this time, to sell into slavery in Barbados. Wroth's venture was the last recorded attempt to supply Barbados with native American labor. Two years later, the Barbados Assembly banned the importation of Indian slaves, effectively halting the immigration of American Indians to Barbados.[31] Shortly thereafter slave traders competing with the Royal African Company won concessions to increase their imports of Africans to Barbados and the temporary decline in the supply of slaves ended.

The labor crisis in Barbados, precipitated by the declining number of white indentured servants, the high mortality among all labor sources, and the Royal African Company's monopoly of the African slave trade, was resolved somewhat by an increasing supply of slaves transported across the Atlantic from Africa after 1676 and a slow natural increase in the native-born African slave population. American Indian slavery, never very popular, lost all support with those changing labor conditions and the total population of Indians continued a rapid decline.

It is also possible, but less likely, that Tituba could have been the daughter of two Indians who arrived in Barbados sometime during the 1660s. Nonetheless, the continuing high mortality of slaves in seventeenth-century Barbados, combined with a lack of Indian men to father children, hampered any possibility of a natural increase among American

Indians, except as mixed ethnic-racial groups.[32] Such offspring rapidly lost their identity as Indians and are virtually impossible to separate from the developing African slave society.

There are no references in the seventeenth-century records to people of combined African-Indian heritages. The children of mixed matches in Barbados were absorbed into slave society as African children. Those children were considered Negroes and their descendants merged with the larger African-American community. Tituba, however, was not the result of any racial mixture. All extant Massachusetts references to her clearly specify that she was an American Indian. In New England as in Barbados, children of mixed Indian-African parentage were described as Negro and not Indian. Their experiences paralleled that of children of African-white couples, merging into a black rather than a white community.[33]

Given the pattern of the slave trade in that area of the West Indies and the structure of Anglo-Dutch relations, it seems reasonable to conclude that Tituba and most other Amerindian slaves living in Barbados during the 1670s probably came from one of the Arawak-related tribes of northeastern South America, that is from Venezuela or Guyana (the English-speaking country sandwiched between Venezuela and present-day Suriname). Tituba would have been among the small contingent of American Indians forcibly transported to Barbados from the South American coast, the Spanish Main, and shipped to the island no more than ten years before moving to Massachusetts in 1680. An Arawak-Guiana background seems to be the most likely explanation for Tituba's origins.

Although the evidence is circumstantial, Tituba, transported to Boston six years after that 1674 kidnapping event, may well have been one of the children in Wroth's cargo that September day in 1674. Evidence uncovered in the Barbados records suggests that Tituba was just a child, somewhere between nine and fourteen years old, in 1676. While still a child she was in all likelihood sold in Barbados as a slave and subsequently brought to Massachusetts by Samuel Parris.

Further evidence of a South American origin for Tituba is her name itself, which has a Spanish flavor and thus a possible association with the part of America first explored by the Spaniards. The Spanish verb to stagger or to stammer for instance is "titubear."[34] The name also resembles that of an Indian tribe living at the mouth of the Orinoco in the sixteenth century; it was called by the Spanish "Tibetibe" and supposedly related to the ferocious Warou tribe. Sir Walter Raleigh noted a group of Indians at the mouth of the Orinoco he called Tivitivas; he assumed them to be a branch of the Warous and probably the same group identified by the Spaniards.[35] Of even more significance is a branch of the Arawaks living in that area of the Amacura River and identified by anthropologists as the Tetebetana.[36] The name Tituba is most likely a Spanish derivative of that Arawak name, reasonable grounds for assuming South American-Arawak roots for the Indian slave woman later brought to Massachusetts.

Arawak names had regular endings to indicate sex and number. The collective ending was "na" or sometimes "no." Tetebetana would have been the name of the group itself. The masculine ending was "die" or sometimes "tie"; the feminine was "do" or "to." Thus a male in the tribe would be called Tetebetadie and a female Tetebetado.[37] A Barbados planter, hearing this Spanish-sounding name, may well have dropped the ending syllable and called a member of the tribe by the name of Tetebe, with its variant spellings including Tituba, Tattuba, and Titeba.[38]

Slaves had little control over names chosen for them although they may secretly have identified themselves by another name. Personal names for slaves usually reflected planter values and interests. They might be given a "racial tag" such as Joseph Indian or Maria Negro or even a translation or Anglicized form of an Indian or African name.[39] A "Tetebe" would have had a familiar ring to a Barbados planter not only because of its Spanish quality but also because it is closely related to the type of African-Caribbean name that was commonplace in Barbados. The suffix "uba," for instance, appears among the inventory lists of female slaves as Altuba or Occuba or Arucuba or as Uba alone.[40] The "ba" ending is found in many African feminine names. So clearly associated with an Indian tribe, Tituba's name would not require any other identifying geographic or racial nomenclature.[41]

The planter in Barbados may also have been encouraged to call the slave by that shortened form of her tribal-family name if the girl had followed Arawak custom and refused to reveal her proper name to him. Such proper names expressed an "identity not only in form but in essence," and were seldom used by Guiana Indians for fear that the identity could be lost if the name were revealed to outsiders.[42] Arawak groups usually addressed each other by relationships using the word for brother, sister, companion, or mother, rather than their given names. Since relationships with Europeans were not always definable, Indians accepted whatever term was suggested to them by the strangers. Thus it was not unusual to hear Indians dubbed Peter, Jack, John, or Mary.[43] Whatever her proper name was, Tituba would have refused to disclose it to her kidnappers, but may have revealed that she was Tetebetado, a female of the Tetebetana clan. To call her Tetebe would also have the convenience of identifying her origin or point of embarkation, making a racial tag or surname unnecessary. The name Tituba, then, is a probably a shortened form for one of the clans or families—the Tetebetana—of an Arawak-speaking group located in the Amacura/Orinoco River area, a section of the world called by Europeans the Spanish Main.

As an Arawak, Tituba, to use the more conventional spelling, came from a people in South America known for their good humor and generosity, qualities born from an easy subsistence. An unidentified visitor to Guiana in 1665 remarked on the abundant food supply of the Amacura area: fish in the lakes and rivers; buffalo, elk, and deer on land; and of the root vegetables cassava and sweet potatoes. The local people made very practical use of that abundance in a varied diet and took advantage of the leisure time to enjoy various forms of entertainment. The Indians, he noted, "are great lovers of fine Gardens, Drinking, Dancing, and divers other pleasures."[44]

Those pleasures included a penchant for running, wrestling, and ball games as well as regular all-night sessions of energetic dancing, singing, and drinking. The dancers usually included both men and women who sometimes danced together and sometimes separately, in lines facing each other. In between dances all would drink copious quantities of a fermented cassava drink until they collapsed from fatigue or drunkenness. Accompanying the dancers were musicians who played on drums, rattles, flutes, and an instrument that resembled castanets. Both men and women chanted songs that had been learned in childhood, taught by the men of the tribe.[45]

Columbus, who had first met a Taino-speaking Arawak group in Hispaniola, described them as a more benign and civilized people than the fierce Indians he called Caribs because of their cannibalism. Vespucci reinforced this view of the Arawaks as a gentle people who enjoyed lavish meals, dances, and singing. At the time Arawak villages were large and permanent, with specialized structures used for ceremonial purposes. Primarily agriculturalists, they seldom instigated warfare with neighboring tribes.[46] Arawaks thus early on had acquired a reputation for being easygoing, less threatening than Caribs, familiar with sedentary living patterns, and more amenable to European influences.

To Peter Wroth and the Barbados planters who wanted domestic servants, these gentle and generous people were a convenient source of labor. The Arawak women in particular were valued for their skill in preparing food, caring for domestic animals, and weaving cloth, in addition to cultivating root crops. The men were very successful hunters, although that talent would not be appreciated in Barbados. They also brought important skills in weaving baskets and fishing.

The Arawak fondness for children may have enhanced their usefulness for domestic work in English eyes. Arawak children were treated gently and with great affection by both parents. Moreover, child care was not a gender-specific task among the Arawaks. Men played important roles in child care as the teachers of songs, customs, and rites; they encouraged boys to play hunting and fishing games from a very young age. Kindly and amiable, Arawak men appeared less threatening to the Barbados planters than alternative sources of domestic workers from either Europe or Africa.

With brownish skin and black hair, Arawaks resembled other Indians of Central America and the Caribbean, but were described as shorter in stature and lighter in skin color than their immediate neighbors. Their dress, however, was typical of the area. The men wore only a single piece of cloth drawn between the legs and held up at front and back by a rope around the waist. Women wore a strip of cloth hung from a rope belt at the waist in front, like an apron, and called a queyu. Scarring and mutilation for decorative or identification purposes was not common. For special occasions men and women decorated their bodies with necklaces of animal teeth or seed and paint and men wore feather headdresses (see Fig. 2). Arawaks were especially noted for personal cleanliness and meticulous attention to their appearance. Bathing in rivers or ponds occurred several times a day, upon awakening as well as after each meal. All were notably good swimmers. Thus Peter Wroth, familiar with Arawak customs, expected the women he wanted to capture to attempt to flee by swimming and had prepared his men for the eventuality.

Daily routines for women in Guiana left little time for leisure. Their

Figure 2: Guiana man and woman.

industriousness probably impressed the English who viewed their own working class as lazy and undependable.[47] Arawak women seemed to be perpetually at work. After a morning bath, they cleaned the houses, fetched water and firewood, cooked the food, prepared the fermented drink of cassava (called paiwari) or sweet potatoes (called casiri), planted the fields, collected the produce, and, when the men prepared to go on a hunt, carried the supplies for them. Women also wove the hammocks used for sleeping and trade. The most frequent occupation was cooking, particularly the making of bread from cassava, which required a complicated process of removing poisons, preparing the flour and baking the cakes in the sun, and the preparation of a stew that is still widely consumed in the West Indies called the pepper-pot.[48] The physical stamina and domestic talents of the Arawak women were especially attractive to Barbados planters in need of household slaves.

Arawak religious practices were of less immediate concern to the English. Those captives from South America, however, carried with them distinctive concepts of the supernatural that would awe and continue to fascinate their English captors. Some aspects of those beliefs would be absorbed by the English in Barbados. Tituba's confession in Salem in 1692, combining as it did elements of those Indian beliefs with that of English folklore, would heighten the fear of a Satanic conspiracy in Massachusetts.

Most Indians of the Guiana area believed in the existence of a large number of spirits of the bush and of the dead.[49] A special feature of Arawakan religion was the worship of effigies that represented personal guardian spirits. The effigy could be given animal or human form but was most often geometric in shape. Although they were often made of different materials, the usual was a three-pointed stone carved with elabo-

Facing page:
The two figures, drawn probably in the nineteenth century, are Anglicized views of Indians from the area of the British colony of Guiana (including present-day Guyana, Suriname, and French Guiana). The facial features are European but the clothing and other artifacts resemble those of the South American Indians. The women wore their hair long, used decorative necklaces of beads, and wore a queyu, an apron sometimes of cloth or of beads held up by strings around the waist. The basket carried on her head was made from the stems of a reed-like plant. The house in the background would have been constructed of poles and thatch and open at either end. The man's bow and arrow were used for both hunting and fishing. (*Photo courtesy of the Barbados Museum and Historical Society.*)

rate designs. The zemis served a variety of purposes and represented a hierarchy of personal spirits associated with the social status of their human protégés. Each member in the tribe had at least one zemi and individuals provided offerings using various narcotic and stimulant drugs during the prescribed rites.

The Arawak world was also inhabited by a variety of malevolent spirits. The spirit of the dead, called opias or hubias, wandered in the bush after dark causing evil. The most feared of all evil forces, however, were real persons called kenaimas. These beings could constitute a danger to any lonely wanderer because they were compelled to kill, cause sickness, or bring about other grave misfortune. To the Arawak of Guiana, the kenaima, although human, could appear with "monstrous characteristics; they may be hairy or they may have protruding eyebrows or two heads; they may have no articulation at the knees, or they may be linked together like Siamese twins."[50] The spirits of these monsters could inhabit the body of any animal and thus change shape at will. Such enormous power to cause suffering, it was believed by the people of Guiana, was unique to the kenaima. Ordinary people were also capable of evil but to a lesser extent.

Nonetheless, a kenaima was a real person, albeit one with special supernatural power used exclusively for evil purposes. The Indians believed he could act either on his own or at the behest of another human agent or of the spirit of a dead person. This malevolence was at such variance with Arawak norms of behavior, which abhorred violence within the group, that a kenaima was always identified with foreign tribes or unfamiliar animals and plants. Such a view of the evil spirit as an outsider may have contributed to intertribal warfare but it also helped foster more amicable relations within the tribe. Arawaks did not expect danger to the group from within; they assumed that only a stranger would bring about great misfortune to an individual. People did not curse members of their own village. Thus visitors or unknown shamans were particularly vulnerable to accusations of sorcery.

The greatest evil to these Indians of the Guiana area emanated from sources outside the immediate family, clan, or village.[51] This concept of an outside evil force, when introduced by Tituba, would play havoc with Puritan notions of the Devil and sin in Salem, Massachusetts.

Birds were often suspected of harboring kenaimas and were held in great awe. They could communicate with the dead and bring messages to the conjurers. Bird calls were also omens, foretelling a potential kenaima appearance. Arawaks paid close attention to the presence of birds, especially those with peculiar or disturbing sounds, fearing most the shrieking sounds of the goatsucker, the nightjar. Their calls inevitably presaged terrible events.[52]

To counter the kenaimas, Indians of Guiana turned to the piaiman, the name given to the shaman in that area. The duty of the piaimen or shaman was to ward off the evil of those malevolent beings. His or her main power was an ability to "converse with the spirits or depart from his own body in deep trances" in order to fight the kenaimas on their own ground.[53] It was believed that the piaiman's supernatural power, unlike that of the kenaima, was an acquired trait. During his or her long apprenticeship, the piaiman was trained to bellow in a loud voice and learned ventriloquism in addition to acquiring knowledge of the properties of herbs and poisons. Much of this knowledge was not exclusive but was shared by others in the tribe, both men and women. But the piaiman's power, gained through the long period of training, was assumed to be more effective than that of ordinary people.[54]

Dreams also had special meaning for Arawaks, as for most American Indians. Dreams, particularly nightmares, were not just omens of evil to come, but real adventures and existential occurrences. They were experienced not by the physical being but by his or her soul, nonetheless becoming "part of the history of each man's life." Events envisioned during sleep and the behavior of people in those dreams were actual events. So real was this dream content that South American Indians believed that people should be held responsible for the consequences of actions dreamed by others.[55]

Indian folk of Guiana devised various methods to protect themselves from the evil powers.[56] One method was avoidance of all new and strange foods and places, or if that were not possible, not calling attention to some suspect natural topography. An extreme measure of avoidance was temporary blindness by rubbing their eyes with a hurtful substance such as hot pepper or merely closing their eyes. Blinded, the individual could hide from the evil spirit. Red paint was also used as a talisman against sickness or diseases, a practice derived from an earlier use of blood for ritual purposes. A father's blood was believed to cure a child or impart courage. Some memory of these blood rituals and avoidance practices would surface during Tituba's ordeal in 1692.

Tituba's young world was informed by these beliefs, practices, and fears. She brought the mental images of kenaimas, the value of trances, and the reality of dreams with her to Barbados from South America and did not lose them completely after her arrival in Massachusetts. Elements of these beliefs would surface later and with great consequence during her interrogation in Salem in 1692.

My Own Country: Tituba in Barbados

Tituba . . . said her Mistress in her own Country was a
Witch, and had taught her some means to be used for
the discovery of a Witch, and for the prevention of being
bewitched, etc.
　　　—John Hale, "A Modest Inquiry Into the Nature of
Witchcraft"

According to local legend, Tituba, along with Indian John, her
husband, had been brought by Parris from Barbados. It was
assumed also that Parris had acquired the two Indian slaves "in
some of his Commercial transactions."[1] Since Parris's commercial contacts came from his sojourn in Barbados, it seems logical for the local
people to have concluded that the two slaves had been in Barbados at
some time before Parris appeared in Massachusetts. Tituba herself during
her questioning in Salem acknowledged that she had lived somewhere
other than New England. She had learned techniques of divination, she
said, from "her Mistress in her own Country."[2] In addition to the nine-
teenth-century conjecture regarding Tituba's origins, there is some fragmentary written evidence in the land transactions of Barbados to support
the local legend. Tituba's "Country" was most likely the English island
colony of Barbados.

A name similar to Tituba appears in a Barbados document of 1676, in
an inventory of a plantation owned by Samuel Thompson in St. Thomas
Parish, five miles inland from the west coast community of Holetown
and about six miles by road from Bridgetown (see Fig. 3). Thompson and
his mother, the three-times widowed Elizabeth Pearsehouse, had jointly

inherited a sugar plantation that contained almost three hundred acres of land and in 1676 held sixty-seven slaves.[3] One of the children on that plantation was called "Tattuba," a name so similar to Tituba's that it would appear to be merely a variant spelling.[4] Whether they were the same person cannot be proven conclusively, but the fact that the name is so rare, combined with the timing of the inventory and other transactions relating to the estate, provide strong circumstantial evidence that the Tattuba in the Barbados inventory was the same person as Parris's Indian slave woman, Tituba. Scattered pieces of evidence also help to link Samuel Thompson to Samuel Parris through friends, family, and business acquaintances.

Samuel Parris, who would bring Tituba to Massachusetts in 1680, had arrived on the island in the mid-1670s to settle the family estate after his own father's death. But instead of living on his father's sugar plantation near Jamestown (Holetown), he took up residence in Bridgetown where he established himself as a credit agent for other sugar planters.[5] He was unmarried and his household, according to a census taken in October 1679, included two other people—a single slave (gender and race unspecified) and an apprentice or hired servant who was probably white.[6] In 1680 Parris left Barbados, presumably taking that slave and possibly one other with him to Massachusetts, but leaving the apprentice behind.

In the light of Samuel Parris's movements, the timing of the public appearance of a slave named Tattuba is most suggestive. Thompson and his mother had inherited the plantation from his father Edward Thompson who died in 1659 when the boy was only four years old.[7] At the age of twenty-one in 1676 he took control of his own two hundred acres and his mother's ninety-seven-acre dower right, one-third part of her husband's estate. She was only a "tenant for life" and at her death the land would revert to Samuel.[8] For reasons that can only be surmised, Samuel took steps immediately upon reaching adult status to convert his legacy into cash and to divest himself of the responsibility to manage the estate for his mother. Perhaps he had the first symptoms of the disease that would bring about his early death in 1680 and felt inadequate to the task of administering the plantation, or perhaps he planned to leave the island.[9] In any event, he felt it necessary to make some provision for the support of his mother and the management of both his and her inheritances.

One of his first acts in November of 1676 was to sell a small St. Thomas plantation of about one hundred acres to Captain Anthony Lane, his mother's father-in-law by a former marriage to Ralph Lane (d. 1669).[10] Her dower rights of thirty-three and one-third acres in that parcel were included in this transaction. She was to be supported by this tenancy and at her death, as payment for Captain Lane's work in managing the property, the land would be given to Captain Lane.[11] The following month Samuel acted on their larger property and in a similar transaction leased one-half of his 200 acres and half of his mother's "moiety" or interest in her ninety-seven acres to his friend, the Bridgetown merchant Nicholas Prideaux.[12] He sold the rest of the estate to Prideaux with the proviso that all of Elizabeth's Pearsehouse's land would be used for her support until her death. When she died Prideaux could take possession of the entire plantation. To complete the sale and lease, Thompson inventoried the contents of the plantation and listed the names of all the slaves. The name "Tattuba" appears on the two inventories taken in 1676 (Fig. 3).

The presence of an Amerindian slave on Samuel Thompson's plantation would not be a mere accident. Only a few miles away was the residence of his grandfather, John Reid, a prosperous landowner and clerk of the local court in St. James Parish, which abutted St. Thomas Parish. Reid had taken part in the early Amerindian slave trade and included Indian slaves among his property.[13] His daughter, Elizabeth, had married Captain Edward Thompson, her first husband.[14] Samuel was the eldest son of that marriage and in 1676 the sole heir to two-thirds of the plantation that was Tattuba's home, his mother retaining her one-third share. The presence of an Amerindian slave on the Thompson plantation then would not have been completely fortuitous. John Reid's involvement with American Indian slaves lends additional credibility to the idea that there could be such a slave at his daughter Elizabeth's and grandson Samuel's home. The Reid-Thompson-Prideaux associations also brought Samuel Parris within that circle.

Whether Samuel Thompson left the island at the conclusion of these 1676 transactions is not known, but he was present in Barbados in January of 1680 when he was noted on the muster rolls among Captain Robinson's troops with one horse. He does not appear among the list of landowners in the census taken shortly before.[15] Richard Ford, the mapmaker, however, included Thompson's name on his map that was

Figure 3: Thompson Inventory of slaves (two illustrations), "A Particular List or Schedule of all and every the Negroes Stock Cattle and Utensils belonging to the plantation of Samuel Thompson Son and Heir of Captain Edward Thompson late of this island deceased." Barbados Archives Recopied Deeds RB 3/10.

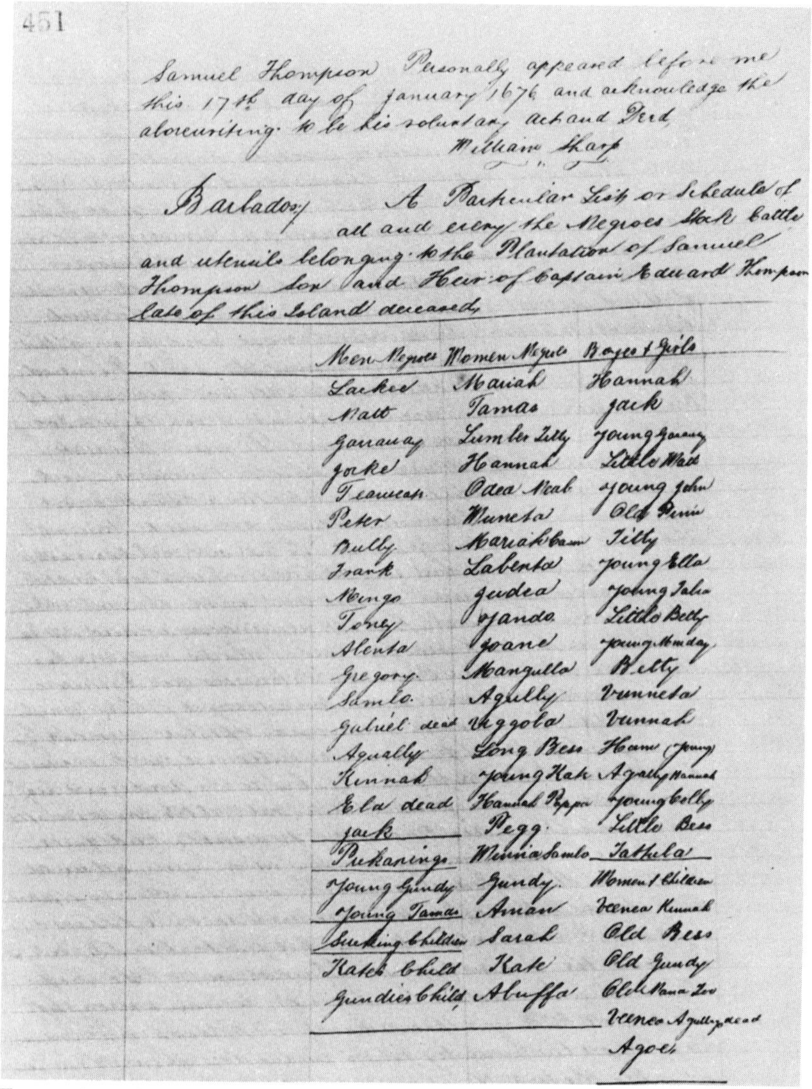
451

Samuel Thompson Personally appeared before me this 17th day of January 1676 and acknowledge the aforewriting to be his voluntary act and Deed,
William Sharp

Barbados A Particular List or Schedule of all and every the Negroes Stock Cattle and utensils belonging to the Plantation of Samuel Thompson Son and Heir of Captain Edward Thompson late of this Island deceased

Men Negroes	Women Negroes	Boyes & Girls
Lackee	Mariah	Hannah
Natt	Tamas	Jack
Garaway	Lumbler Lilly	young Garaway
Yorke	Hannah	Little Natt
Teaweah	Odea Neah	young John
Peter	Muneta	Old Denis
Bully	Mariah [illegible]	Tilly
Frank	Laberta	young Ella
Mingo	Judea	young Jaba
Tony	Yanda	Little Betty
Alenta	Joane	young Monday
Gregory	Mangullo	Betty
Samlo	Agully	Vunneta
Gabriel dead	Uggola	Vunnah
Agually	Long Bess	Hanne (young)
Kennah	young Kate	Agally Hannah
Ela dead	Hannah Pepper	young Betty
Jack	Pegg	Little Bess
Pekaningo	Minna Samlo	Tathela
young Gundy	Gundy	Women & Children
young Tamas	Aman	Venea Kennah
Sucking Children	Sarah	Old Bess
Kates Child	Kate	Old Gundy
Gundies Child	Abuffa	Old [illegible]
		Venea Agully dead
		Agoes

Two versions of the inventory of slaves on Samuel Thompson's plantation taken in December of 1676–77 and acknowledged as his "voluntary Act and Deed." The documents were signed in January 1677 but not registered by the court clerk until October of 1679. In the interim some changes were added regarding deaths. The list on page 455 (the earlier version) notes the death of only one adult man, Ebla. The list on page 451, revised, notes that death and those of another man and a woman—Gabriel and Agully. The name "Tattuba" appears, underlined, on both inventories at the end of the list of girls and boys in the right-hand column. The list on page 455 also includes a "young y John" among the girls and boys. He is described as only "young John" on the revised list. (*Courtesy of the Barbados Archives. Photo by E. Benjamin.*)

published in London in 1680 in recognition of the Thompson-Prideaux partnership.[16] In November of 1679 Samuel Thompson, now twenty-four years old, wrote a will in anticipation of his early death. In it he distributed the rest of his property, provided for the freeing of one slave, and the gift of another one to Prideaux.[17]

Thompson's soon-to-be fatal illness may have triggered additional changes in the ownership of his former plantation amidst concerns that the land might be divided. During the summer of 1679, Prideaux sold his part of the Thompson-Prideaux plantation to John Hothersall, intending to "keep it in the family," although whose family and whether Prideaux and Hothersall were related is not clear in the records. This contract, signed in July 1679, was registered in October of that year.[18] Thus between December 1676 and October 1679, the plantation that was home to the slave named "Tattuba," had exchanged hands twice and was still in flux.

It was within that period, between the time when Samuel Parris first returned to the island in the mid-1670s and December of 1679, that he acquired at least the one slave noted in the census taken that month. A second American Indian slave was acquired shortly afterward. Tituba could have been either one. John Indian was probably the other slave.[19] The Thompson plantation, with its shifting ownership and leaseholds, would have been a likely source for Parris when ready to acquire domestic workers. As land changed hands, new owners reevaluated labor needs and might dispose of superfluous workers, especially teen-aged domestic help.

There is no clear indication in the Barbadian papers that Hothersall or Prideaux or Thompson or his mother sold the slave Tattuba from the Thompson plantation to Parris or even that she was an Amerindian. No Amerindians were identified in any of these transactions—an omission that seems to have been common at the time. But the coincidence of this unusual name with its clear Indian connotations making its appearance at the moment when Samuel Parris acquired a slave with such a similar name is a curious and suggestive event. Parris quite likely was acquainted with John Hothersall and Samuel Thompson whose lives touched his through their mutual acquaintances in St. Andrews and St. James Parishes. John Hothersall's father was soon to marry the widow Sparkes who was living on the old Parris plantation called "Springhead" in St. Thomas.[20] The dense network of kin and commercial contacts in Barbados gave Samuel Paris opportunities to take advantage of a variety of business transactions.

Samuel Parris's connection to Barbados goes back to the 1650s when his father, Thomas, bought land there. The older Parris moved his family to the island from England after he inherited some scattered but substantial holdings from his brother John in 1660. That inheritance consisted of parts of three plantations in the central and western sections of the island, a storehouse at Reid's Bay on the west coast near Jamestown (now Holetown), and a house in Bridgetown. Among the three plantations was "Springhead," which extended from the landlocked St. Andrews Parish to St. James nearer to the coast, a small estate in St. Peters Parish leased out in 1656, and unnamed seaside land near the Reid's Bay storehouse in St. James. By the time of his death in 1673, Thomas had sold off most of his and his brother's property except for the 20 acres in St. Peters Parish and a plantation of 170 acres near Reid's Bay on the west coast.[21] "Springhead" had been sold to John Sparkes, whose widow later linked Samuel Parris to John Hothersall and to the slave listed in the Thompson inventory as Tattuba (see Fig. 4).[22]

Samuel Parris, who had been sent back to Massachusetts to attend Harvard, was still there when his father died in 1673.[23] Thomas had willed his real estate, including the one remaining plantation in Reid's Bay, to the now twenty-year-old son, but Samuel probably never lived on the plantation nor was it likely to have been Tituba's home. The property, a relatively substantial tract of 176 acres, was leased to and occupied continuously throughout the 1670s and 1680s by Edward Elding, a respected planter and the son-in-law of one of the larger landowners of the area, James Nore.[24] Due to Elding's efforts, most of that leasehold was under sugar cultivation worked by a labor force of seventy slaves and three indentured servants.[25] Nothing in the record indicates that any of those slaves was an Indian. Toward the end of 1680, just as Samuel Parris was preparing to leave Barbados, he transferred title to the land to Elding.[26]

It is unlikely that Tituba would have come from Elding's leasehold. Barbados suffered from a labor shortage during those years, and few people could afford to purchase or lease a plantation without a secure hold on the workers—both slave and servant. A landowner would hesitate to claim any of the slaves on previously leased and occupied land. The

Figure 4: "A New Map of the Island of Barbados by Richard Ford, ca. 1680, Wherein every Parish, Plantation, Watermill, Windmill & Cattlemill is described with the name of the Present Possessor, and all things, els[e] Remarkable according to a Late Exact Survey thereof."

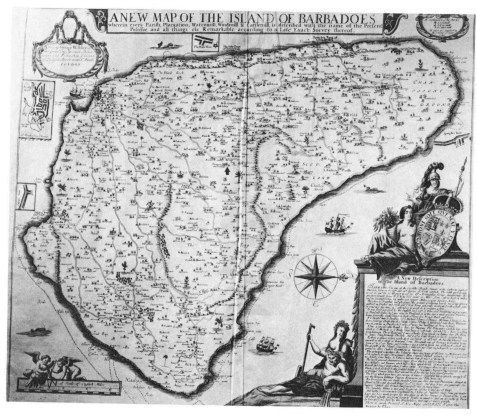

A more accurate rendering of the island than Ligon's earlier map (Plate 6) with representations of houses, windmills, and roads. The perspective is from the east. North is on the right. Much more of the interior of the island had come under cultivation in the last twenty-five years as a result of the booming sugar industry. The Elding-Parris plantation is noted at Reid's Bay on the west coast (top of the map). Samuel Thompson's plantation, Tituba's home, is identified as Thompson and Prideaux in the western part of St. Thomas Parish in what appears to be the very center of the island (arrow added). It is marked with two windmills. The Thompson land had the advantage of being near one of the roads leading to Bridgetown. In the absence of such a road, Thompson would have had to rely on donkeys to carry the sugar over rough land to Holetown on the west coast, thus increasing his costs.

The legend on the lower right corner, "A New Description of the Island of Barbadoes" gives details about the geography, political divisions, towns, agricultural, military size, and government of the island. (*Photo courtesy of the Barbados Museum and Historical Society.*)

general practice evident in the records of contracts of sale and lease was to treat slaves as real estate in land transactions; slaves were accordingly transferred along with the buildings and equipment on working plantations.[27] Elding needed all the servants and slaves he had to work the 176 acres. Parris, on the other hand, as a merchant in Bridgetown, had other opportunities to purchase domestic slaves through his commercial connections. Although Nicholas Prideaux's name does not appear in any of the Parris transactions, they probably knew of each other in the small Bridgetown commercial network. The Thompson-Prideaux partnership was in the process of change and the slave population in St. Thomas Parish would feel the effect of these shifts.

Unfortunately, the second set of transactions, the July 1679 Prideaux-Hothersall bill of sale, does not include a list of slave names, so it is not possible to trace the individual slaves any further than the 1676 transactions or even to know if Tattuba was still there at the later date. The new deed of 1679 records only that the eighteen Negro men in Thompson's original lease had been reduced to fourteen by 1679 (at least two had died) and the twenty-four women increased, probably from the list of girls who had become women during that time, by four. The number of working children, which had been nineteen in 1676, was now twenty. The four infants and very young children in 1676 had either died or were old enough to work. The schedule on the deed notes that two more slave children had been born and several other slaves purchased since 1676.[28] The acquisition of new slaves and the loss of a part of the original labor force during this period may indicate that Prideaux was selling off some slaves and acquiring new ones more useful for his plans. Some may have died, grown too old, or lacked important skills. Regardless of his reasons, unlike the Elding plantation, changes in the Thompson-Pearsehouse inheritance were taking place during the time that Parris was in need of household servants.

The Tattuba of that 1676 inventory was listed among the working boys and girls, a category that usually included children between nine and fourteen years of age.[29] At the time that Parris was getting ready to leave Barbados in 1680, Tattuba, therefore, was somewhere between the age of thirteen and eighteen, certainly old enough to take on the domestic duties as housekeeper to a young man with few family responsibilities. She had time to mature and acquire more skills as Parris's fortunes improved. Twelve years later, during the Salem trials, this Tattuba of the Thompson plantation would have been between twenty-five and thirty years old. Assuming that Tattuba and Tituba were the same person, Parris's Indian woman servant was a relatively young woman when she was accused of witchcraft.

The circumstances of age, name, legal status, and timing, therefore, point to a connection between the Tattuba living on Samuel Thompson's land in 1676 and the Tituba Samuel Parris brought to Massachusetts in 1680. The appearance of the unusual name Tattuba in a Barbados deed, and one so similar to that of Tituba does confirm, at the least, a Barbados association for the accused Salem witch. But were they the same person? Logic and the circumstances of the time would seem to indicate that they were.

The slave named Tattuba on the Thompson deeds is not described as an American Indian. She is listed as one of the Negro girls and boys. If she were an Amerindian, the absence of such a designation requires some explanation. Thompson may have been careless or just indifferent. Or he may have assumed that the name clearly indicated an Indian background. After all, Tituba or Tattuba denoted an Arawak Indian tribe in South America—the Tetebetana. No additional descriptive surname or "racial tag" would have been necessary.

Given the fearful conditions of the time, it is also possible that Samuel Thompson was being circumspect about the presence of an Indian on his plantation. He was not alone in that practice of omitting the term "Indian" on contracts during the years between 1676 and the early 1680s. In fact, all the official records strangely ignore the presence of Indians on the island during the critical years between 1675 and 1684 and only during those years. The practice in earlier years was to clearly recognize the Indian presence.

Amerindians in pre-1675 property transactions, for instance, are often specified as such, even though they appear at the end of the list of Negro slaves and not under a separate heading as the indentured servants did. For instance, John Beeke sold to Thomas Sturt (*sic*) ten acres near the south coast of Barbados on March 1, 1674/75 and included on the list of 10 slaves were eight Negro men followed by the names of two other people, Jack and Mary, identified as Indians.[30] On May 23, 1662, William Browne sold Hugh Agton land in St. Peter; listed after the names of the Negro men slaves is one "Indian."[31] On William Hilliard's plantation in 1656 were fifty-eight adult slaves and eighteen children; listed last in this inventory of girl slaves is "Syminige ye Indian."[32]

In most of these early deeds, when names are given, however, Indians do not stand alone as a separate category as do "Christian Servants," the indentured whites. All non-whites, including the Amerindians, are listed under the rubric of "Negroes," a term which was intended to connote the condition of enslavement and not necessarily color or ethnicity. Within those "Negro" slave schedules the only distinct categories are age and gender, with Indians mentioned last in each group. Occupations and special skills are seldom recognized in these seventeenth-century inventories, nor are price valuations given. Thus by the 1660s American Indians were becoming, in the eyes of the planters, merely slaves, and, over time, gradually lost their distinctive ethnic identity. The process was accelerated as a result of a series of crises in the mid-1670s.

The year 1675 had been a difficult time in Barbados. The discovery of a slave conspiracy in St. James Parish on the west coast in May sent out spasms of fear throughout the island for years afterward.[33] Although the conspirators were captured and executed with public displays of extreme cruelty, rumors of new threats continued to disturb the plantocracy.[34] The execution of the presumed culprits was interrupted on August 31 by a severe hurricane that practically wiped out the buildings and crops along the west coast. Two hundred people were killed and about one thousand homes were destroyed.[35] Food crops and sugar cane were equally devastated and many faced starvation. Planters still recovering from the shock of the threatened 1675 slave rebellion lost most of their equipment and homes. The Assembly adjourned in the face of the catastrophe.[36]

Fears for their safety in Barbados became more worrisome to whites in November 1675 when word arrived of Indian uprisings in Massachusetts and the Chesapeake Bay areas of North America.[37] In the absence of an indigenous Indian population, Barbados had escaped the large-scale retaliation experienced by the mainland settlers when local Indians attempted to eject the interloping Europeans and regain their lost lands. Perceptions of native Americans in Barbados retained echoes of the earlier European view of a wild man amenable to the influences of "civilization" and Christianity. But now the terrors of the mainland frontier infected the islanders and were joined to the usual uncertainties of life in the West

Indies. The crisis mentality demonized the American Indians as it had done elsewhere in America.[38] Planters feared that Indian uprisings on the mainland colonies could spread to Barbados; they imagined a threat existed as long as any Amerindians lived there. Many settlers left the island in the wake of these crises in anticipation of even more troubles ahead.[39] Samuel Thompson may have anticipated such a move when he received his inheritance and thus turned to his friends for his mother's care.

When the Barbados Assembly reconvened in 1676, it took steps to protect the island against further man-made havoc: new laws tightened the slave codes, attempted to slow the outward migration of poor whites, and prohibited the further importation of Indian slaves. The Assembly also proposed to "send away those already brought to this Island," lamenting that the Amerindians were "a people of too subtle, bloody, and dangerous nature and inclination to remain here."[40] The events in mind were, of course, mainland hostilities—King Philip's War in Massachusetts, the war against the Susquehannocks in Maryland, and then Bacon's provocations in Virginia. They also worried that New England Indian captives would be sent to Barbados as slaves. And there was the additional possibility that Indian slaves would be sent from Carolina, where Barbadians recently arrived in North America had discovered a new source of wealth in the Indian trade in furs and slaves.[41] Coming on the heels of a potential insurrection of rebellious Negro slaves, the planters in Barbados were not willing to risk an infusion of new rebels in their midst from their sister colonies to the north.

Although there is no evidence that any official steps were taken to systematically dispose of the island's Amerindian slaves in later years, the kidnapping of South Americans had ended with the passage of the 1676 law. Moreover, the servant labor crisis that precipitated an interest in Amerindian domestics at mid-century had eased by 1680 with an increase in the number of native-born Africans. They were considered more tractable than the African born and now served both house and field.[42] The events of 1675–76 thus suggest why Hothersall or Prideaux was willing to sell and why Parris chose American Indian slaves when leaving the island. Wary of the remaining Indian presence in Barbados, planters encouraged emigrating whites to take them elsewhere. To facilitate those sales of Indian slaves, the prices may have been lowered. The young Samuel Parris, struggling with unfulfilled mercantile ambitions, was able to acquire a household staff at a relatively low price. Parris, Tituba, and possibly John, his man servant/slave, joined the exodus from Barbados in 1680. By 1684 the total number of American Indians in Barbados had diminished to a minuscule group—given as seventy-two out of a total of 46,600 slaves.[43]

Significantly, no Indians were counted in the census taken at the end of 1679 while Tituba and Parris were still living there.[44] The hostility toward Indians following 1675 is clearly reflected in a refusal to acknowledge their existence in Barbados during those perilous years. There is, for instance, only one reference to an Indian slave in all the extant contracts signed between 1675 and 1684.[45] This was for a plantation that had been mortgaged in 1675 and had to be returned intact in 1678 with all the slaves and items listed in the earlier inventory and thus the necessity or carelessness of leaving in the descriptive term for the sole Indian slave.

And yet it is obvious that Amerindians were living in Barbados between 1675 and 1684. The census taken in 1684 identified seventy-two Indians on the island, and they were not all new to Barbados that year.[46] There is no evidence that Peter Wroth's 1674 cargo of eight women and two children from the Amacura River had been removed and it is unlikely that they had all died during those five years.[47] Quaker leader George Fox, when visiting his fellow Quakers in 1671–72, noted the presence of native Americans and remarked on the need for instructing those people he called "Tawnies," as did Morgan Godwyn in his diatribe as the "Negro's and Indian's Advocate" of 1680.[48] Godwyn, particularly, published his appeal for humane treatment of Amerindians at a time when the official records stubbornly refused to recognize them in the census.

Other evidence for an Indian presence can be deduced from the extant legal records. The deeds in the Barbados archives are incomplete, and only a small number of contracts at any time provide inventories giving the names of slaves on the plantations. Those that do are suggestive of the continuing practice of American Indian slavery during those years when no Indians are mentioned either in deeds or the census.

The presence of Amerindians can sometimes be inferred from their location on the inventory lists or in conjunction with their surnames. Some transactions in the late 1670s, for instance, include names such as "Jack Surrinam" and "Peter Tobago" and "Maria Surrinam."[49] Since slaves throughout the Americas were sometimes given surnames indicating ethnic or geographic origins or port of embarkation, it is likely that Jack and Maria came from Surinam and Peter from Tobago. Quite possibly they were Arawak Indians.[50] A refusal to reveal their personal names would have resulted in the use of the English nomenclature of Jack, Maria, and Peter.

It is significant that these names all appear at the end of the list of Negro slaves in the usual manner of indicating Indians but without the distinguishing label. Tattuba's name appearing at the end of the 1676 Thompson schedule of boys and girls may reflect this same common practice. The absence of the designation "Indian" does not prove that a particular slave was African, even though listed under the rubric of Negroes. Godwyn noted that the words "Negro" and "slave" had become synonymous by 1680.[51] All slaves, regardless of ethnic background, could be listed as Negroes. During the last quarter of the century, slaveholders no longer considered it necessary to distinguish their Indian slaves from the Africans. Nonetheless, the location of a name at the end of the list, where American Indians were usually noted, coupled with a reference to an American locale known to be the source of Indian slaves at that time, does provide verification that a particular slave was of Indian rather than of African background.

The scarcity of references to Amerindians in deeds and the census taken in late 1679 reflects a politic discretion following the crises of 1675–76. Those who harbored Amerindian slaves did not want to call attention to the presence of those now demonized and therefore fearsome people. But they were there and the practice of locating the names of Amerindians at the end of the schedules of slaves continued without the descriptive term.

It is very likely, then, that the Tattuba of the 1676 Thompson deed was an Amerindian. The name is too reminiscent of the Tetebetana clan to be discounted. Whether spelled as Tetebe or Tituba or Tattuba, it is a name that appears to be a uniquely American Indian derivative and not African.[52] For the merchant Prideaux, the quiet sale of this Amerindian girl to an unmarried merchant in need of an experienced domestic servant, and who was relocating to the mainland, would have made good sense and have been a relief to his neighbors.

The Tattuba inherited by Samuel Thompson was probably the same person as the Tituba that Samuel Parris brought to Massachusetts and who figured so prominently in the early phases of the Salem witchscare of 1692. She had come originally from an Arawak-speaking group in South America, an area that formed part of what was vaguely identified as the Spanish Main. Tituba's behavior in Salem suggests nothing to the contrary, but rather supports these conjectures regarding her ethnic background. Parris's Indian woman was, therefore, no more than thirty years of age in 1692 and possibly as young as twenty-five. She carried with her memories of life in an Arawak village as well as the image of an emergent Creole society in the Barbados of the 1670s.

The Barbados that Tituba would have seen in the seventeenth century did not differ too dramatically from the landscape of South America. It too had a tropical climate and familiar vegetation. The topography, insect life, number of daylight hours, nuances of seasonal change varied little from the mainland. The sudden disappearance of rivers during the early months of the year may have been startling, but once the rainy season started in June, the deep rapid rivers sometimes overflowing their banks offered a challenge to swimming abilities.[53]

The concentration on agricultural pursuits in Barbados also dimly echoed the economy of the Arawaks. The scattered plantation units and small size of the Barbados towns, however, were in sharp contrast with Arawak villages which sometimes contained as many as three thousand persons.[54] More confusing to an Amerindian girl would be the appearance of the population. By the middle of the century slightly less than half the population of about fifty thousand was of darker skinned people from Africa, most of the rest European. Of American Indians, she might see none at first, the numbers were so very small.[55] Thus the human landscape would have presented the most disturbingly different visual quality to Tituba.

By 1679 the island began to undergo a change in its racial composition. The 21,725 Europeans counted that year were now outnumbered by 32,473 Africans, almost all slaves.[56] The number of Indians, who were probably all enslaved, is not known, but by the 1670s could never have been more than 0.2 percent of the total. An early observer noted both their servile status and small numbers: "The Negros and Indians (of which latter there are but few here) they & the[ir] Generation are slaves to their owners to perpetuity."[57] A later 1684 census confirmed a rapidly growing African population that reached 46,204 and, for the first time, a reference to 326 Mulattos. The white population continued to decline and numbered 19,568 people. Only seventy-two Indians could be counted in that 1684 census.[58]

Although Barbados had few rivers of the kind familiar to Guyanese people, it was surrounded by water and one did not have to walk too far to see the ocean. Barbados is a small island of 167 square miles, somewhat pear-shaped—twenty-two miles long on its north-south axis and fourteen miles wide at its widest point in the southern section. By mid-seventeenth century it was the most densely settled area in the English-speaking world. Unlike many other islands of the Caribbean, it is not of volcanic origin; the soil is porous, which makes drainage more effective, and the island was blessed with a good underground supply of drinkable water that would not be as easily polluted by the English habits of waste disposal in nearby rivers. It is located at 13 deg. 10 min. north Latitude. The most easterly of the West Indian land masses, at 59 deg. 30 min. west Longitude, it more properly sits in the Atlantic Ocean than in the Caribbean.[59]

The eastern coast feels the effect of the Atlantic swells and currents; it is too dangerous for use as a landing place for ships or bathing. Population density along that coast was sparse compared to other parts of the island. The south coast was and is more hospitable to shipping and the west coast even more so. Most agricultural pursuits were concentrated in these areas and in the interior of the island.

The main port and city, Bridgetown, developed in the southwest sector of the island, and was protected by spits of land around a navigable inlet called Carlyle Bay (Fig. 5).[60] By 1654 that town had a population of only two thousand. The small metropolis with some three hundred or four hundred houses, many of which were taverns, no doubt provided sustenance for the mariners moving in and out of the port, as well as meeting places for the rural planters. Taverns and households were just beginning to depend on African female labor serving as cooks, nannies, nurses, maids, chaperons, seamstresses, and laundresses. An analysis of the 1680 census indicates that by that time 48 percent of Bridgetown households had no white maids and only 9 percent had no black ones. Black maids, therefore, lived in 90 percent of Bridgetown households.[61] Bridgetown was also the site of government buildings and thus an important social-political center. Standing prominently in the market area, and a warning to the unruly, was a large barred cage, fourteen feet long, used to house runaway servants and slaves. Two other ports, Jamestown

Figure 5: Prospect of Bridgetown by Samuel Copen.

A view of Bridgetown as it looked in 1695. This major city in Barbados is seen from the south across Carlyle Bay. Although painted sometime after 1695, the painting accurately reproduces the buildings, streets, and activity at the end of the seventeenth century and re-creates what Tituba could know of the area. The tall, narrow, gable-roofed houses and some smaller squat houses are tightly clustered on narrow streets. In the background, the hilly interior of the island is dotted with the windmills used to power the sugar-cane processing. Tituba's home would have been close to the right-hand side of the picture, in the far distance where two windmills stand alone. *(Photo courtesy of the Barbados Museum and Historical Society.)*

(now called Holetown) about halfway up the west coast and the larger Speightstown, a few miles further north in the parish of St. Peter, served as landing places for smaller craft and as a convenience for more northerly sugar and tobacco plantations.

As the demographic profile of Tituba's "country" changed from white to predominantly black, so too did the basis of the economy shift. Sugar cultivation was introduced by the 1640s and twenty years later had almost replaced the earlier diversified economy of tobacco, cotton, ginger, and foodstuff production.[62] Sugar planters depended heavily on African slave labor and a declining number of indentured servants in this mono-culture economy. It was in the interior sugar-growing area with its large African population that Tituba would have lived and worked.

Before Samuel Parris's planned return to Massachusetts, Tituba would experience a vastly different world from the one she would find in that northerly colony. She lived in tropical Barbados on a sugar plantation with its peculiar daily and work routines. She had also been subject to a variety of African cultural influences as well as the direct supervision of her English mistress in the big house. Her life would have had a quality far removed from that known to the Arawaks of South America. She, therefore, had to learn to adapt to this new Barbados world, before she was again forced to a third and even more radically different environment in Massachusetts.

Strange New World: An American Indian on a Barbados Plantation

As for the *Indians*, we have but few. and those fetcht from other Countries; some from the neighboaring Ilands, some from the main, which we make slaves: the women who are better vers'd in ordering the Cassavie and making bread, then the Negroes, we imploy for that purpose, as also for making Mobbie.
—Richard Ligon, *A True and Exact History of the Islands of Barbados*

Although enslavement was a common thread in the experience of both Africans and American Indians in Barbados, the texture of life for each group differed in several significant aspects. Indians did not perform the same chores as Africans, nor were they, at first, subject to the same demeaning repudiation of their cultures by the planters. Planter perception of native American abilities in the early years was quite different from the perception of Africans. Because Indian work routines were less demanding physically, they may have been less of a health hazard. On the other hand, because of the very small number on the island, native Americans had fewer possibilities to establish families or to maintain customs that required interaction with others of like background.

In some ways Tituba experienced a sharper break with familiar societies and was more alienated from her cultural roots than most African children. She lived in a society that offered few of the comforts of familiarity except for the geographic setting. Tituba would have recognized the plant and animal life and knew how to convert those raw materials into food and other necessities of life. The Arawak economy depended more on agriculture than fishing and hunting, and the women were responsible for the growth as well as the production of food, particularly the cassava and sweet potatoes.[1] Such Indian domestic skills were encouraged and exploited by the Barbados planters and Tituba would feel more comfortable in the role of cook and domestic drudge than as field worker. Tituba's other memories of how one should conduct one's life, of traditions and values learned from her parents and kin, received scant attention and certainly little encouragement for further development.

There is no evidence that the planters in Barbados made any systematic effort to find and use native American labor for the tobacco or sugar plantations. They assumed, based on the high mortality of Indian workers in Spanish possessions, that the Indians were of little use as field hands. Instead, as Ligon noted in the late 1640s, the small contingent of Amerindian slaves on the island was employed as domestics. Amerindian women, since the appearance of the Arawaks in the 1630s, were respected for their talents as cooks and the men for their skill as fishermen and potential footmen.[2] Nevertheless, they remained only a small part of the labor force.

During the formative years of Barbados society most domestic work was performed by indentured servants. Only after mid-century, as the number of English servants declined, did planters turn to Amerindians as a potential replacement for that household labor. The planters disdained other potential sources; they were dissatisfied with what they considered unruly Irish servants and were, temporarily at least, reluctant to divert Africans from the field.[3] Only American Indians, particularly Arawaks, seemed to offer an acceptable substitute, even though they too were in short supply. Peter Wroth's kidnapping ventures in South America noted in chapter 1 were obviously an attempt to capitalize on that need.

Relations between the planters and the Indians during the first fifty years of the colony were marked by a relatively benign respect for the Indian way of life, particularly as it could contribute to the quality of life for whites in Barbados. During the earliest contacts, even though based on an exploitive master-slave relationship, planters had shown little fear of or dislike of native Americans and, therefore, felt no need for repressive measures.[4] The seventeenth-century Englishman may have perceived Indians as rude, barbarous, uncivil, and savage, but they thought that only a temporary state. Before the violent encounters of the late seventeenth century, native Americans were perceived as capable of ultimately being tamed and turned into copies of Englishmen.[5] Therefore, at first contact with the English in Barbados they were not treated with the same disdain and attempt to degrade as Africans were.

Early on the Barbados planters had actively encouraged the Amerindian slaves in Barbados to retain some elements of cultural identity. Slave owners promoted the establishment of separate communities so that Indians would live apart from Africans in their own quarters on the plantations. At least until 1650, Arawak slaves had maintained customs of dress, food preparation, food production, and other cultural patterns followed in their native habitats with little interference from the English. Ligon's map of the island in the late 1650s (Fig. 6) portrays an Indian named Salymingoe, drawn with a canoe and in the distinctive dress of an Island Carib or Trinidad Arawak.[6] These pictorial representations of cultural artifacts are a recognition of distinctive Amerindian cultures on the island and a respectful acceptance of their customs that was very unlike the continuous brutal treatment of Africans.[7]

By the 1670s, however, English treatment of the Indians began to show marked changes. In fact, the practice of a separate Indian society did not continue beyond the early 1650s.[8] It may not have been a conscious change of heart; conditions on the island mitigated against a permanent separate native American community. From the beginning, segregation had not prevented close contact and early sexual encounters with the other servants and slaves.[9] Those interracial alliances, combined with declining imports, led to the absorption of resident Amerindians and those of mixed genetic heritage into a syncretic, African-dominated, slave society. As the Indian women married and had children, fathered in most cases by African slaves or perhaps by the rapidly declining number of white servants, separate native identities began to disappear.

Plantation owners did nothing to discourage this process of amalgamation. They may well have looked on the integration of Indian and African societies as an asset, as a way to insinuate Indian domestic skills into the larger slave society in the absence of a sufficiently large self-sustaining Indian population. In his investigation of Indian cultural contributions to Barbados society, the anthropologist Jerome Handler con-

Figure 6: Richard Ligon's map of Barbados, ca. 1657. "A topographicall Description and Admeasurement of the Yland of Barbados in the West Indyaes with the Mys. Names of the Seuerall plantacons."

This oldest extant map of Barbados shows the locale of plantations, hills, and roads on the island at mid-century. Typical of the time, the map is oriented for an approach to the island and Carlyle Bay from the sea, in this case from the southwest looking northeast. Neither the scale nor the shape of the island is accurately drawn, but it does illustrate the dense settlements and plantations along the west and south coasts. The Indian presence is acknowledged with a drawing of an Indian man wearing a loincloth and holding a bow. Nearby is Salymingo's 35-foot canoe. Sugar had not yet overtaken the early diversified economy and Ligon noted the presence of cattle, sheep, and swine. The transport of goods from the interior was by donkey and camel tended by both African slaves and European servants. The Africans are wearing loincloths similar to that of the Indian; the indentured white servants are dressed in the European fashion. *(Photo courtesy of the Barbados Museum and Historical Society.)*

cludes that by the beginning of the eighteenth century, "deaths, escapes, miscegenation, and acculturative processes had combined to all-but-eliminate them [Indians] as a distinctive ethnic group."[10]

The process of assimilation had begun much earlier. The numerical decline in the Amerindian population, its dispersed demographic pattern, and the process of absorption into the African slave culture that in all likelihood shaped Tituba's life in Barbados can be traced in the extant seventeenth-century legal records between 1650 and 1680. The Hilliard plantation is one illustration of this development.

On William Hilliard's plantation, which was home to several Indian families, native Americans were merging into the larger slave population as early as the 1650s. Richard Ligon, who lived on Hilliard's plantation from 1647 to 1650, noted at the time the presence of three Indian women with their children in a separate Indian house.[11] But none of the women observed by Ligon was found in the later land sales. In two transactions involving sections of his land, only one Indian girl is mentioned in each deed. The 1654 transaction lists Simy the Indian among the Negro girls; in 1656 the one Indian identified as Syminge is also listed under Negro girls.[12] Although the number and categories of servants and slaves changed over time and the two transactions did not include all of Hilliard's property, it is still surprising that so few American Indians—and no adult Amerindians—are identified in those inventories.[13] Hilliard had either sold them by 1654 or was no longer distinguishing between Negro and Amerindian slaves when inventorying his property except in rare cases.

Hilliard's 1654 deed also includes a woman slave named Simy, but she was not identified as an Amerindian and, because she appears in the middle of the list of slaves, was either an African or one of mixed race background. On the other hand, the girl Simy at the end of the same list is described as an Indian.[14] It may be that Hilliard recognized as discrete groups only newly acquired Amerindian slaves who could contribute native cultural skills and were clearly different in behavior from those born on the plantation. Young Simy then, as an identifiable American Indian, was given the name of an adult female African, or an African-Indian, who may have acted as her substitute mother. Tituba's experience may have been similar. As a solitary young Amerindian, she would have lived with and been nurtured by an African family in a slave society.

In recognition of her slave status, her name, like Simy's, was placed last on a list of Negro girls.

Both Indians noted in the Hilliard inventories were girls, pointing to a preference for recently arrived young female Amerindians. Ligon, significantly, makes no mention of adult male Amerindians on Hilliard's plantation in 1650 but specifically describes the kidnapping of one of the women, named Yarico. She had been tricked into leaving Guiana on the coast of South America then sold by a treacherous English sailor pretending to be in love. He then sold her into slavery in Barbados.[15] Yarico's tale is one of betrayed romance, but her experience illustrates that a demand for American Indian female skills was present even at mid-century. Many other women continued to be captured without the lure of male promises.[16] Peter Wroth's 1674 expedition described in chapter 1, during which he chose to capture eight women and two children rather than boatloads of men, points to the continuing, and possibly exclusive, interest in female Indian slaves.

The fact that there is such a small number of Amerindian men mentioned in Barbados inventories and depositions, and the scattered nature of the Indian presence in those legal records, combined with what is known of Indian slave-catching expeditions suggest that there were, in actuality, few Indian men on the island. Such a gender imbalance could account for the declining number of clearly identifiable Amerindians and the consequent absorption of the succeeding generations into the larger African community.

It is pretty clear that the practice of including Amerindian slaves on the list of Negro slaves was a harbinger of the future. Even though planters expected Indians to retain the passive quality and special talents that made them so attractive as household servants and so different from the overtly rebellious Africans, they also came to expect those domestics to be part of the larger slave society. No attempt was made to nurture a separate Indian society after the 1650s, and by 1676 the possibility of such a development absolutely appalled the planters who now feared any Indian presence. It is unlikely therefore that Tituba would have lived apart from African slaves on her plantation home or have been isolated from African cultural patterns in the Barbados of the 1670s. Her new world was numerically dominated by African slaves, but shaped by the interests and concerns of Europeans who held political and economic power. Severed from her cultural roots, Tituba was subjected to increasing influences from those other cultures, becoming part of the Creole world emerging on the plantations.

This process of amalgamation, adaptation, and cultural syncretism occurred throughout the Americas wherever a variety of cultures met under conditions new to all.[17] Barbados was no exception. The cultural exchange that contributed to the phenomenon of a distinct African-American way of life in Barbados drew its inspiration from the three resident ethnic groups—American Indian, European, and African, with varying degrees of emphasis. But none of these larger groupings represented homogeneous societies. Each one contained within itself varieties of cultural forms, traditions, and behavior patterns. Europeans in Barbados, for instance, included Scots, Irish, Welsh, as well as the dominant English. Indians may have included Arawaks from the islands and the mainland as well as a small number of island Caribs; and Africans revealed even greater diversity, with immigrants from the Senegambia region on the extreme west coast of Africa to the Guinea coast and further south to Angola.[18] Out of this bewildering mixture, some cultural patterns seemed to prevail at different times and in different locales. Why particular traits and behavior patterns appeared to dominate the emerging Creole societies at any one time or in any one place cannot always be explained in terms of numbers of people present.[19] Similarity of traits in the different groups, the early presence of particular individuals with special skills, the volume of African imports at a crucial moment, the nature of work routines, the size of the social units, and the degree of separation from white society all contributed to the African-American Creole culture that shaped Tituba's social world.[20]

The Barbados planters' determination to maintain a psychic, if not physical, distance from their slaves especially influenced the developing religious culture of plantation society, one area of life that no doubt had a major impact on Tituba's mental world.[21] Slave religions early on acquired distinctive syncretic qualities derived from a variety of African forms and possibly American Indian practices. Very little of slave religions was influenced by European religion, and the dominating concept seemed to have been that of Ashanti magical practices that focused on the obeah man or woman.[22]

The seventeenth-century planters, with a few exceptions, had denied slaves access to information on Christianity and barred them from the

Anglican church.[23] Their reasons for doing so are complex. They certainly feared the revolutionary implications of Christian doctrine and were suspicious of missionaries who promoted the radical notion that conversion would make more tractable slaves.[24] But probably of equal importance was the planters' concern to establish a clear psychological distinction between themselves and their slaves. They needed cultural differences to reinforce their sense of superiority and to justify the continued enslavement of non-Europeans. To have admitted slaves into the Anglican community might have required an open recognition of their humanity. Quakers were an exception and when the Friends included their slaves at meetings, they were reprimanded and fined. Under pressure from the non-Quaker planters, the Barbados Assembly declared that Negroes were "wholly incapable of conversion" and officially barred their attendance at church services.[25]

In the absence of Christian instruction or the forced conversions practiced by the Spanish, Barbados slaves followed the religious practices of their own cultures. Although deplored by powerless representatives of the various churches, both African and Indian religious beliefs and ceremonies were tolerated by the English authorities by default. The African slaves were free to borrow ideas from each other, adapting old traditions to new conditions and possibly retaining elements common to all, while incorporating Amerindian beliefs and European rituals as desired.[26]

In Barbados a substantial African population early in its history, and a continuing large importation from Africa during the seventeenth century, produced a variety of African ceremonial practices that alternately puzzled, repelled, and fascinated European observers.[27] One horrified Calvinist visitor in the 1660s, Felix Sporri, condemned slave behavior related to religious rituals he did not understand as "idolatrous ceremonies and customs in honor of their God who is mainly the devil." The ceremonies, he noted, consisted of a series of all-night "dances" with "drumming on a hollow tree trunk over which an animal skin is stretched, making clapping noises by knocking two rocks together, and accompanying this with terrifying shrieks and bodily movements" (Fig. 7).[28] To Sporri the physical aspects of worship—the dancing, the trances, the vigorous body language of the Africans—resembled play more than piety. Like most other Europeans, he did not understand that dancing and physical movement were integral features of African and Indian religious rituals.[29]

Occasionally an Englishman did report on these ceremonies with a

Figure 7: Slaves in Barbados.

Although depicting a period in Barbados history long after Tituba lived there and showing the more acculturated Africans wearing European-style dress, the picture does illustrate the private domestic life of slaves and the kind of physical environment that Tituba would have known in Barbados. The oblong thatched-roof hut was also typical slave housing in the seventeenth century. The one-room interior held very few personal possessions. Beds consisted of wooden platforms with mats rolled out for sleeping. The big house where Tituba learned about English manners was set off some distance from the slave huts. The windmills that powered the sugar production share the landscape with lush vegetation. (*From John Augustine Waller,* A Voyage to the West Indies, *1820. Photo courtesy of the Barbados Museum and Historical Society.*)

more objective eye. One unidentified visitor to the island in the 1650s admitted that although the practices were unfamiliar in that he "could never yet come to know what Religion they are of," yet he observed that before indulging in some "sports, which they have every night," the slaves went to their homes and "mumbled over some prayers." He admitted to being unfamiliar with their concepts of the supernatural: "what they are or to whom directed I cannot tell."[30] Ligon, writing at about the same time in the mid-seventeenth century, also assumed that the rituals were related to a belief in a deity because of motions and gestures when Africans raised their hands and looked up at the sky, in spite of the fact that the slaves were dancing.[31] Thus some Englishmen did grasp the idea that these behaviors were part of a pattern of religious ritual rather than mere revelry.

Thomas Walduck, a military officer stationed in Barbados, associated the slaves' activities with "diabolical Magic." Apparently a witness to many of these events, Walduck provides the most detailed description of slave religious practices. He noted that the ceremonies were led by a man called the "obia." This "obia," he said, functioned as a healing priest and leader of religious rituals, but was also capable of bringing harm. The obeah was known to torment others with pain in their bodies and cause "lameness, madness, loss of speech, loss of the use of all their limbs."[32] The obeah concept "may have developed in a broadly comparable fashion from various supernatural practices and beliefs founded in different African ethnic traditions."[33] It embraced, as Walduck noted, a system that included both socially valuable and anti-social practices. The obeah were people who were assumed to be capable of both curing illness or causing harm through the use of supernatural magical practices.

Walduck observed too that both Amerindians and Africans in Barbados used image magic with such materials as clay, wax, and dust fashioned into a form which they then stuck with a variety of objects to cause pain. Such techniques, he thought, were known only to blacks native to Africa, but Amerindians, he said, used similar "Magick and ways of Divination." The planters, Walduck thought, occasionally participated in these ceremonies.[34]

The similarity of beliefs and techniques in Barbados with learned lore in Europe surprised Thomas Walduck. He marveled that such "simple creatures" as the Indians and Africans he met could have devised these powerful means of destruction. The techniques described by Walduck were also carried to the mainland as the population—African, Indian, and European—moved to the newer colonies, taking with them the techniques of this syncretic culture. In Salem during the 1692 witchhunt, Candy, the African-American slave transported from Barbados, demonstrated occult practices that had "clear African and Afro-American parallels."[35] She showed the Massachusetts investigators a piece of cheese, some grass, and two pieces of cloth tied into knots resembling dolls, claiming they had magical powers. One of the pieces of cloth was knotted in an African fashion. In a demonstration of image magic, Candy set the "puppet" on fire. Some in the audience complained of a burning sensation, blaming it on Candy's magic; they gasped for breath, fearful of drowning when the material was put into water.[36] Candy, not denying any African association with these objects, claimed that such techniques had been taught to her by her white mistress who also came from Barbados.[37] This was no secret ritual practiced only by Africans; many on the island were sharing information about occult techniques all during the century.

The exchange of witchcraft lore among Africans and whites in the West Indies was facilitated by the many similarities between African and European beliefs. Thus in both areas the witch is generally female. She can separate from her body and does so at night to meet in an assembly with other witches flying as an owl or an animal or on a stick of wood. The witch preys on people, sucking the blood or eating the body of her victim. For Africans, any disease may be a sign of the evil one's stratagem. The English blamed witches' actions for inexplicable diseases and deaths.[38] Everywhere in the seventeenth-century world, death, disease, or misfortune could be attributed to supernatural causation.

Walduck's letters written in 1710 described practices that already had a long history in Barbados. The lore of the obeah, a carryover from African rituals, and his Amerindian counterpart, identified by the English as a conjurer, went back at least half a century. The local obeahs in Barbados were sometimes accepted and addressed by that name. In 1676 a slave in St. Michaels Parish was called "Obeah" by a planter in a legal document. A few years later in St. Georges Parish, "Jack Surranam," boatswain, slave, and probably an Amerindian, was described as a "Conjurr."[39] Tituba, therefore, could have been introduced to the healing practices and occult techniques of the obeah by either her white mistress or her slave family or even another Indian. African magico-religious practices were sufficiently widespread to be known by all segments of the population on the island.

Tituba did not have to be genetically African to be familiar with a variety of African magico-religious practices so well-known in Barbados. She may have observed the obeah man or woman manipulate objects meant to kill, cure, or procure someone's love, or, as she testified in Salem, the techniques used to identify the source of misfortune and to uncover a witch.[40] Nor had she necessarily lost all sense of her Amerindian culture, which, even if she did not remember a time among her people, was kept alive by two almost contradictory impulses—the indifference of the planters to the slaves' religious and cultural interests and their concern to preserve Indian domestic skills which meant encouraging the retention of some tribal knowledge.

Transition to an African-Barbados society was somewhat eased for Tituba by the similarity between some African cultural features and those of American Indians. The African association of music and dance with religious ceremonies, the use of drums and other beating instruments, the nighttime occurrence of these rituals with many engaging in social interaction, all would have resonated with familiarity even if the peculiarities of musical rhythm and body language differed.[41] She would have found companions for bathing, a daily routine among the Arawaks, who were in the habit of going into water several times a day. Africans also took advantage of the few ponds and the seasonal flow of the rivers on the island to wash regularly by immersing their entire bodies in the water. They too were observed to be good swimmers.[42] Hammocks, baskets, cooking utensils, mortars for grinding corn borrowed from Indian crafts were already ubiquitous on the island, although gradually undergoing changes shaped by African skills.[43] Clothing too was similar. Slaves, whether African or Amerindian, wore few clothes compared to the Europeans. African adults, both men and women, wore loincloths reminiscent of the covering used by the Indians of South America.[44]

Both groups believed that sickness and misfortune were brought by supernatural forces and could be cured by magical means; religious ritual was closely associated with medical practice. Native Americans and Africans shared a belief in a curing ceremony that often included the seeming extraction of a foreign substance such as a stick or stone from the body.[45] The Arawak shaman might have sucked out the disease and produced a stone to prove the effectiveness of his healing power; the obeah had other means of "extracting" an offending object from the ailing body to heal it. The form of the cure differed but the function would have been familiar. One wonders if Tituba or some other Indian of her time might have instructed an obeah about the practices of the piaiman regarding insect poisons unique to America and thus subtly help shape the African treatment of illness along the lines of her tribe. Africans, for instance, probably learned from some unidentified American Indian how to extract the egg sacs of the deadly chigger that embedded itself in human skin.[46]

Tituba's daily life would, no doubt, have brought her into close contact with the other slaves on the plantation. She would have lived in one of the slave houses, little oblong huts lined up in a row and built of sticks and sugar cane trash. Inside, the meager furnishings included mats for sleeping, a pot for cooking, and eating implements of calabash gourds cut open (see Fig. 7).[47] Emotional satisfaction and socialization to her new world would have come through that African slave community. In both African and American Indian societies, kinship defined one's place in the world. With those links dissolved by the forced migration across the water, new bonds were created on the plantations.[48] Deprived of her own family in South America, Tituba may have been adopted and nurtured by an African family that introduced her to the routines of plantation life and helped her to forge new kinship links to replace the bonds broken by her captivity.

The Barbados planters had no objection to the development of slave family life, as long as it did not interfere with the work schedule. They often recognized the desires of their human property to establish intimate family relations. In the seventeenth century, planters were tolerant of the African system of polygamy and some of the African men may have had several wives, although monogamy was probably more common.[49] Ligon explained the importation of a large number of African women as a response to the desire of the men to continue polygamous practices.[50] It is more likely that planters had economic reasons for wanting female slaves. They found the women easier to handle as well as cheaper to purchase and, since some African women were already inured to agricultural labor in Africa, they could adapt to the demands of tobacco and sugar culture in Barbados.[51] Whatever the reason, the presence of a large number of African women meant that children and slave family life became a possibility early in Barbados history, in spite of a continuing high mortality rate.

By the beginning of the eighteenth century there was a fairly equal number of male and female slaves in Barbados, with the females slightly outnumbering the males. On Tattuba's plantation in St. Thomas the females of all ages outnumbered the males. By the end of 1679 there were twenty-six men and thirty-six women, eight boys and twelve girls in the labor force.[52] The number of women on the Thompson plantation had gradually increased over the years, even though more male slaves were purchased than females. Women obviously had some advantage over men in spite of the dangers of pregnancy and childbirth.[53] They managed to endure the hazards of disease and accident far better than their male counterparts, especially where Tattuba lived and worked in the interior of the Island.

The Barbados records provide some evidence of early family formation and suggest what kind of family life an Indian slave would have experienced. Naming patterns and inventory groupings indicate that these slave families in Barbados were usually monogamous and often patrilineal.[54] As early as 1654, a Catholic priest arriving in Barbados from Surinam noted the sale of a plantation that included three African men "each of whom had his wife and child."[55] In many of the existing deeds and wills, slaves are grouped together as nuclear families. In spite of several seventeenth- and eighteenth-century comments about polygamous practices, the slave families in those extant records of the second half of the century seemed to have followed the European practice of monogamy. When John Jemmott of St. Peters Parish died, his inventory listed almost all his slaves as married couples with children. Sampson and Hannah, his wife, are listed along with their three children. Samboe and his wife Aconah and their two children were another family. There was also Black Tom and his wife Oboe and their two children; and "great Bess otherwise called Acoe" who had no resident husband but did have a daughter.[56]

So too Richard Howell inventoried his plantation and many of the slaves are listed as nuclear families. One couple called Tom and Mary had four children named Betty, Mary, Mingo, and Tom. All the other children in this inventory are identified by the name of at least one parent, sometimes the father and sometimes the mother. Quite possibly one parent had died; more likely he or she lived on a neighboring plantation and therefore did not appear in the Howell inventory. Another Tom on Howell's land was listed as Judge's boy, meaning his son, and Samson was Rose's boy. The absence of a parent was also noted. Howell indicated that Sambo's parents had died.[57] On another plantation, purchased by Timothy Thornhill from Andrew Afflick in St. James, almost all the slaves were listed as part of nuclear families: Orgator's Maria and three children, Peter and Maria with one child, Bally and her child Dick, Robin and his wife and three children.[58]

Godwyn's 1680 statement regarding the "barbarous" African manners in practicing polygamy is often used as evidence that such was the custom in Barbados. But Godwyn, like Ligon, probably exaggerated the extent of the practice of polygamy to support his arguments for the need for instruction and baptism of slaves. Later in the century a French cleric repeated the condemnation of the planters who refused to promote Christian practices among the slaves. He too pointed to the practice of polygamy as evidence of the lack of Christian instruction.[59] That some slaves had several wives and that planters looked upon such liaisons as a means of breeding a labor force, as Ligon suggested, is quite possible. Indications of a polygamous family structure appear in the pattern of runaways in the eighteenth century.[60] Thus both polygamy and monogamy, like Christianity and traditional African/Indian religious practice, could exist side by side in seventeenth-century Barbados society.

Regardless of which system predominated, planters especially recognized the importance of mothers in the lives of their young children. When Timothy Thornhill leased a plantation in St. Peters to George Harst, he noted that there were fifteen very young children living there "both unfit for work and also unfit to be taken from their parents."[61] Invariably on these lists, very young children, certainly all the children still nursing, were identified by their mothers' names. Sometimes the babies were merely identified as a particular woman's child. As on the Thompson plantation, those infants had no individual names as yet.[62]

The strong bond between mother and child was recognized by planters. Hans Sloan, visiting the English-speaking islands early in the eighteenth century, remarked on the love slave parents had for their children and that in Jamaica no master dared separate them too early.[63] There was a line of degradation and inhumanity beyond which no master dared cross in the seventeenth-century English Caribbean world.

Occasionally the inventory listing individual children added the father's name as an identifying family name, according the African family a patrilineal quality. On the Hawley plantation in St. Michaels, Ogu and Jane Mannuell were the children of Mannuell; and young Mingo Pharrock was the son of Mingo Pharrock. So too the small boy Mingo Cormante was the son of another Mingo Cormante.[64] George Payne also noted family associations in his inventory. He owned Tom Pawpaw and his son Harry Pawpaw; Jackoe and his daughter Mariah Jackoe; and Tony and his son Dickie Tony.[65] It is possible, however, that these were polygamous families. The wives and mothers are not noted and, therefore, the family line was associated with the father.

Not all inventories identify family groups as clearly as the above illustrations. Sometimes the use of just first names can supply a clue to family formation. When children were called by the parents' given names

they can sometimes by identified by a same sex diminutive   as young
Mingo, Little Bessie, and little Jug or Little Moll or Peg Little.[66] Plantation owners recognized and accepted the association of children with at
least one parent.

Indian slaves, however, are seldom noted in family groups because
there were probably too few on any one plantation. John Stewart owned
one Indian named Jack.[67] He was not associated with any women or
children on the plantation. When Peter Wroth sold some slaves to John
Kellicott in 1670, he included one Indian woman called Semo.[68] When
William Pettye sold his plantation in St. James to John Reid, he included
only one unnamed Indian.[69] There was also one unidentified Indian on
William Baldwin's land and another on Peter Hancock's plantation.[70] On
Hilliard's plantation was the Indian girl named Simy but no others.[71]
There are only occasional references to Indian couples: Jack and Mary in
1679 on Thomas Sturt's land, for instance.[72]

On Samuel Thompson's plantation where Tattuba lived there are too few
clues to family arrangements even for the more numerous Africans (see
Fig. 3). Similarity of names helps to connect some of the children to a
parent of the same sex. Young Garaway was probably the son of Garra-
way, as little Mott was Mott's son. Both Kate's child and Grundy had
infants. Young Grundy, another one of Grundy's children, was listed
with the pickannies and thus was between four and nine years old, as was
young Tamas, the child of Tamas. Old Bess, Long Bess, and Little Bess
may have been related, as were the adults Kate and young Kate. The
only woman on the plantation who could be associated with a particular
man is Minnah Sambo. She was either the daughter or wife of Sambo.[73]

Of particular curiosity on the list of children is the name "young y
John." There is no adult called John on the plantation and, therefore, no
ostensible reason for the qualifying word, young. The extra "y" in one
version of the inventory is especially tantalizing. The second list refers to
him only as young John. Is it possible that this is Indian John and that
the "y" was intended to signify his ethnic background as an American
Indian? Additional research on symbols used in the inventories may
provide evidence to support this view. In light of present knowledge, it
will have to remain a mystery.

Tattuba's distinctive name appears at the end of the list of boys and
girls and just before the pickannies and suckling children. Her name, like
young y John's, cannot be connected to anyone else on the plantation.

No adults have a similar name, nor do any other children. Similarity of names makes it possible to link African slaves to their kin; Tattuba's unusual name with its Indian origins prevents such a linkage. We cannot know whose household was her home or which adults offered her sustenance. The only conclusion possible is that, since there were no identifiable adult Indians on the Thompson plantation, Tattuba, as with the other slave children during their earliest years, was probably adopted and through her years as a "pickannie" or young child had lived with one of the African families.[74]

Because she is listed among the boys and girls, Tattuba was probably between nine and fourteen years of age at the time of the first inventory taken in 1676. Even if she had lived in a family group before that time, by the age of nine she would no longer be under the continual care of an adult slave. Mothers lost control over the socialization of their children by the time the young ones reached nine and often earlier. By the age of five children were already part of the economic unit. They were in the first work group—the pickannie gang—and by nine or ten were expected to contribute fully to crop time production.[75]

Once she was old enough to participate in the labor force, Tituba's life would differ radically from the experience of African youngsters. Unlike other children of her age, she would be spared the arduous work in the fields. As an American Indian, she would be more valuable in the plantation house where she worked under the direct supervision of the white mistress. On Tattuba's plantation that mistress was Elizabeth Pearsehouse, the mother of Samuel Thompson. Samuel had just passed his twenty-first birthday in 1676 but never married. He died early in 1680, leaving neither a widow nor children.[76] His mother, the only other white presence on the plantation, would have been the mistress of his house, the supervisor of the household slaves, and Tattuba's main source of information about English habits and behavior.

During the years of Samuel's tenure, the labor force on the plantation had increased to at least eighty-eight slaves. The death of at least three slaves listed in the 1676 transactions was more than balanced by the purchase of another twelve men and eight women and the maturing of several small children by 1679. Only two babies had been born and were still alive after three years.[77] There were now only twenty children of working age, and Tattuba had probably moved into the adult category and was busy learning about English household ways.

An Indian slave may have spent her sleeping and few leisure hours with the other slaves, but by day she came in close contact with English society in the big house. The widow Pearsehouse instructed her in the Anglican beliefs, since Indians in the seventeenth century, unlike Africans, were considered worthy of an education about European society.[78] She certainly learned to speak English under the tutelage of her white mistress, and Elizabeth Pearsehouse may also have introduced her to English witchcraft practices, supplementing the traditions of the slave society. Tituba claimed that she had learned how to identify and protect herself from witches by using techniques taught to her by her white mistress in Barbados.[79] That mistress, of course, was Elizabeth Reid Thompson Lane Pearsehouse, the three-time widow and now dependent of her eldest son, but also the daughter of the respected St. James planter and court clerk John Reid.[80]

Tituba's duties in the Thompson household may also have extended to satisfying the sexual needs of the young master, Samuel. The housekeeper-concubine was not unusual in Barbados where slave owners commonly and openly kept black mistresses. In a society where the law did not recognize the rape of a slave as a crime, those who hired or owned female workers often expected sexual favors.[81] And Samuel Thompson was in his twenties and unmarried. A young, female household servant without the protection of law or custom was easy prey for any sexual advances he chose to make.

The Thompson sugar plantation in the eastern part of St. Thomas Parish (Fig. 8) consisted of some three hundred or possibly more acres by the mid-1670s, jointly occupied by the youthful Samuel Thompson and his mother. Until her eldest son Samuel reached legal age in 1676, the St. Thomas acreage was under the legal control of her brother-in-law Robert Thompson.[82] As soon as he could, Samuel took charge of the plantation with its sixty-nine working slaves. The eighteen adult men and thirty-two adult women were barely enough to handle the sugar production, household chores, and child care. That adult labor force was aided by the nineteen children considered fit for less arduous labor. Two infants and two very young children called pickannies completed the enslaved residents on the plantation, making a total of seventy-five people including the two white owners living on the three hundred acres. There were no white indentured servants at the time.[83]

But Samuel was not well and the slaves might have realistically feared that with his death and that of his aging mother, there could be little

Figure 8: Barbados Parish boundaries.

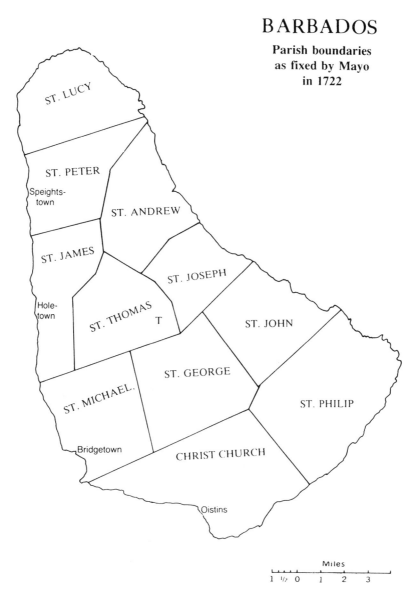

BARBADOS

**Parish boundaries
as fixed by Mayo
in 1722**

ST. LUCY

ST. PETER

Speights-
town

ST. ANDREW

ST. JAMES

ST. JOSEPH

Hole-
town

ST. THOMAS   T

ST. JOHN

ST. GEORGE

ST. MICHAEL

ST. PHILIP

Bridgetown

CHRIST CHURCH

Oistins

Miles

1 ½ 0   1   2   3

The Thompson-Prideaux plantation is located in St. Thomas Parish. Its location is indicated by a "T." *Adapted from a map in P. F. Campbell,* Some Early Barbados History *(St.
Michael, Barbados: Caribbean Graphics & Letchworth, 1993).*

security for the future. Samuel attempted to provide some measure of stability for his mother by establishing special conditions for a leasehold of half of their inheritance in St. Thomas. He gave it to his friend, Nicholas Prideaux, a leading merchant in Bridgetown, with the stipulation that Pearsehouse be supported by the rental income.[84] The arrangement might also keep the plantation families intact. The slaves could only hope that they would not be sold off to pay Samuel's debts after his death.

Samuel lived for several years after those 1676 arrangements and he probably began courting Prideaux's daughter Ann during that time. Thus marriage and a continuation of the family line may have improved the gloomy atmosphere of 1676. By the summer of 1679 Prideaux and his wife Elizabeth were getting on in years too and he thought it prudent to turn some of the property over to another planter, John Hothersall, a move that would keep the land within the family.[85] Thus in these complicated land transactions some attempt was made to maintain the land and slaves as a unit. Thompson's poor health and preparation for death by the fall of 1679 would undermine that stability.

In the meantime life in the big house educated Tattuba on the intricacies of English styles and standards of decoration, food, drink, and clothing, qualities that served to distinguish the white planter class from the mostly non-white servile population of the island.[86] It is very likely that Tattuba was forced to wear European-style clothes, to conform to the outward trappings of the English ideal of proper servants. She would have to give up the traditional apron that covered only her genital area and instead cover breasts, trunk, and legs with layers of clothing: smock, petticoat, and waistcoat and cover her head with a coif or cap and wear shoes.[87] Such attributes of English civility no doubt served to set her apart and above the field labor and to help the planters maintain the appearance of the English hierarchical system. Some planters even required that servants wear English livery.[88] But the clothing could also serve as a camouflage, a protective coloration for Indians who could then appear as white.[89] To what extent this mimicry of English ways also obliterated her Indian identity would be evident in Salem.

An Indian slave's daily work was devoted to household chores, most likely in the preparation of food. From the time that the Arawaks had first appeared in Barbados, the planters and their wives had developed a taste for American Indian food and drink and assumed that the Arawak women were especially talented in that particular domestic chore. Even though they preferred European bread and beer, they could not grow wheat and barley in the Caribbean. Trade with the North American colonies and England and Ireland brought those precious edibles to Barbados, but the supply was not always dependable. Distance and sailing conditions could mean that grains and other European food arrived moldy and rancid. The hazards of shipping and the vicissitudes of warfare could and did interrupt that trade. As a substitute for wheat they could eat bread made from local cassava or corn. The Indians had learned to extract the poisonous juice from the cassava roots, which they then grated and baked into cakes.[90] It was a process that Tituba knew from South America and was an expected skill of Arawak women.

For the same reasons that they preferred European grains and meats, the planters also craved the drinks of the old world—Madeira from the Portuguese wine islands and claret from France. The more affluent could afford to purchase the expensive imported wines as well as cider from England. But they also drank fermented drinks made of local products. One such concoction called perino by the English was made of cassava root. Arawak Indians called it *paiwari* and prepared the drink by first chewing the root and then putting the residue into water to ferment for several hours. Ligon described the resulting brew as somewhat like English beer that would "keep for months in a barrel." The more popular and more potent Indian drink was "mobbie," made of sweet potatoes which Ligon compared to wine. Tattuba, who would have known the drink as *casiri*, could have made the mobbie (from the Carib word for sweet potato, *ma bi*)[91] from red-skinned potatoes, producing a red-colored drink that to the English resembled French claret. When made from white-skinned sweet potatoes, the result was a white wine-like drink.[92]

Although planters much preferred imported food, many of the local fruits and root plants, familiar in some cases to both Africans and Indians, eventually became staples of the table. Oranges, lemons, limes, watermelons, muskmelons, guavas, papayas, mangos, pineapples, and cassava dishes would be served along with salt beef, pork, and wheat products from England and North America.[93] Indian techniques of preparation continued to be valued, even though by the end of the seventeenth century it had become difficult to distinguish between African and American influences on the local diet. The ubiquitous pepper pot stew, for instance, which is still a popular dish, resembles both African and Indian stewed meat and vegetables.[94]

When Samuel Parris arrived in Barbados—a young bachelor in his early twenties—and set up his living quarters in Bridgetown, he would have wanted an experienced housewoman to cook, wash his clothes, keep his house in order, and tend to the needs of his apprentice. He found that English female servants were scarce. Until the 1670s, Africans were given few opportunities to learn the necessary skills in "an ideology of white supremacy," that separated the roles of white and black female labor and relegated blacks to mind-numbing field work.[95] The possibility of purchasing an Amerindian girl who had probably served as a maid in a big house, was familiar with the local foodways, dressed and spoke in the English manner, and was considered amenable to Christian education, was not to be ignored. Her availability as a sex partner could also enter into his decision. The price may have provided an additional incentive to Parris, as Indians cost less than Africans.[96] Indian slaves may have been considered superior for domestic duties, but, because they could not be put to work in the fields to cultivate sugar, their market value was below that of Africans of comparable age. The opportunity to acquire such a house slave came some time in 1679.

By the summer of 1679 Samuel Thompson's illness became more threatening and he prepared to die by completing the arrangements for his mother's upkeep. By October he had divested himself of all his landed property. He prepared his will in November of 1679, leaving most of his other property to a variety of female relatives.[97] He had not married and had no children to inherit his valuables. His mother was provided for in the many leases and arrangements made with his friends Prideaux and Anthony Lane.

In spite of Thompson's careful attention to maintaining the plantation intact for his mother's support, as his death approached he began to pay off his debts and disperse the labor force through manumission and gift. He decided to free a slave named Jack, probably his valet, to whom he also gave both land and money. To his "loving friend Nicholas and his daughter Ann" he gave as a gift, or as payment for a debt, another slave named Gregory, probably also a house servant.[98]

Thompson's deathbed move to break up the plantation labor force may have encouraged Prideaux or his partner in this plantation venture, John Hothersall, to sell more of the slaves, particularly those they considered superfluous or dangerous. The household staff may have been the first to feel these changes. Tattuba, not only a part of the household but also identified with a feared ethnic group, was earmarked for such a sale. A likely customer would be someone leaving the island and willing to remove an Arawak from Barbados to a more distant land. Thus the Indian girl, formerly a welcome addition to the Thompson plantation, was now rejected. She would be uprooted once again. Parris's plans to return to Massachusetts at about the time that Samuel Thompson was dying would have given his fellow merchant, Nicholas Prideaux, sufficient reason to part with the Indian girl.

On the other hand, it is possible that Samuel Thompson had inherited a debt due to Samuel Parris's father and Tituba was sold to discharge that obligation. The younger Parris, after all, had returned to Barbados to settle his late father's affairs and to collect debts due the estate. He had proceeded to do so shortly after returning to the island. Although there are no extant records of a business transaction between the Thompsons or Prideaux and the Parrises, the transfer of slaves or servants from one person to another is suggestive of just such an agreement. Once those debts had been collected, Parris could retire to Massachusetts ready to capitalize on his inheritance and continue to enjoy the services of a female slave.

There are then several possible explanations for why Tituba moved from the Thompson plantation to the household of Samuel Parris. None can be proven conclusively, but the very multiplicity of possibilities strengthens the likelihood of such a scenario.

Assuming that the transfer of Tituba, as the name came to be spelled in Massachusetts, was completed sometime in 1679, she would have been between twelve and seventeen years old when she entered Samuel Parris's household—old enough and strong enough to handle most household chores and most likely an experienced concubine. Whether she found Parris attractive and was willing to satisfy his sexual needs or if she dreaded her new role in his household can only be surmised. She came from a South American society in which chastity was not valued and girls were occasionally given to men to pay off debts.[99] If she had previously satisfied Samuel Thompson's sexual urges, his death would have ended that relationship and her transfer to the control of another man meant a continuation at least temporarily of that exploitation. Parris's decision to go to Massachusetts and their residence in a much more restrictive sexual climate would finally end those demands. Instead, Parris would find a husband for her and a wife for himself in order to comply with the sexual mores of Puritan-dominated Massachusetts.

If Tituba had not yet received instruction in Christianity, it most likely would have been started once she entered Parris's household. He did not teach her to write. He may have taught her to read. The events in Salem in 1692 indicated that Tituba recognized the significance of books and had a minimal ability to read or at least recognize names.

Parris, fulfilling the Barbadian planters' expectation, did not stay in Barbados for long after acquiring his Amerindian slaves. By the end of 1680 he, Tituba, and possibly Indian John, had arrived in Boston, Massachusetts. Tituba's life was about to take a dramatically different turn as she faced an even stranger new world in the Puritan Bay colony.

Massachusetts

Figure 9: Chart of Boston, ca. 1700.

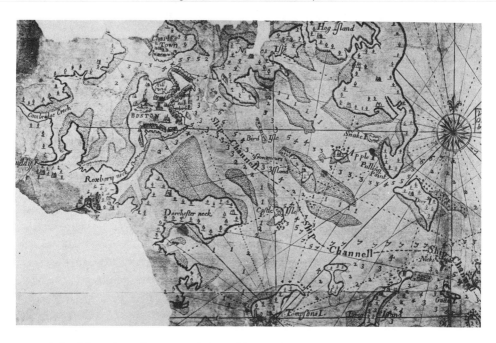

A detail from the earliest engraved chart of Boston Harbor, offering a view of the land and buildings as seen when approaching from the ocean. Such a sight would have greeted Tituba when approaching Boston Harbor during the winter of 1680. The crowded appearance of the tall narrow houses and long warehouses was not too different from that of Bridgetown. *(Courtesy, Boston Public Library.)*

CHAPTER FOUR

An Incomplete Transformation:
A Tawny Puritan

. . . imprudent zeal in the magistrates of Boston to
Christianize those heathen before they were civilized
and injoining them the strict observation of their lawes,
which to a people so rude and licentious, hath proved
even intollerable.

> —Edward Randolph, "Report on the Indians in
> Massachusetts, 1676"

As the vessel from Barbados approached Boston Harbor late in 1680, Tituba could have seen the low buildings at the wharves and the hustle and bustle of a busy port (see Fig. 9). Some forty-five hundred people lived within the boundaries of this most important international market center in New England. Ships plying the Atlantic trade entered the harbor carrying goods and human cargo—paying passengers, servants, and slaves—from the West Indies, Africa, Southern Europe, and the British Isles. The accents of the seamen, the sounds of ships unloading, and the smells would not have been too different from those of Bridgetown. Parts of the town itself resembled the chief Barbados port, with its many small, low-roofed wooden houses interspersed with taller, narrow buildings clustered tightly together on narrow, mostly muddy, streets.[1] In Barbados that architectural style was inappropriate for the climate—the low roofs and small window openings retaining heat and preventing the movement of air. But in the cooler climate of New England, residents were grateful for the warmth of such close quarters.

The cold of the New England winter could be a shock to those

65

coming from the Caribbean. Arrival at that time of the year was surely uncomfortable for anyone who had rarely if ever experienced temperatures below fifty degrees Fahrenheit. The many layers of clothes on Tituba's back and the covering of her head and legs would have been appreciated for the first time. And the winter of 1680–81 was an especially cold one, further adding to her discomfort. The harbor iced over. Residents complained of the many snowstorms and the "constant continuance of cold weather," that made living and travel conditions worse than during any winter in recent memory.[2] Tituba must have longed for the familiar humid heat of the tropical islands and felt despair at the short, dark days of the Massachusettes winter. By the beginning of the next year she may have had even more reason to suffer wrenching homesickness for a tropical landscape when news was heard of Captain Samuel Legg's plans to sail to Barbados in February of 1681.[3] But a slave had no choice in this matter. She could not return to Barbados. Parris had decided to move to Boston and this was to be her home as long as he wished to keep her there. A major adjustment on her part was absolutely essential for survival.

As Tituba looked over her immediate environment, a closer inspection of the dock area revealed a number of brick warehouses and nearby some substantial brick and stone houses, all newly constructed. Beyond was a major highway paved with stone and dotted with the larger stone and brick homes of the merchants. Behind those houses, Tituba learned, lay well-planned gardens and orchards.[4] That vista was in sharp contrast to the untidy and impermanent look of Bridgetown's commercial center.

Tituba and Samuel Parris saw a new and more elegant Boston than Parris had known before he left for Barbados. A disastrous fire in August of 1679 had destroyed many wooden warehouses and shops in Boston, several ships at the dock, and some eighty homes. It was the most recent of several fires that plagued the city during the seventeenth century when wood was the material of choice. After the fire of 1679, the Massachusetts General Court ordered that, in the future, new buildings were to be built of brick or stone. Not all residents could afford to comply with those regulations, but many did and the more elegant newly constructed shops and warehouses that Tituba saw, added to the scene of the larger merchant homes, gave the city a more substantial and settled appearance than Bridgetown in Barbados.[5] It was an awesome sight and a harbinger of the future experiences Tituba could expect (see Fig. 10).

In her observation of the people on the docks, Tituba would have

Figure 10: A detail from "A Southeast view of the Great Town of Boston in New England in America," ca. 1730.

From a print sculpted by I. Carwitham of Boston early in the eighteenth century. Neither ship design nor architecture changed between Tituba's time and 1730. The crowded houses and narrow streets, the warehouses and churches, the many ships under sail all give an impression of motion and commercial activity that would have been reminiscent of Bridgetown but on a much larger scale. Boston was Tituba's home for about eight years (1680–88) before Parris took her to Salem with his family. *(Courtesy, American Antiquarian Society.)*

noticed that the workers did resemble the interracial labor force in Bridgetown—white and black shared the chores of seamen, ordinary laborers, coopers, caulkers, and rope makers; but unlike Barbados, the African faces were very much outnumbered by the white workers. Only 3 percent of the Boston population was African in 1690; the proportion was somewhat, but not much, less at Tituba's arrival in 1680.[6] Although in all occupations black faces appeared in smaller numbers than they did in Barbados, their roles would not have differed considerably in the two cities. Some Africans held responsible jobs in Boston as supervisors of businesses. The manager of Roger Darby's warehouse, destroyed in the great fire of the previous year, had been a hired slave called Mingo.[7] The black presence may not have been as dominant as in Bridgetown, but it was a visible reality in that northern city. By 1687 a visitor could comment on the scarcity of white labor and the ubiquitous presence of Africans so that "not a house in Boston; however small may be its Means, . . . has not one or two" African workers.[8]

Of Indians, Tituba would see even fewer than she did of Africans. Native Americans were no more welcome in Massachusetts than they were in Barbados after 1676. Bostonians, like other New Englanders, feared the proximity of this newly acknowledged threat to the very existence of the colony. Memories of King Philip's War, just four years past, lingered in the memory of all. That conflict, which had dramatically altered even the most innocuous and naive perceptions of native Americans, resulted in "an intense hatred and suspicion of all Indians."[9] Only a few hundred would live within the Massachusetts English communities as servants or tenant farmers, and those few had only a meager interaction with whites outside of their immediate households.[10]

Soon after Parris arrived in New England with his Indian servants, an Irish woman was found dead and scalped in Boston. Indians were implicated in the crime and Samuel Sewall reported that the incident set off "Great Rumours and Fears of trouble with the Indians." Men began to carry weapons with them when going to the church. In January an Indian broke into a Braintree, Massachusetts, house and the owner justified his shooting and killing of the burglar by comparing him to a dog.[11]

The horrors of the 1675–76 warfare that led to the death of thousands of the English settlers, nearly a tenth of the adult population, and perhaps twice that number of Indians, forever ended the schemes of Puritans to "civilize" and Christianize the native population. Edward Randolph blamed the uprising of 1675 on the "impudent zeal" of the Boston leaders to convert the Indians to Christianity.[12] John Eliot's "praying villages," originally envisioned as the vanguard of evangelical work among the Indians in the 1640s, became, by 1680, nothing more than reservations of Indians struggling to maintain some vestige of tribal cohesion. The warring Indians who survived the crisis of 1676 were shipped out to the Caribbean and the Mediterranean to be sold into slavery. Children and the less threatening remnants of the tribes were committed to servitude in New England; some found a meager livelihood as tenant farmers. Those clinging to tribal connections were confined to praying towns under the supervision of the English.[13]

Whatever goodwill some Puritans may have felt toward Indians before 1675 evaporated in those bloody encounters. In 1677, the General Court ordered that no one in the colony was to buy or keep any Indian men or women above the age of twelve because they "causeth much trouble and fear to the Inhabitants where they reside," and could be a danger to the town.[14] As the level of hostility intensified in Massachusetts, the mere presence of an Indian suspected of a crime could touch off a riot. Indians had no assurance of physical safety within a Puritan community. In Marblehead in 1677 two Indian prisoners accused of stealing a fishing vessel were assaulted by a crowd. The women of the town inflicted a cruel revenge that mimicked the Indian methods of torture:

> the whole town flocked about them, beginning first to insult them and soon after, the women surrounded them. . . . Then with stones, billets of wood, and what else they might, they made an end of these Indians . . . we found them with their heads off and gone, and their flesh in a manner pulled from their bones.[15]

Little of that enmity would be immediately apparent to Tituba when she arrived in Boston during that winter of 1680–81. Her status as a servant provided sufficient protection from any overt acts of hostility. Colonists were accustomed to Indians as house servants whose behavior could be closely monitored. She, as a individual, would not be perceived as a threat to the community because she was already enslaved, had no local tribal connections, was subject to the supervision of an Englishman, and, equally as important, was a woman. The few Indians she would meet would all be indentured to white masters or enslaved like her. They did not arouse the same fear as tribal Indians or free persons who could act independently.[16] Her presence, therefore, would go unnoticed until circumstances and her love for Betty Parris forced her to participate in a ritual that thrust her into a completely new and fearful role.

Local customs and regulations in Puritan New England reinforced and rewarded those accomplished in the expected deferential behavior that

Tituba had learned in Barbados. Transported so far from her roots in the tropical Caribbean and lacking any other supportive social institutions, she did not question, and probably welcomed, the protective invisibility granted by her gender and servant status.[17] She spoke English, dressed in the European manner, and behaved with the correct deference expected of a servant and a woman. She could only hope to make herself inconspicuous by her continued imitation of the deportment and dress of an English bound servant.

Once settled in her new home, Tituba would find that law and tradition gave her greater protections of her civil rights and left her less vulnerable to the arbitrary will of her master than in Barbados. Very few Indians in Massachusetts were actual slaves, but the law did not distinguish between ethnic groups, nor was the treatment of servant and slave much different. The enslaved person in Massachusetts was either a black person from Africa or the West Indies, or an Indian captured during warfare in America. Tituba, as an American Indian from the Caribbean, was an unusual sight, but her status was defined by the same laws and obligations imposed on all other servile men and women. Moreover, whether African, Indian, or white; whether legally a slave (that is bound for life), an indentured white servant with a stipulated number of years of service, or a wage laborer, all such bondsmen and women were considered a part of a family and subject to a more general set of laws and obligations to the head of the household and the community.[18]

Enslavement was well known to the Massachusetts Puritans by 1680.[19] The first slave documented in New England was in 1637 when, after the Pequot War of 1637, captured Indian men were sold into slavery in the West Indies and the women and children enslaved in New England. The following year the first African slaves were brought to Massachusetts from the Tortugas in the West Indies. The seventeenth-century slave laws in Massachusetts applied equally to African and Indian: in 1641 slavery, defined as perpetual servitude, was legalized; in 1662 new laws allowed the child of a slave women to follow the condition of the mother rather than following the common law practice of the father's status; laws first requiring military service and then prohibiting military training of slaves applied to both black and "tawny" men. Special laws applied to slaves, regardless of color, established penalties for running away, drunkenness, theft, destruction of public property, and assault on a white person.

In spite of this legal discrimination, the law provided the same procedural protection for slaves as for free persons, although subtle distinctions in actual treatment reminded Africans and Indians that they were not English. In criminal cases a grand jury presentment preceded imprisonment for all, regardless of class or social status. Conditions in the jails were usually the same for both the free and the unfree. Although slaves and servants did not appear on juries, they did participate fully as witnesses in trials. There were no legal restrictions on the testimony of Indians, slave or free, and thus, as Tituba's experience demonstrated in 1692, she could bear witness against whites and her testimony, theoretically, had the same force as that of free persons.[20]

Stories of the treatment of Indians in court were probably common gossip in town among the servants and within the Indian community. Free Indians did sometimes sit on juries involving other native Americans. When the miscreant Joseph Indian of Martha's Vineyard was accused of murdering his wife, "a squaw," in Boston in February of 1685, half of the jury were Indians and the others Englishmen. If Tituba heard the details about his trial and the evidence presented, she would know that Indians took part in the court procedure. Joseph did not speak or understand English well enough and an Indian interpreter stood by ready to translate for him. In spite of the evidence that Joseph had killed his wife by beating her on the head, dragging her through the streets, and then abandoning the badly battered woman, the jury found him guilty not of murder, but of "unnaturalnes and barbarous Cruelty towards his wife." The court, believing that Indian custom condoned wife-beating, refused to condemn Joseph for a capital crime. He was sentenced instead to thirty stripes and told to pay forty shillings or face being sold into servitude.[21]

Indians and whites usually received similar punishments for the same crimes, but occasionally whites were fined and Indians subjected to more severe physical punishment.[22] When Jonas and Abraham Indian were convicted of stealing a hog and cider in October of 1675, they were each whipped with thirty stripes and had to compensate the owners for their loss in the amount of fifty-four shillings for the hog and twelve shillings for the cider. The same court also sentenced a group of white men who stole two sheep to a similar punishment. They were to receive thirty lashes each and had to pay forty-two shillings to the owner of the shop. For a burglary in 1685 Sam Indian was fined, branded with the letter

"B," and had an ear cut off. Two white men convicted of a similar offense were merely branded and fined. But Sam's mutilation may have been due to the fact that he committed the crime on the Sabbath.[23]

Popular prejudice against the word of an Indian could subtly affect their credibility in court. Few whites would rely on the word of an Indian who, they assumed, did not have the same degree of Puritan self-control. Lying, along with "Idleness, and sorcery, and a notorious want of Family Discipline," were, according to Cotton Mather, vices associated with Indian behavior.[24] Sarah Goode attempted to draw on that prejudice in 1692 to discredit Tituba as a competent witness against her. That Goode failed to undermine Tituba's testimony was a surprise to her and possibly to Tituba. Generally the word of a native American witness was more acceptable only "in the trials of other natives in the colonial court," rather than against whites.[25] Tituba's ability to convince her tormentors to accept her testimony with no reservations was a rare occurrence in Puritan New England. Her credibility as a witness may have been due to her successful absorption of English behavior patterns, aided by her knowledge and understanding of Puritan religious beliefs and shrewd insight into Puritan psychology.

In spite of the apparent equality before the law, Indians as a group were often treated differently by the legal system. Thus although English servants committed the crimes of theft, promiscuity, and disorderly conduct at the same rate as Indian servants, such antisocial activity was more clearly identified with native Americans. Traditional Indian behavior was also closely tied to criminal tendencies. Indian impatience with the restraints of servitude, as evidenced in their running away or drinking, was taken as proof of loose morals.[26] Sometimes cultural differences were taken into account and punishments were less severe, as happened to Joseph of Martha's Vineyard described above. This was the case especially for those crimes where Indian tribes had different methods of dealing with offenders as in murder, crimes committed while under the influence of alcohol, and sexual offenses.[27]

Other indications of racial differentiation can be found in court records in which Indians were always identified by race (as were Africans) and whites by social status. Clerks in court records often referred to Indians as "it" or "which" or "that" rather than "who," depersonalizing them. Regardless of the law, Indians were never considered or treated as equal to whites, nor was there an intent to fully assimilate them into English society.[28]

That Puritans could believe Tituba was both in league with the Devil and sincerely penitent for her past actions in 1692 reflected the ambiguity of their attitudes toward Indians. The clergy's attempt to "reduce" Indians to "civility" by changing their behavior was never followed by acceptance of them as full members of Puritan society.[29] As long as lying was associated with Indians, they could not be true Puritans and their conversion would continue as an incomplete transformation. In Tituba's case, some of those informal rules regarding testimony were suspended as she bore witness against white people and took center stage during the early phase of the witch scare. She thus came closer to a full transformation than most other native Americans.

The credibility of Tituba's testimony discussed in chapter 8 bears tragic witness to that paradox of Puritan perceptions of American Indians. Tituba the Indian woman would always remain an outsider in that closed Puritan society. Her camouflage as a household servant afforded only tenuous protection against persecution. During a crisis when scapegoats were wanted, any deviation from conventional behavior could put that facade in jeopardy. That protective coloration almost failed her in February of 1692 when she participated in a magical ritual that forced her to emerge again as a visible Indian presence.

Until that terrible time, Tituba found that the law sometimes protected slaves and servants against excessive abuse from masters. Those laws may have eased her work load. To safeguard the health of these dependent peoples, slave owners were expected to provide sufficient food and clothing. In May of 1685, for instance, Benjamin Mills was ordered to explain why his Indian servant was so poorly clothed.[30] Adequate shelter generally came as a matter of course; there were no separate living quarters for slaves and servants in Massachusetts households. Unlike the Barbados plantation arrangements, in New England Tituba ate and slept under the same roof as the master's family. She knew also that little physical labor was expected in inclement weather and Parris was expected to allow his servants to rest during the extremely hot days of the summer.[31]

Life in Boston may have offered greater legal protections and physical comforts, but these advantages were offset by fewer opportunities for personal freedom compared with those Tituba had enjoyed in Barbados. Massachusetts masters were forbidden to force their servants to work on Sunday. Servants were, however, expected to accompany the family to church services, which left them with minimal free time. Slaves and servants had no liberty to indulge in enjoyable or personally productive leisure activities on meeting days. Like everybody else in Puritan New England, they were forbidden to take part in any games or sports, to fish, plant, or hunt on the Sabbath.[32] Whatever freedom she had enjoyed in the slave compound in Barbados to sing, dance, worship the deities of her choice, or to take her daily swim disappeared once she arrived in Massachusetts.

Tituba had also lost the advantage of leisure time during religious holidays celebrated by the Anglican church. In Barbados slaves were granted free days for Christmas, Good Friday, and Easter Monday.[33] Puritans frowned on the revelry of such holidays as innovations of the Roman Catholics carried over by the English church that they wanted to purify. They had outlawed public religious festivals early on in an attempt to eliminate such "profane" customs.[34] As a result of these new restrictions and prohibitions, Tituba was subject to continuous scrutiny of her activities during both working and leisure hours.

As a servant, Tituba had no right to a private life or the freedom to express herself in personal adornment. She was warned against idleness, swearing, and cursing, excessive drinking and profaneness. But the "seminal sin" was "refusing to subject to order" by violating sumptuary codes or demonstrating a contempt for authority. She was expected to maintain a strict modesty in dress that marked her calling as a member of the lower class.[35] The law thus imposed a standard of behavior and clothing that could help Tituba blend into the background. With few alternatives or opportunities to deviate, she probably maintained a modesty appropriate to her station in life. Although the evidence is very circumstantial, the absence of complaints against her before 1692 would indicate that the neighbors had little reason to fear any threatening behavior from Samuel Parris's servant woman.

The restrictions on Tituba's activities were not much different from those on any other servant, child, or female in a Puritan household. Religion in New England, more than any other factor, shaped relations between parents and children, among adults, between servant and master, and between the ruled and the rulers. To obey the commands of the master or father of the family was a Godly injunction and all members of the household were expected to be obedient, faithful, and to show due reverence to those in authority. Tituba, like other servants in Boston, was expected to consider her master's welfare above all others.[36]

Samuel Parris, in turn, had religious obligations to his servants. He would have been especially encouraged to pay heed to the religious instruction of his slaves because of an early Massachusetts law (1644) that called for the Christianizing of Indians.[37] Within the household, every head was responsible for the spiritual welfare of all members of the family, including servants and slaves. Every morning upon rising and every evening upon retiring, as a good Puritan master Parris led his entire household in prayer, Bible reading, and the singing of psalms, duly instructing his slaves in the signs of redemption and the strictures of the Puritan covenant with God.[38] Because full understanding of the process of salvation came only from thorough study of the Scriptures, literacy was a minimal requirement for Puritan sainthood and a given necessity to enter the Kingdom of God. Following his calling to instruct his family, Parris or his wife may possibly have taught Tituba to read. She certainly understood the importance of reading and of books to people in the Protestant-English world.[39]

Shortly after arriving in Boston, Tituba faced dramatic new challenges in the household when Parris acquired a wife and then began to consider a ministerial vocation that would eventually take the family to Salem. Sometime during that first winter of 1680 Samuel married Elizabeth Eldridge. When they began courting is not known. They may have become acquainted during his days at Harvard or through his aunt and uncle, Susannah and John Oxenbridge. Susannah was the widow of his uncle John Parris in Barbados. After the Oxenbridges married they had moved to Boston where John Oxenbridge served as pastor of the First Church from 1671 until 1674.[40] Parris was also related to the Hulls and through them to the distinguished Sewall family. And there were many connections with other Boston families who had had commercial dealings with both Samuel's father and uncle.[41] Samuel Parris was neither a stranger to Boston nor without the social connections necessary to establish himself as a merchant and family man.

His youthful merchant ambitions had brought him back to Massachusetts in 1680 and he quickly established his shop and household in rental quarters in Boston. He had acquired sufficient financial advantage from his dealings in Barbados to give himself a comfortable living from that income and to provide the capital for his new ventures.[42] That income permitted Parris to acquire the trappings of respectability—as a church member, head of household, public servant, husband, and father in Boston. It was not sufficient for his needs, however, and Parris was never satisfied with either the respectability or uncertain financial rewards of the commercial life. That unhappiness eventually led him to consider the church as a more satisfactory calling.[43]

Within a year of their marriage, Samuel and Elizabeth became parents. Their first child, a son Thomas, was born in October of 1681. By November of 1682 a second child was born, a girl named Elizabeth and subsequently called Betty.[44] That child would be the source of much consternation in Salem. The year of Betty's birth Parris purchased some property for his shop and had embarked on a series of financial investments that failed to adequately fulfill his ambitions to find a secure economic hold on the commercial world. Parris, however, did not turn to thoughts of a vocational change until 1686. That year he began to substitute for absent ministers and to speak at informal gatherings in various churches.[45] He muddled along as a merchant until after the birth of their third child, another girl in January of 1688 named for Samuel's aunt Susannah, when he began formal negotiations with Salem Village.[46]

At some time the household was increased by the addition of another slave, a young African this time.[47] Thus by the middle of 1688 when Parris gave serious thought to serving the Salem Village congregation, there were at least eight people living in his Boston household: Samuel, his wife Elizabeth, their children Thomas (7), Elizabeth (6), and Susannah (under a year), and three slaves: John Indian, Tituba, and an African boy of about fourteen.

In the meantime imperial politics threatened the destiny of the Puritan colony and upset the tranquillity of the Parris household. Puritans faced the most severe threat to their control over social and political life after 1684. Complaints about the Massachusetts government, combined with the accession of the autocratic James II to the throne and a growing awareness of the economic importance of the American colonies, were leading the English government toward more determined efforts at control of the empire. During the summer of 1685 news arrived that the original charter for Massachusetts had been recalled and that a new, more centralized government was to be established. Joseph Dudley would serve as interim governor. Moreover, an Anglican priest arrived to conduct services according to the Book of Common Prayer, with plans to use the meeting house for his church ritual.[48]

The arrival of Sir Edmund Andros in December of 1686 signaled the end of Puritan hegemony. The Dominion of New England was to unite the New England, New York, and New Jersey colonies into one political jurisdiction. The new governor abolished all elected assemblies, restricted town meetings, and attempted direct control over militia appointments. A portent of things to come was the first public Christmas service permitted in the Town House and conducted by the Anglican priest.[49]

The ban against the celebration of that holiday by the Puritans was never completely successful and traditional English popular culture in caroling, feasting, and the "forbearing of labor" was not lost completely. Legal prohibition of such festivities kept the populace under some control but Andros increasingly violated Puritan customs and law to the delight of the less Calvinistic New Englanders. He permitted celebration on Sabbath evening, revelry on Sundays, and the ringing of bells to mark special occasions.[50] Parris's move to Salem by the summer of 1688 had at least removed him from the sight of these flagrant exhibitions of Anglican customs. But political events continued to unsettle life for all in New England.

The 1688–89 Glorious Revolution in England—the overthrow of James II and the accession of William and Mary as monarchs—left the way open finally to dispose of Andros. Increase Mather, one of the leading Boston ministers and a vocal opponent of Andros's regime, immediately set off for England to lobby against the governor.[51] In April of 1689 the Andros regime was "cast out" of Massachusetts and, led by the mercantile community, Simon Bradstreet and twenty-one other prominent citizens established a temporary government. New elections established a lower house and the old Massachusetts government of 1686 was temporarily restored. In an attempt to conciliate the new monarchs, the lower house, the General Court, made a radical break with the past by eliminating the religious qualification for voting and opening political participation to all adult males who paid four shillings in taxes and owned a house and lands worth at least six pounds. The following year Plymouth colony was absorbed into the Massachusetts governmental structure. At the end of 1691 Massachusetts, acting under the uncertainties of this ad hoc government, still awaited the arrival of a new charter and a new governor. The colony was disturbed even more by threats of enforced religious liberty, particularly for the protection of Quakers.[52] Contributing to the anxieties of the time was renewed Indian warfare in 1690.

The Parris move to Salem had occurred the year before the removal of Governor Andros. It was not until the spring of 1689 that Samuel Parris completed negotiations with Salem Village over his salary and other income, but the family may have moved there the summer before. Parris's name is absent from the Boston tax assessment list for August of 1688 and he began to keep a record of deaths occurring in Salem Village on June 24, 1688.[53] By July of 1689 the family had definitely settled in the Salem parsonage and Samuel was preaching in the village.[54] The household was also reduced in size when the African boy died in that year.[55]

Housing in the parsonage for the many members of the family was comfortable in accordance with the standards of the time. The building measured 42 feet by 20 feet, with two rooms upstairs and two rooms downstairs. The front door was placed on the long, south side, of the building (see Fig. 11). There was also an unfinished attic and a lean-to at the back of the house. Below, a cellar ran under half of the building (see Fig. 12).

On the ground floor, one of the two rooms was kept as a parlor that held the best bed for Elizabeth and Samuel Parris and the baby; a second bed in the corner provided a sleeping place for the other children, Thomas now eight and Betty seven.[56] They might have been joined by Parris's niece Abigail Williams. The other downstairs room, the hall, contained a cupboard or chest, a table, and backless benches. Parris used it as a study to prepare his sermons and conduct Bible readings for his household. The hall also served as the kitchen where Tituba and John and the African boy probably spread pallets at night to sleep. The upstairs chambers were set aside for the storage of foodstuffs and out-of-season tools, but might also have served as a sleeping space for the slaves and servants in the family. Necessary cooking and washing implements — pots, kettles, buckets — were stored in the lean-to, an area in which Tituba seemed to spend much of her time.[57] All rooms served a multiplic-

Figure 11: Parson (Joseph) Capen House, Topsfield, Massachusetts.

Built in 1684, this house, in size and style, most closely resembles the Salem Parsonage where Tituba lived from 1688 to 1692. Built of wood, it has the typical seventeenth-century four-room plan with attic and gable roof, but the overhang of the second floor makes it somewhat more high-styled than the one used by Samuel Parris and his family. Upon entering the house from the door on the long side of the building, the Great Hall, which served as the kitchen, would be to the left and the parlor to the right, with the chimney between. The second floor was divided into two chambers and the attic or garret was left unfinished. *(Photo courtesy of the Topsfield History Society.)*

ity of purposes and the living arrangements made no provision for personal privacy for anyone.

For Tituba the growing family and unfamiliar surroundings meant new and varied responsibilities and some emotional stress in adjusting to new conditions. Her work routine continued its usual round of cooking, washing, starching, and cleaning, in addition to caring for the children, and, possibly, the more specialized crafts of spinning, sewing, and dairying.[58] But there were decided differences between Barbados and Massachusetts in the materials she worked with. The food supply in Puritan communities was more predictable and somewhat unfamiliar. Most of it was locally grown produce, which meant she had lost access to both

Figure 12: Parsonage site.

The archeological site of the 1681 Salem Village Parsonage located off Centre Street in present-day Danvers, Massachusetts, and home to Tituba from 1688 until 1692. The photo was taken looking to the west and revealing the half cellar under the Great Hall. The foreground shows the interior passageway to the cellar and to its right the location of the original central chimney stack. The front door was left of the cellar stairs. Built as a four-room, two-and-a-half story structure, the house faced toward the south and measured 42 feet long and 20 feet deep. The room area to the east of the chimney, the parlor (lower edge of the photo), did not include a cellar under it. By 1692 the kitchen lean-to mentioned by Tituba had been added to the north (right side) of the building. *(Photo and descriptive information by Richard B. Trask.)*

cassava and sweet potatoes, the mainstay of her diet in both South America and Barbados. Neither of those root vegetables, so high in calories and vitamins, was grown in Massachusetts. Nor would she see much of lemons, limes, or melons.[59]

New Englanders, like the Barbados planters, preferred the English diet of meat, wheat, and European vegetables, but in Massachusetts they were able to reproduce much of those agricultural and animal sources in their own soil. It had not been possible in Barbados and much of the desired European foodstuffs had to be imported, but there Tituba could also depend on the availability of familiar tropical foods.[60] The Massachusetts farmers produced sufficient food for their own use as early as the 1630s and it was not necessary to import most foodstuffs.[61] They certainly did not hunger for the tropical plants as Tituba did. However, the wheat that they craved was in short supply. The crop was attacked by a stem rust that damaged the crops from the 1660s on and had to be imported just as it was in Barbados. In the 1680s it was a luxury item along with the imported French, Spanish, and Portuguese wines carried by the New England merchants into the Massachusetts ports. Trade with the West Indies brought in the sugar and molasses used to flavor foods and produce rum.[62]

It was necessary for Tituba to learn some new ways of handling food and also producing drinks more compatible with Massachusetts tastes. Indian corn gave her a familiar substance to work with and New Englanders consumed the same loblolly or corn meal mush that she knew in the Caribbean. She had to learn to eat her new bread made from rye meal and corn. Fruits came from the more traditional European trees: apples, pears, quince, cherry, plum, and barberry. Instead of mobbie made from cassava, she learned to ferment apples to make cider, or to brew barley and malt to approximate the English beer.[63]

Her own diet was probably more varied than in Barbados where servants and slaves were limited to corn, plantain, cassava, sweet potatoes, peas, beans, salt fish, and occasional salt pork.[64] New England servants shared the table with masters and their families, enjoying a more varied and nutritious diet. She and Elizabeth Parris would also have tended their kitchen garden with turnips, carrots, peas, beans, and leafy green vegetables to cook for sauces and "sallats" in the summer and fall. Tituba also learned to dress the local turkeys, large birds weighing forty or more pounds.[65]

Other foods on the table reflected a seasonal character. Winter meant salt pork, dried cod, peas, and brown bread of rye meal and corn, all washed down with beer produced by the women. Autumn harvest and killing time gave an abundance of grains, peas, and fresh meat from newly slaughtered swine and steer, as well as butter and cheese. Spring might be a scarce time. Farmers wintered cattle with little feed and the animals provided neither milk nor meat. Colonists subsisted on the dried and salted meats of the fall and possibly some root vegetables preserved in the cellar along with pickled and sweetened vegetables and fruits. After spring grasses began to grow, cattle could be fattened and local farmers again brought meat into Salem daily. Fresh fish would also be available in port towns. As a result of this abundance, Tituba probably enjoyed a "comfortable subsistence" along with the Parrises in New England.[66]

By 1692 John and Tituba were married, but their marital status in 1689 is not known. There were no legal impediments to their union at any time and Parris's decision to purchase a male Indian slave may have been with the intention of providing a mate for Tituba. However, it was not essential that Tituba marry an Indian man. Interracial marriages were not unusual and not illegal in New England. After 1705 only black-white unions were forbidden. And the marriage of Indians and Africans was commonplace due mainly to the shortage of male Indians and female Africans. The African labor force in Massachusetts was predominately male, while male Indians captured in warfare were usually transported out of the colony.[67] But Parris chose to find a native American mate for Tituba. Or the reverse situation may have been the case. For reasons that can no longer be surmised, he may have purchased Tituba as a potential mate for Indian John.

In either event, any sexual relations between Parris and Tituba, if such had been the case, would have ended before they arrived in Massachusetts. Parris's marriage to Elizabeth and another consort for Tituba would end any speculation about a possible illicit relationship between master and female slave. Marriage for Tituba and John would halt any potential gossip and prevent any scandalous behavior on the part of the servants.

That Parris intended his slaves to marry is a very likely scenario. He recognized, as most Puritans did, that sexual needs were as natural as other bodily functions and needed to be satisfied. Without the sanctions of marriage, slaves would not have any lawful means to satisfy the lust that Puritans assumed was a universal human frailty.[68] Marriage, therefore, was the only acceptable outlet for that sometimes inconvenient human need and Parris may have planned ahead when he bought the Indian girl Tituba. But there is no record of when she and John married. The seventeenth-century records make no mention of Indian marriages and it is possible that records for racial groups other than for whites were not kept during that period of time.[69] In the absence of vital records for Indians, Tituba's age in 1689 and New England marriage customs may suggest a possible date.

There is no research on the age at marriage for slaves in Massachusetts, particularly Indians. Lorenzo Greene has noted that, in many of the advertisements for runaway slaves in New England, the few women who had children had become mothers by the age of eighteen.[70] This number is small and it may well be that these were women without husbands running away from a potential whipping for fornication. Slaves suffered punishment for bearing children outside wedlock, just as whites did.[71] Slave owners had practical reasons for encouraging lawful unions among their slaves if they were to avoid public censure and the loss of work time.

On the other hand, early marriage for the breeding of slave children was not a practical goal in New England because no economic purpose was served. A large slave-labor force was not suited to the economic needs of the Puritan communities and infants could be burdensome. As a result, slave children in New England, unlike their counterparts in the West Indies, carried little value. There were too few Africans present to impress the Puritans with the strong bond between mother and child that prevailed throughout the Caribbean and some masters sold the children of their slaves as young as a year or two.[72] Perhaps this was a reflection of the general custom of binding out the children of the poor or negligent parents.[73] The treatment of slave children thus paralleled that of some white children who were taken from parents and put into other households to learn a trade or be disciplined.

Patterns regarding age at marriage for slaves probably followed the social norms of the larger society rather than conditions related specifically to enslavement or economic necessity. Information on marital practices in New England among whites is available and the custom for slaves probably was not much different. Research in Andover, Massachusetts, for the years 1680 to 1704 indicates that there was a gradual increase in the age of first marriage for women during that period. The average was twenty-two but some 25 percent of the women married after age twenty-five and many older still. Plymouth girls married slightly younger. Between 1650 and 1675, the mean age was 21.3 but it too was rising. Investigation of Dedham points to twenty-two as the average age of marriage in the seventeenth century.[74] Over time the trend was for delayed marriage and both men and women married at an older age as the century drew to a close.

In 1689 Tituba was probably between twenty-two and twenty-seven years of age, a time when most young women were betrothed. It is very likely that Tituba was married about the time the Parris household arrived in Salem or shortly before. Parris may well have delayed the sexual union of his adult slaves because he did not want to be encumbered by an early superfluous offspring of a slave. Tituba and Abigail, Parris's niece, were sufficient to assist Elizabeth Parris in the household work. Even John Indian's labor was not required in the parsonage in Salem. He was hired out to work in the local tavern run by Ingersoll.[75] Only Tituba's death or removal from the household would necessitate additional domestic labor.

The move to Salem and Parris's new responsibilities as a model for the community may well have precipitated the marriage of Tituba and John. The union probably occurred shortly after leaving Boston during the summer of 1688 and before Parris took over the leadership of the Salem Village congregation in the spring of 1689. The marriage was certainly before he began to keep records in Salem. It may have become important at that moment for Tituba and John to marry, to prevent the occurrence of a scandal in the house of a minister if the slaves did give way to their expected sexual desires and were caught.

But there is no documentary proof of this union for that time. The Boston records of all marriages during the 1680s are very sparse, and none at all was recorded in the decade before 1679.[76] Nonetheless, the absence of such a record does not preclude the possibility that the marriage occurred during the late 1680s rather than earlier or while they were in Barbados. Tituba's youthfulness when they left the island would indicate that marriage was delayed until she had reached her early twenties at least.

The interests of Tituba and John, unless forced on the master's consciousness by a pregnancy, would not have entered into the decision-making process. Marriage was a civil affair and served specific social purposes, although religious sanctions governed marital behavior.[77] The choice of a mate was the prerogative of the head of the household. Although girls were seldom forced into unwanted marriages, there was little they could do to marry without the consent of a father or a master short of becoming pregnant and causing embarrassment to the family. Parris may also have been less concerned about his slaves' behavior before he had taken on ministerial duties or the more crowded urban household in Boston may have acted as a deterrence for any unwarranted sexual activity.

Did they have any children? There is no documentary evidence that

Tituba had given birth, but the absence of such a record is not conclusive evidence that she was not a mother. It is theoretically possible that she had had a child or more that were not recorded or mentioned in any record of the time. She may have given birth but lost the baby very early. In those times of high infant mortality, early death could explain the absence of a child. Although infant survival rates were better in America than in Europe, the crowded living conditions of a town and the danger of epidemic disease made life in the urban areas more precarious than in the rural areas. Even under the best of conditions, prospects for infant survival were tenuous. In Plymouth in the seventeenth century, one of the areas with the fastest-growing natural increase in the population and the best chance of survival in the English-speaking world, one in ten infants died.[78] Measles, for instance, was a dreaded disease in seventeenth-century New England. The first recorded epidemic there was in 1657. Thirty years later a measles epidemic attacked both children and adults in Boston while the Parrises and their servants were in the city.[79]

Salem, as a port, was subject to epidemics sparked by diseased human cargo. A smallpox epidemic broke out in Boston in 1689 following the arrival of a ship from the West Indies and slowly spread to surrounding towns including Salem. Diphtheria was a continuing problem in New England, as was malaria during the seventeenth century.[80]

The death of a slave infant would not be a notable event except in the minds of the parents. Such a death would not be an economic loss to the slave owner; there was little reason to comment on such an event. Even among whites, an unknown number of infants died leaving no trace in the records.[81] Although Parris did make some attempt to list infant deaths in his Salem records, he did not begin to do so until October 1694. That year he noted a stillbirth for the first time when he wrote that the "abortive daughter of John Wallcott lived not an hour." In the spring a son of Joseph Pope was listed as stillborn and he noted a Negro child in the household of Mary Putnam died shortly after his mother in February of 1694.[82] But no such record provides a clue to Tituba's pregnancies or losses.

It is possible, however, that Tituba and John had had a child who survived but does not appear in the public record. The major source of information on Tituba comes from the documents recording the witchcraft episode in Salem between 1691 and 1693 and not all persons resident in the Village appear in those papers. The Parrises for instance had three living children at the time. Only Betty, the middle child, was affected. The other children, Thomas and Susannah, are not mentioned in those transcripts at all. Nor is Samuel's wife, Elizabeth. Nonetheless, they were all present in Salem at the time and living in the parsonage. Thomas and Susannah probably witnessed their sister's tormented illness, but played no role in the events as victims or accusers. So too, Tituba and John may have had a child, one probably too young to be implicated as five-year-old Dorcas Good was following the accusation against her mother Sarah. If the Indian couple had been married within three years of 1692 as I surmise, any child of that union would have been no more than two or three years old and easily ignored by those observing the events.

Samuel Parris's will provides evidence that there may have been such a child, a daughter named Violet. Strangely, no mention of the woman is made in any of the histories of the Salem events. Parris's will probated in 1720 left to his son Samuel (son of his second wife) the "Indian woman Violet" appraised in the inventory at thirty pounds.[83] She was subsequently sold to cover debts against the estate and one of the executors made two trips to Sudbury in order to do so.[84] After this short appearance in the public record, Violet, the Indian woman slave, disappears from notice. It is an extraordinary oversight that she not been linked to the other Indians who had lived in Parris's household twenty-eight years earlier or even considered as Tituba's daughter. And yet there is enough circumstantial evidence to make that connection.

That Violet, the Indian woman, has not been identified as Tituba's daughter is possibly due to the existence of another woman also named Violet but who was an African-American. The repetition of the name has led to confusion over whether they were the same person. This second Violet appears in Betty Parris Barron's estate in 1754 as one very sick Negro maid named Violet, "of no value."[85] She was about forty-five years old at that time of Barron's inventory and therefore would have been only eleven years old at the time of Samuel Parris's death thirty-four years earlier.

It is unlikely that the African-American Violet Barron was the same Violet of the Parris household. Betty Barron's Violet was only a child in 1720, no more than eleven years old, whereas the woman in Parris's will was valued at close to the price of an able-bodied man.[86] It is not very probable that a girl before the age of puberty would be worth as much as thirty pounds. Moreover, the will refers to an "Indian woman," an unlikely designation for an eleven-year-old African-American child, even one of mixed racial parentage.

The most likely explanation for the Indian woman Violet's presence in the Parris household in 1720 is first that she was an Indian as described and second that she was the daughter of his Barbados slaves. It is reasonable to assume, in light of the practice of separating parents and children, that the daughter would not have been sold away with Tituba and John in 1693. She could have remained in the Parris household. Moreover, any daughter of the two Indians in the parsonage would have been born about 1690, reasonably an adult in 1720, and quite possibly worth thirty pounds.

That this elusive reference in Parris's will to an Indian woman named Violet has been ignored by the scholarly community is not surprising in light of the many distortions that exist regarding Tituba's life itself, particularly the determination to transform her into an African. Logically there is more reason to assume that the Indian woman Violet mentioned in Parris's will was the offspring of Tituba and John Indian than that Parris purchased another Indian servant after 1693 or that Violet was really an African even though described as an Indian woman! To confuse this Indian woman with the African American with the same name parallels the misunderstandings regarding Tituba's background that have plagued scholarship since the nineteenth century.

The most likely explanation for Violet's appearance as an adult Indian in 1720 is, therefore, that she was an Indian as described and not an African. It is very likely that she was a daughter of Tituba and John. Parris rejected the Indian couple, but had little reason to sell or dispose of their daughter. As she matured and learned household skills, her labor would substitute for that of the disgraced Tituba.

Thus on the eve of the 1692 witch scare Tituba was married to John Indian and both were living in the household of Samuel Parris, his wife Elizabeth, and their three children, Thomas, Betty, and Susannah. Tituba's and John's daughter called Violet may have been about two or three years of age. Tituba's work centered on the household, the cooking, cleaning, and care of all the children. John spent much of his time hired out to Ingersoll to assist in work at the tavern.

On the surface there was little to distinguish the Parris household from others in the community, except for the presence of the Indian slaves and, possibly, the family's more diligent attention to spiritual matters.

But they had reasons to be less satisfied with their lives than their neighbors. As 1691 drew to a close, the minister began to face considerable opposition from the community. The generally favorable response to his ministerial style and efforts had begun to fade by 1691 and the village dissatisfaction was reflected in the erratic payment of his salary. Other external events also impacted on their lives as warfare with Indians and the French, in the conflict dubbed King William's War, brought new refugees and horror stories to town. A serious drought in 1691 also jeopardized the food supplies.[87] The number of deaths during the 1690s due to clashes with the Indians stands out among the Village records.[88]

Events came to a head for the Parris family when a new Village committee, elected in October of 1691, refused to impose the usual taxes to support the minister and Parris was denied both his salary and firewood for the winter. His sermons reflected the "stress and crisis" atmosphere, with increasingly bitter jeremiads regarding an evil that had infected the Village. His preoccupation with a conspiracy against him personally was projected onto the larger society as a conspiracy against the Church and by inference against the Godly community. He linked his opponents to the forces of Satan and publicly proclaimed that Salem Village was under siege.[89]

Parris's children and servants heard not only the sermons that hinted at a diabolical plot but more informal complaints of ungrateful communicants and fearful retribution. Members of the household began to reflect those anxieties in different ways. Tituba had a dream that an evil man with the appearance of a respectable-looking clergyman had approached her with enticements to hurt the children in the village.[90] Little Betty began to fall ill with inexplicable pains and hallucinations. Parris's weekly warning that the Devil had infected the Village was about to become a reality.

The Devil in Massachusetts: Accusations

> The affliction . . . never brake forth to any considerable
> light, until diabolical means were used, by the making
> of a cake by my Indian man, who had his directions
> from this our sister, Mary Sibley; since which appari-
> tions have been plenty. . . . But by this means (it seems)
> the Devil hath been raised amongt us.
> —Samuel Parris's Statement, March 27, 1691/92, in
> Paul Boyer and Stephen Nissenbaum, eds.,
> *Salem Village Witchcraft*

Salem, late 1691. Two of the girls in the Parris household, Betty, age nine, and Abigail Williams, her cousin, age eleven, curious about their future, and, drawing on a cultural tradition that was centuries old, were playing fortune-telling games. They dropped the white of a raw egg into a glass. The shape of the blob, they hoped, would reveal something about their future lives. The girls thought they saw tragedies in the form of an egg white that took the shape of a coffin.[1] It was an unsettling, possibly frightening, experience. But alone that vision was not enough to touch off the extraordinary physical symptoms that brought the activities of the younger children to the attention of the adults.

During the winter they were joined by two other neighborhood girls— Elizabeth Hubbard, seventeen, and Ann Putnam, age twelve. Elizabeth, like Abigail, was separated from her parents and was living in the household of an uncle, Dr. William Griggs. Ann, living at home, was a highly suggestible child—an overly sensitive daughter of a woman devastated by grief after the death of her infant and the children of her two sisters. The youngsters may have been observed in their play by two other girls in the village, both seventeen years old—Mary Walcott and Mercy Lewis, the latter a servant in the Thomas and Ann Putnam household.[2]

Was Tituba involved in these games? There is no evidence in the record of the Salem events that Tituba participated in or contributed to the childish activities of the girls in the village, although she may have been aware of them. Nor do we know what Tituba thought of the games, whether they were innocent entertainments or ungodly undertakings. She most certainly accepted the usefulness of such practices because, like most seventeenth-century people, she believed that human action could influence the spiritual realm and conversely that spirits could determine or at the least foresee future events.

The magical fortune-telling practices were not unusual in Puritan communities. They were part of a folklore deeply embedded in English life and, as with so many other aspects of New England life, were transported with the colonists from the old country. For the general population, the possibilities of fortune-telling, whether through astral predictions or occult practices, satisfied an emotional need. Magic—particularly divination practices—had a useful purpose in English life as it did in other cultural traditions. These practices offered a sense of certainty and security about the future when people had so little control over, or scientific understanding of, natural occurrences.[3] Thus Sarah Cole of Lynn and others in her town had "toyed w'th a Venus glase & an Egg," to determine "what trade their sweet harts should be of."[4] The Reverend Cotton Mather, well versed in the practices of young people who took part in experiments with "little sorceries," had noted that some also used "sieves and keys, and peas, and nails, and horseshoes," when attempting to divine their futures.[5]

The vast lore of magical practices that informed the folk cultures in England's colonies would be quietly reshaped in the New World by similar witchcraft traditions practiced by Africans and American Indians. None of these techniques, whether sieves or eggs, was exclusive to English folklore. They paralleled the magical practices found among other cultures. The sieve and sheer formula is very similar to divining practices found in Africa. The egg as a part of divining and curing ceremonies has an even more ancient history.[6] As different cultures met in the New World, similarities of form or function would permit an easy borrowing of magical techniques by one group from another. Thus it would not be surprising to find that the English colonists, separated from the roots of their ancient traditions in England, and under the influence of both native Americans and Africans, modified their Old World practices to fit new circumstances and new pressures. Puritan perceptions of Indian religions and the impact of Tituba's subsequent evidence offer an opportunity to follow that interactive process on witchcraft beliefs and its consequences. Traditional English forms would be both reinforced and reshaped by contact with the strange concepts introduced by Tituba.

Magical practices, whether ingrained in English folklore or borrowed from other cultures, usually managed to escape the notice of authorities. Those folk practices were part of the everyday mundane world; they seldom involved diabolical action or even evil intent, called maleficium. Most English people were more interested in witches who could heal the sick, find lost goods through divination, or provide some certainty about future events.[7] At times in old England when maleficium was suspected, some misfortune had occurred and in the absence of a reasonable explanation, the community looked for a likely culprit. They searched for evidence that a witch had cursed or had used some image magic—most often a model of clay or puppet of rags stuck with pins.[8] But even this minimal hardware associated with occult practices was seldom employed in New England. The knowledge and skill of the cunning folk usually required little apparatus. Only occasionally would such implements be discovered on this side of the Atlantic.[9]

Nor did practitioners of the occult in England and her colonies threaten religious practices. The two realms—the occult of the cunning folk and the theology of the leadership—existed side by side, most of the time without conflict or conscious thought. Educated persons officially frowned on these activities, although the elite sometimes took part in other superstitious practices such as astrology for medical "prognostications."[10] In the seventeenth-century world, folk healers and prognosticators operating outside the realm of theology seldom came to the attention of the legal system.

Even more rare in the American experience were stories of night-flying witches attending some diabolical, cannibalistic, and erotic orgy, elements of folklore that could be found in varying degrees throughout the African, European, and Asian worlds, but more characteristic of Europe than of other places.[11] In early modern Europe such witch fantasies were elaborated by zealous witchhunters who found accusations of diabolical pacts and witches' covens useful ploys to stamp out religious dissidents.[12] Those large-scale witchhunts played no role in American history until 1692. When it happened it was because Tituba's confession gave substance and shape to amorphous fears about a diabolical invasion.

What is very clear from the record of the Salem events is the total lack of proof that at Tituba's instigation the girls ran naked through the woods, drank blood, danced to drums, or stuck pins in waxen images.[13] Or even that the girls had done so without her assistance. These are fictional creations of other eras and not part of the seventeenth century record of events. The actual experiences of the girls with the occult is much more in line with traditional English folklore. The Reverend John Hale interviewed Betty Parris at the time and concluded that she and Abigail Williams, her cousin, were merely trying to tell their fortunes by using the egg and a glass.[14] No adult was implicated at first and the girls did not accuse Tituba of sharing their activities or of teaching them occult techniques.

Nor did the Reverend Parris at the end of the witchcraft scare even hint at the possibility that Tituba might have introduced his daughter to those or any other forbidden games. His admission that some members of his household were attempting to raise spirits referred to a single specific occurrence of occult practice on February 25, an event that subsequently led to Tituba's confession.[15] Parris rejected Tituba after the end of the witchcraft trials because she recanted her confession, declaring her innocence in a pact with the Devil, not because of any alleged complicity in occult activities before the crucial month of February 1692.[16]

The stories about voodoo in the forests or initiating the girls into satanic practices, drawing blood or dancing naked in the woods, or of Tituba's involvement in some forbidden African or Caribbean voodoo practices are imaginative creations of late nineteenth- and early twentieth-century writers.[17] Nor did Parris, at any time, even suspect her of such activities. Although Tituba would admit under pressure to knowledge of fortune-telling devices that were a part of English folklore, she did not confess to any involvement in the occult before the frightening events of 1692.[18] Then her confession was a reluctant tale of fanciful dream-like experiences taken from the mythology of several cultures. Before that time she merely watched and worried as the Parris girls suffered the consequences of their forbidden activities.

The particular egg and glass trick used by the Salem girls had its origin in the magical folklore of England.[19] It was carried across the ocean by the colonists, either in their memories or in printed matter, and was probably learned by the young people in Massachusetts by listening to adults or possibly actually observing the actions of the local practitioners. Dorcas Hoar was known to tell fortunes in Beverly, Massachusetts, and Samuel Wardwell did the same in Andover. Both adults learned the techniques by consulting English manuals on the subject.[20] The cunning folk of Salem were no less knowledgeable about such things than their counterparts elsewhere. They would be ready to ease a worried mind about the future, provide protection against evil magic, or cure a case of suspected bewitchment. Such folklore of the occult persisted even in Puritan New England. The subtle distinctions between magic and religion propagated by the learned clergy had little effect on the attitude of the larger population that relied on magical practices to resolve problems that could not be eased through natural or institutional means.[21]

The playful diversions of the Salem girls during the winter of 1691–92 took an unaccountably sinister turn when, probably late in December, Betty, the youngest of the group, began to exhibit bizarre physical symptoms, with bodily contortions and complaints of pains throughout her body—of pinching sensations and of sharp, knife-like pains.[22] Abigail soon followed suit and by the end of February Ann Putnam and Elizabeth Hubbard also began to complain of pain. Ann Putnam described sensations of a knife at her throat and Elizabeth Hubbard hallucinated about wolves trying to attack her.[23] In late March Mary Walcott and Mercy Lewis joined the group of "afflicted" girls.[24]

Why the girls involved in the fortune-telling suddenly exhibited such peculiar symptoms is a mystery. Perhaps the fortune-telling had been observed by others and they feared the wrath of their parents for their unorthodox behavior. Their guilty anxieties were manifested in a variety of erratic physical symptoms, from the temporary loss of speech, sight, and hearing to loss of appetite and sensations of being pinched and bitten.[25] It is possible that they became frightened by their own imaginations that foretold of death when one of the girls saw the egg take on the shape of a coffin. Or perhaps one of the girls in a spiteful mood threatened to tell the parents of the others of their forbidden games. Fearful anxiety could be expressed in bodily symptoms.

Or, even more likely, perhaps Betty, the daughter of the village minister, more sensitive to the nuances of Puritan doctrine, was overwhelmed by guilt because of their forbidden activity. Betty may have suffered a sudden revelation of sinfulness following one of her father's regular prayer sessions or biblical explications. Samuel Parris's warnings of an evil conspiracy may also have affected his daughter's reaction to what had been seen as an innocent game in earlier months. That fall the congregation had been fed a regular diet of reprimands for their sinful behavior in not supporting their church and its minister. Parris, in these jeremiads, had warned that their actions in ignoring his material needs were evil acts, evidence of a decline in their spiritual quest. In sermons and conversations, Betty heard about the conspiracy against God in the village reflected in this lack of deference to the minister, her father.[26] Family anxieties over their lack of income, combined with weekly jeremiads directed against the Satanic forces in the community, may have added to the eleven-year-old's guilt about the fortune-telling.

Such prophesy, divination, or fortune-telling, although deeply embedded in the English cultural heritage, was severely condemned by the Puritan clergy. It belonged in the category of personal revelations, like antinomianism, that challenged not only the authority of the clergy but the power of God who alone had access to "occult realms."[27] Any attempt to divine the will of God through magical means, according to Puritan precepts, to question God's omnipotence, was a blasphemy. Betty, the youngest of the group of curious girls, the most impressionable, and possibly subject to a steadier diet of fearful jeremiads warning of the imminent punishment for sin, exhibited the earliest and most worrisome symptoms.[28]

We can assume that all the girls knew of the sinfulness of their actions, but as with most layfolk of the century, they did not necessarily dwell on the contradiction between their behavior and the strictures of the Church.[29] Consequently, the girls, at first, ignored the contradiction between the orthodox religion of their minister and folklore of the neighborhood. They followed lay traditions, where the widespread use of divination, however loathsome it was to the clergy, was received with more equanimity except in periods of acute social stress. Then evil magic or maleficium would be suspected and cries of witchcraft could turn the popular will against those practitioners of magic and divination.[30]

Betty's bizarre behavior following on their forbidden games frightened her friends and family. Her pain and discomfort appeared real, but with no apparent natural cause. The pinching, prickling sensations she complained of, the sense of being choked, the difficulty in breathing, and the beginning of hallucinations were more than disturbing, they were frightening in their strangeness. Samuel Parris called in several physicians, hoping, if not for a cure for Betty's sickness, at least for an explanation for it. The doctors' efforts failed to ease the child's distress and the suspicion grew that the cause might be supernatural. Finally Dr. William Griggs, recently arrived in town and the uncle of one of the girls involved in the fortune-telling games, was consulted after the other physicians failed to find a remedy. He suggested that because he could find no natural cause of Betty's malady, it was possibly the result of witchcraft, "the Evil Hand." [31]

If the Devil's work was implicated, the responsibility for a cure lay with the Church. It was a spiritual and not a medical matter. For Protestants of the Puritan stamp, only prayer could serve to exorcise the presence of the Devil. [32] The Reverend Parris thus followed orthodox procedure when he initiated a series of prayers and made arrangements for a fast day for the community to repent of its collective sins. He knew of Cotton Mather's widely publicized success in exorcising the devils in the four Goodwin children just a few years before and employed the same rituals of prayer, calls for repentance, and tender loving care of the victims. [33] The situation also offered an opportunity to remind the community again of their collective sin in refusing to support their minister. The bizarre behavior of the girls would get a great deal of attention.

By the middle of February little Betty had been in pain some six weeks, since some time in December. Neither Parris's prayers nor her mother's and Tituba's care and concern seemed to help. [34] Neighbors were well aware of Betty's suffering. As in all Puritan communities, gossip and the habit of prying into the affairs of others kept the community informed about the most serious personal affairs of others. There was no privacy in seventeenth-century New England villages. [35] The suffering of the Parris household would have been a source of communal concern and ordinary conversation among their closest Salem neighbors, particularly Samuel and Mary Sibley just up the road. [36] Talk about remedies would have been part of the local gossip. There may have been some quiet discussion of how to employ more effective techniques and which of the local cunning people could be called on to effect a cure.

Finally, Mary Sibley, their neighbor and covenanting member of the

Church, decided to take more direct action to determine who in the village had bewitched the girl. She hoped that once revealed, the witch responsible could be forced to undo her evil work. Sibley enlisted the aid of John Indian and Tituba, the Parris family cook, to use countermagic to find that witch. Tituba agreed to prepare the witchcake. The little girl's strange illness during the winter of 1691–92 had so mystified and worried Tituba that she willingly collaborated with Mary Sibley to use occult means to ease Betty's pain. She, like Sibley, knew that such practices could work. She had learned of other techniques from people in Barbados but was willing to try the technique proposed by Sibley. Tituba's later bewilderment at the results of her experiment indicated that initially she had not feared any harm to herself or the community from that benevolent action.

On February 25, 1692, after two months of watching Betty's painful suffering and under Sibley's supervision, the two Amerindians prepared a witchcake—a concoction of rye meal and the girls' urine, which was baked in ashes and fed to a dog.[37] Supposedly the dog was a familiar, that is, the animal form of a witch. The dog, bewitched by the cake, according to the folklore, would then reveal the name of the witch causing the problem.[38] The technique was of English origin, but the assumptions behind the experiment were widespread among most peoples.

The taking of a substance from the body of a person—such as hair, nail parings, or in this case, urine—and applying ritualistic procedures were common magical practices in most folk and tribal cultures including the English.[39] These practices, including the use of clay models or puppets of rags stuck with pins, however, had become relatively rare in England. By the seventeenth century most magic there was worked through touch, or invisible emanations from the eyes, or curses rather than through the use of technical aids.[40] On the other hand, sympathetic or associational magic had continued to be common practices of obeah people in the seventeenth-century Caribbean and of Amerindian shamans in both the North and South American world. Puritans imagined Indians as conjurers; they tended to equate Indian spiritualism and religious practices with witchcraft.[41] Sibley's countermagic reflects the older folk practice from Europe reinforced in New England by the Puritan contact with Creoles from the Caribbean and Indians in New England.[42]

Although the use of such "white magic" techniques was fairly common throughout the New England world, more widespread certainly than in old England, Sibley appealed to John and Tituba because sympathetic magic was so closely identified with Indians. It was not necessary that Tituba and John have personal reputations as cunning folk, only that they fit the stereotype of effective witches. As Indians who had associated with obeahs in the Caribbean, they certainly conformed to the popular image of cunning folk, whether or not they had actually dabbled in the occult. Sibley's assumptions regarding Indians and occult practices were confirmed when Tituba, under pressure, admitted to familiarity with techniques used to reveal a witch as well as methods to protect herself against evil magic. But Tituba also denied participating in magical rituals previously, either in Massachusetts or Barbados.[43]

The compassionate gesture to reveal the cause of the girls' infirmities that employed techniques embedded in the magical folklore of so many cultures sparked a ten-month nightmare of intense fear, death, and emotional turmoil throughout Massachusetts. Tituba's protective camouflage as a member of a Puritan household was stripped from her, exposing her as an Indian and demanding another means of resisting persecution. The Salem witchhunt was about to begin.

It is unlikely that Tituba as an individual was actually known for her skill in such white or black magic before 1692. There is no evidence (except in the imaginations of historians, playwrights, and novelists) that she was an active participant in occult rituals before that date. She was probably telling the truth when she denied using witchcraft previous to the witchcake incident: all the available information indicates that she had probably lived an ordinary, low-key life until then. No one suspected that she had been involved with occult practices before.

In the close-knit Puritan world a reputation as a cunning person or conjurer would have come to Parris's attention earlier, or surely a witness would have appeared to testify to such skills in court when Tituba was first accused. But there is no such testimony in those records regarding any alleged occult practices by Tituba nor a single complaint that she was responsible for other misfortunes. No one mentioned occasions of maleficium connected to Tituba, nor was she accused of wrongful behavior toward her neighbors or the members of the Parris household. No witnesses came forth to blame her for committing acts of witchcraft that took place before February 25. All accusers refer to their fanciful tortures at Tituba's hands as beginning after that fateful day in February. Among those early depositions against Tituba, Elizabeth Hubbard claimed that Tituba's specter first came to her on February 25 and Ann Putnam, Jr., dated her torments at the hands of Tituba on the same day. Abigail Williams was less precise in her time sequence but went no further back than several times in February.[44]

In contrast, many of the others accused of witchcraft faced complaints of maleficium and dissatisfaction with their behavior dating months and years earlier. A number of witnesses appeared in court to testify to Sarah Good's magical powers and her supposed bewitchment of many victims over a period of years before 1692. Samuel Abbey blamed Good for the death of his livestock two years before, accusing her of "Spitefully & Mallitiously" harming his cattle, sheep, and hogs after he had turned her and her husband out of his house. Henry Herrick and Sarah Gadge also testified about Good's actions to harm their animals two years previously.[45] In another hearing, Bridget Bishop also elicited complaints dating back many more years. William Stacy accused Bishop of using occult means to steal from him and to destroy his property. He testified that fourteen years ago she had frightened him one night while he was sleeping when she appeared to him in a bright light. He accused Bishop of causing the death of his daughter Priscilla two years before.[46] James Carr accused Mary Bradbury of making him sick and unable to take medicine some twenty years earlier.[47] John Best testified that some years past Ann Pudeator threatened his wife and caused "pinching & Bruseing of her Till her Earms & other parts of her Body Looked Black."[48] Three of those women with previous witchcraft reputations were convicted and executed for the crime of witchcraft. Mary Bradbury managed to escape from jail.

From the absence of such testimony against Tituba, it is likely that no one in Salem remembered a time when the Indian woman was suspected of having or demonstrating occult power, of cursing her neighbors, or causing harm to them. Until the end of February 1692, Tituba had successfully hidden behind a commonplace facade—if not as a saint at least as one of the harmless ordinary folk who knew how to stay in her place. After that day she discovered that her transformation into a Puritan was incomplete and no amount of camouflage could protect her against the identification of Indians with the presence of evil.

That Mary Sibley had asked her to assist in the countermagic of the witchcake can have explanations other than that Tituba was a known many ways Tituba was a logical person for Sibley to approach. As a servant Tituba lived in the Parris household and had access to Betty's urine; she was the family's cook; and she was used to obeying orders from her betters. It may have been customary for those in straightened circumstances to call on Indians to take part in magical rites and Tituba happened to be a convenient ploy. Sibley's request then was in line with the common perception of Indians as practitioners of the occult and fit in with Tituba's usual duties as a household servant. Desperation may have driven both women to draw on generally acknowledged folk tradition that one time alone. The witchcake experiment brought on the first public awareness that Tituba had knowledge of magical techniques. If such activities had been suspected before, no one thought to make reference to it in 1692.

After being exposed as a participant in the witchcake incident, Tituba admitted only that she was acquainted with methods of uncovering witches. She made no mention of Indian techniques. The information was acquired, she said, through her mistress in Barbados.[49] It may well be that Elizabeth Pearsehouse or some other white woman in Samuel Thompson's Barbados household had introduced her to occult practices derived from either English folklore or the developing syncretic practices on the Island. It is also possible that Tituba's attempt to blame an Englishwoman for introducing her to divination techniques was intended to divert attention from her physical presence and the association of Indian beliefs with Satanic practices. She could then shift attention to the more familiar and possibly less threatening language of English folkways, a device she used more than once during the witch panic.

There was, however, nothing uniquely English about the witchcake except possibly the rye flour, which was an important cereal in the new England diet. The dog as a familiar and urine as a substance that somehow maintained a spiritual connection with the original body were ideas universally believed and accepted. Sibley's suggestion to the Amerindian slaves would have been consistent with their own understanding of occult practices, whether they learned about them from their African companions in Barbados or an Indian shaman or even an Englishwoman in Barbados.[50] The significance of this event is not in the particular technique used but the fact that the Puritan woman Sibley turned to the Indians—the personification of occult power—to carry out the action, and that Tituba at first innocently collaborated. Both women acted in accord with popular beliefs regarding the efficacy of countermagic and the supposed ability of Indians to divine and control those powers. Once she realized the tragic consequences of that stereotype, Tituba tried to extricate herself by identifying her occult knowledge with the English tradition—to hide once again behind the camouflage provided by her acculturation.

It was not an unlikely facade. For Puritans, as for many other peoples of the century, the practice of witchcraft was very real. It could, they believed, literally conjure up spirits. The magical techniques of the cunning folk may have belonged to the realm of folklore, but the beliefs regarding the presence of the spirit world were endemic throughout the community. Samuel Parris too sincerely believed that evil spirits had literally been let loose in Salem and that magical means could affect the behavior of those spirits. His conclusion was not unusual for his time. Salem in the seventeenth century was as densely populated with spiritual beings as any African or Amerindian village.[51]

To the seventeenth-century European mind, magic and religion were cut from the same cloth. The line between the material and the spiritual was not always clearly delineated; the invisible world of the deity was a palpable presence to the Puritans. "The people of seventeenth-century New England," notes David Hall, "lived in an enchanted universe. Theirs was a world of wonders."[52] Puritans were intimately acquainted with events they thought of as the wonders of providence. Earthquakes, volcanoes, and personal misfortunes were spoken of as prodigies and portents, the evidence of God's will. The supernatural presence was observed in the death of a child, a sudden epidemic disease, a drought, or a case of bewitchment, and prayer had real existential power.[53]

As God existed, so did the evil presence Christians called the "Devil." Cotton Mather could write of his experiences with evil spirits as "Illustrious Providences," or "Memorable Providences," and as the "Wonders of the Invisible World." He believed that people, with the aid of the Devil, could work magic. He recognized that in his world there was no clear division between the spiritual and the material or between magic and religion. These "Remarkable Providences," phenomena such as witchcraft, diabolical possessions, and strange apparitions, confirmed God's existence. After all, history, to a good Puritan, was providential, the working out of God's will. Magic and the affairs of the Devil were part of that will and to deny the existence of the Devil was tantamount to admitting to atheism.[54]

Tituba was no stranger to these concepts. In a similar fashion among African and American Indian societies, the invisible world of wonders was just as real and spirits could also be manipulated through magical practices for both good and evil.[55] Although there were major differences in the explanation for the existence of evil, in the nature and number of gods, and the rituals associated with the supernatural, the common belief in the existence of this invisible world permitted the comfortable transference of witchcraft practices from one ethnic group and set of religious beliefs to another. Individuals, whether of Amerindian or African ancestry, could easily integrate the ideas and techniques of English witchcraft without violating essential qualities of their own worldview.[56] Or conversely, they could introduce new forms without necessarily affecting the substance of English religious ideas. In the seventeenth-century world, the supernatural omens, the magical techniques, and other practices associated with witchcraft could be and were understood and adapted regardless of origin. The function of the practice might vary. The function was much more susceptible to the evolutionary process than the form. The form, the techniques themselves, provided a universal language slaves often used as a strategy for survival.[57]

The result of the late February attempt at countermagic in Salem was a disaster for all concerned. The girls, already visibly disturbed by Betty's response to their previous sinful involvement in the occult, were frightened even more by this countermagic practiced on their behalf. The appeal to supernatural powers, regardless of purpose, was still heresy because they knew it depended on a Satanic influence. Now aided by Tituba, John Indian, and Mary Sibley, they worried that they had inadvertently conspired to let an evil spirit loose in Salem. Their physical responses certainly indicate that a new quality of fear had entered their lives. They expected retribution and the heightened fear brought on what can now be diagnosed as hysterical fits.[58] In the days following the witchcake incident Betty developed even more violent and bizarre symptoms, and the peculiar behavior spread to the other girls. Abigail and Betty complained of torture by invisible hands. They began to see apparitions of allegedly murdered people. The other two girls involved, the younger Ann Putnam and Dr. Grigg's niece Elizabeth Hubbard, also began to complain of similar symptoms.[59] Their bodies assumed strange postures. John Hale observed that they

> were bitten and pinched by invisible agents; their arms, necks, and backs turned this way and that way, and returned back again, so as it was impossible for them to do of themselves, and beyond the power of any Epileptick Fits, or natural Disease to effect. Sometimes they were taken dumb, . . . wracked and tormented so as might move an heart of stone.[60]

Their distress became so great that Parris looked for more advice and decided to consult with the leaders of the community and ministers from the surrounding towns. After some discussion and observation of the girls' behavior, the leaders agreed that the sickness was the work of the Devil and advised Parris to continue his prayers.[61] The ministers hoped to follow Cotton Mather's example of success in calming the Goodwin children in 1688. But Parris also impatiently decided to question the children about who was tormenting them, much as Mather had done in the earlier cases of witchcraft.[62] The result was a terrifying series of events.

Parris may have been encouraged to question the girls at the end of February because he had found out about the witchcake and he believed that the countermagic would work. Much as he condemned the actions of Sibley, John, and Tituba, it is possible that Parris assumed that their occult power would reveal the names of the Devil's handmaidens. Parris, like the other literate people in the seventeenth-century world, accepted the reality of evil magic. Thus he noted in his Salem records that Daniel Wilkins had been "bewitched to death." He did not doubt that when the daughter of Ann Douglas died the cause was "by witchcraft."[63] How easy it was to blame Betty's pains and the discomfort of the other girls on the same witchcraft that had sporadically plagued the community.

In spite of their belief in the reality of magic, Parris, Mather, and other theologians denied that ordinary people could manipulate occult forces without assistance from the Devil. According to Edward Phillips's 1671 lexicography, witchcraft was "a certain evill art, whereby with the assistance of the Devil, or evill Spirits, some Wonders may be wrought which exceed the common Apprehension of Men."[64] In European folklore, as among Amerindian and African cultures, witchcraft, or the evil actions of cunning people, helped to explain otherwise inexplicable strange happenings; but to the educated part of the Christian community, the ultimate source of evil power was beyond human control and had to be traced to a diabolical force.[65] The presence of those practicing divination and the suspicion of deaths due to witchcraft could only mean that the Devil was the unseen instigator. But more direct, verifiable proof was necessary to confirm those omens.

The girls did confirm Parris's suspicions regarding the presence of witches as well as the efficacy of white magic and identified their tormentors as two somewhat disreputable and socially outcast women—Sarah Goode aged thirty-eight and the more elderly Sarah Osborne.[66] They also pointed to his servant woman Tituba, who had made herself more vulnerable to such an accusation with her involvement in Sibley's attempt at magic.[67] The three were likely targets for such an accusation because each one deviated from the norm in some way, Tituba particularly because of her ethnic identification.

The three women were immediately accused of bewitching the girls. Warrants for their arrest were prepared on February 29. The following day they were arrested for alleged witchcraft activities, questioned over a period of several days in Salem, taken to the jail in Ipswich, and finally sent to jail in Boston to await trial.[68] Those arrests should have but did not end the witchhunt. It was merely the beginning of the worst witch-scare experienced in America. It was followed by six months of accusations, arrests, examinations, jailings, and finally trials and multiple executions involving people from distant towns and including strangers with no ties to Salem.

The scope of the witchhunt that followed Tituba's arrest defies any simple explanation. Accusations of witchcraft were not unusual in the seventeenth-century world that believed in divine providence and worried incessantly about the state of each soul. The social tensions and personal misfortunes blamed on occult powers, and that often preceded a witchcraft scare, were common occurrences. Historians have noted that the sequence of events before a witchscare usually involved the existence of prior animosities among neighbors and a denial of assistance to a needy person. The soon-to-be accused witch leaves the premises mumbling a malediction. In due course something goes wrong with the household of the uncharitable family and the woman who has cursed them is accused of wrongdoing.[69]

These were invariably face-to-face events, involving only a few persons, and may have functioned as a means of controlling the deviant behavior of particular individuals, especially women. As the English historian Keith Thomas points out, potential assaults on the witch could serve as a means of enforcing communal values. They

> constituted a check upon outbursts of temper, swearing and cursing, or similar expressions of malignity. In sixteenth-and seventeenth-century England, no less than in some modern African societies, witch-beliefs could thus inhibit the expression of vicious feelings, and help reinforce the prevailing ethic of neighbourliness and communal solidarity.[70]

But events somehow went awry in 1692. Instead of bringing the community together and reinforcing the ethic of neighborliness, the New England Puritans almost destroyed their sense of communal purpose. Why this happened has led to a vast library of studies that has put Salem and its environs under a literary microscope. Every aspect of social and psychological life has come under scrutiny, from the quality of food consumed to the unusual manipulation of the legal system, from the hidden agendas of the examining magistrates to the extent of personal and social conflicts in the colony, from the methods of rearing children to blaming individuals.[71] The problem faced by historians is not about witchhunts and witchcraft. Such "wonders" were integral aspects of New England life. The historiographic problem is to understand why the Salem incident deviated from earlier episodes.

A major clue to an understanding of what happened, why the Salem experience was unique, and what Tituba's specific role was in this incident, is in the sequence of the early events. It is particularly important to sort out what happened between the end of December and the beginning of March, and to concentrate attention on the week between the witch-cake incident and the conclusion of Tituba's testimony a few days later. The conventional description of those events following the accusations of the girls in late February has been confusing and the progress of the girls' "afflictions" somewhat telescoped by most scholars. The truth has been obscured by assumptions of Tituba's supposed connection to voodoo activities.

A careful extraction from the various firsthand accounts and the earliest accusations in the extant legal records indicates that from December until February 25, the complaints of the girls were limited to inexplicable pains and sensations that affected only four girls: Betty Parris, Abigail Williams, Elizabeth Hubbard, and Ann Putnam. After the witchcake incident on February 25, the girls began to exhibit some of the more bizarre physical symptoms that involved disjointed limbs, choking sensations, convulsions, and possible hallucinations. They huddled under chairs, and attempted to bury themselves in holes, and, as Calef described these peculiar behaviors, they began "to use sundry odd Postures and Antick Gestures, uttering foolish, ridiculous Speeches, which neither they themselves nor any other could assign no [any] reason for."[72] The witchcake experiment and Tituba's participation in it were significant factors in exacerbating their hysterical symptoms.

The epidemic of strange behaviors and accusations did not spread to other victims until after Tituba's arrest and her several testimonies beginning on March 1. March 5, the conclusion of Tituba's remarkable confession, marked a new chapter in the witchhunt episodes of New England.[73] By the time the first ministers invited by Parris arrived in Salem on March 11, the hysteria had spread to many more people, including several adult women—Mrs. (Bethshaa) Pope, Ann Putnam's mother called Ann Sr., Goodwife (Sarah) Bibber, and Goodwife Goodall[74]—and the symptoms of the accusers had become extraordinarily bizarre, with visions of witches' meetings and animal familiars, and specters harassing and murdering people.

This magical experiment with the witchcake can explain the beginning of the witchhunt but not the extraordinary atmosphere of social tension that permeated Massachusetts for the rest of the year. It is events following the discovery of countermagic that brought on the epidemic of hysterical symptoms, wild accusations, large numbers of arrests, trials, and executions. Those March events set off the hunt for culprits far beyond the geographic boundaries of the early events to include many strangers and people not ordinarily involved in such accusations.

There is no doubt that a peculiar combination of social tensions, exacerbated by the factional conflict within the community of Salem Village, contributed to the atmosphere of fear so necessary for the advent of a witchscare. Charles Upham suggested this as a major cause and Paul Boyer and Stephen Nissenbaum have provided a brilliant analysis of the Salem community to support that argument.[75] Indian warfare and the uncertainties related to the arrival of a new charter and new Governor in the two years before the witchhunt also added to the level of social stress. But other towns in frontier Massachusetts that experienced the same socio-economic-political difficulties did not spark a similar witchscare. Several communities suffering from less stress did suffer from contact with Salem as the witchscare virus spread.[76] This contagion too was a unique aspect of the 1692 episode.

The "witchcake" concocted by Mary Sibley, Tituba, and Indian John merely set the stage for the most dramatic act in this early American tragedy. It was a crucial moment in that the "diabolical means" used to help cure Betty Parris, and Samuel Parris's response to that countermagic, put Tituba in the limelight. How she and her supposed co-conspirators, Sarah Osborne and Sarah Good, responded to the accusations of the girls was of even greater importance to the course of events in March and the following months. Tituba's confession is the key to understanding why the events of 1692 took on such epic significance.

The Reluctant Witch: Fueling Puritan Fantasies

> Titiba an Indian woman brought before us by Const[a-
> ble] Jos Herrick of Salem upon Suspition of Witchcraft
> by her Commited according to the Compl't of Jos. Hut-
> cheson & Thomas putnam etc. of Salem Village as ap-
> peares p Warrant granted Salem 29 febr'y 1691/2 . . .
> —In Paul Boyer and Stephen Nissenbaum, eds.,
> *Salem Witchcraft Papers*

On the last day of February 1692, a leap year, Joseph Hutchinson, Edward and Thomas Putnam, and Thomas Preston appeared before Salem magistrates John Hathorne and Jonathan Corwin to make complaints against the three accused women for "suspition of Witchcraft." They charged that Sarah Osborne, Tituba, and Sarah Good had been using occult means to injure four girls over a period of two months. Four girls—Betty Parris, Abigail Williams, Ann Putnam, and Elizabeth Hubbard, all under eighteen years of age—added their testimony to support the complaints. Thus began the legal process that focused attention on Tituba and would eventually lead to the imprisonment of more than one hundred people over a period of nine months and the execution of twenty between June 19 and September 22. A few more would die in prison from exposure and disease, adding a gruesome note to the death toll from this witch scare.[1] Tituba would escape with her life, but she would spend thirteen months in a crowded, foul-smelling, and filthy Boston prison, unsure of her fate.

Tituba's subsequent testimony confirmed the worst fears of a diabolical presence and gave the Salem worthies reason to launch a witchhunt. She supplied the essential legal evidence required to begin the process of communal exorcism, to purge the community of its collective sin. Without her testimony the trials could not have taken place. Thus it was only after Tituba began to confess that the witchhunt began in earnest. In her fantasies of an evil power, the Indian woman confirmed that the Devil was now among them.

Witchcraft was a crime against God in the European world and, therefore, a heresy, but in England it was treated as a social crime. English laws of 1542 and 1604 made it a capital offense to invoke an evil spirit, to use magic to hurt or kill people, find lost treasure, harm cattle, or to "provoke unlawful love," among other anti-social activities. The penalty for such acts was a year's imprisonment for the first offense and death for the second.[2] As in all criminal cases in the English world, the legal process in identifying and prosecuting persons accused of witchcraft followed a standard sequence. It began with a formal complaint presented by members of the community, a preliminary hearing to investigate the charges, the presentation of an indictment against the accused, and finally trial by a jury of freeholders of that county. The somewhat vague Massachusetts laws of 1641 and 1642, which governed events in 1692, were seemingly based on a combination of the English laws and Old Testament prohibitions. They prescribed death "If any man or woman be a witch (that is hath consulteth with a familiar spirit)." Massachusetts generally followed English procedures; a jury trial was mandatory before the punishment could be inflicted.[3]

Magistrates John Hathorne and Jonathan Corwin, after hearing the complaints of Joseph Hutchinson, Edward and Thomas Putnam, and Thomas Preston in Salem, followed the standard procedure and issued warrants on February 29, 1692, to arrest the three accused women (see Fig. 13). Constable Joseph Herrick was also ordered to search Tituba's and Osborne's possessions for "images and such like" as evidence and to bring the women to Ingersoll's Tavern at 10:00 the next morning for questioning. No incriminating artifacts were found in their possession. Constable George Locker was sent to arrest Sarah Good and bring her too to the tavern.[4]

Samuel Parris must have felt a certain satisfaction when Joseph Herrick appeared at his door to arrest Tituba. He was angry at her defiance of his authority by participating in an occult ritual. A day or two before he had beaten his servant woman to force a confession about her role in the making of the witchcake.[5] She contritely admitted her guilt in that ritual and hoped that the matter would end there. Parris was not satisfied with that minimal confession and demanded more details about her knowledge of occult practices and of others involved in this incident. She told him of Mary Sibley's participation. His immediate response to the imputations of witchcraft on the part of one of his supporters in his conflict with the Village has not been recorded. At first Parris appeared to ignore the implications of Sibley's role. But Sibley was not forgotten; he would deal with her later and in a less punitive fashion.[6]

When questioned later about her familiarity with witchcraft practices, Tituba admitted to having learned about occult techniques in Barbados. Her mistress in her own country, she said, had taught her how to reveal the cause of witchcraft and also how to protect herself against that evil power.[7] Such knowledge was intended to help defend herself against the malevolence of others, but not to do harm herself. To Parris she denied being a witch or taking part in the pain experienced by the girls, even though she had admitted to participation in an occult ritual.[8] Tituba did not understand Parris's insistence that she was responsible for the children's distress. She had not meant to hurt Betty, but to help the little girl. Why, when her intentions were good, was she accused of causing Betty's illness?

Tituba's initial reluctance to respond to Parris's accusations of witchcraft followed from a difference between folk and Christian theological notions regarding magic. Tituba, drawing on folklore, made a distinction between protective and healing powers and evil intent, between white magic and black magic, or what could be perceived among some tribal cultures as the difference between sorcery and the magical work of healers and curers like obeahs and shamans.[9] In Tituba's mind witchcraft was equated with the European idea of maleficium, the commission of an evil act. Because she had no evil intent in manufacturing the witchcake, Tituba denied that she was a witch.

Parris, on the other hand, assumed evil intent. In his mental world all occult powers were evil because they were derived from devilish associations. Tituba, in the tradition of most ordinary folk, as well as Indians and Africans, focused on the effect of the ritual rather than the origins of her power. Parris, concerned with the assumed Satanic source of her

Figure 13: Arrest warrant for Tituba and Sarah Osborne dated February 29, 1691/2.

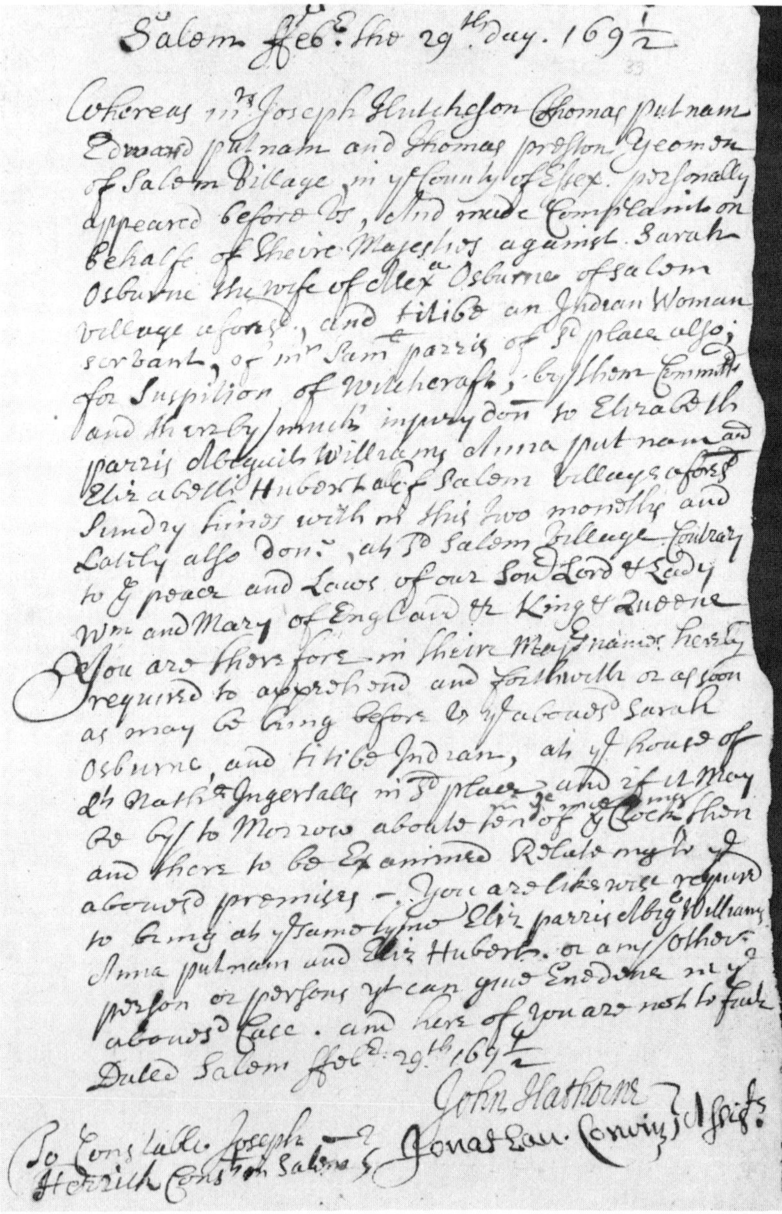

magical power, began with a different set of premises. Participation in magic was a form of blasphemy—it violated God's commandments—that could not be left unchallenged.

This "disjunction" between theological and popular notions of witchcraft did not matter until people turned to the legal system for protection against the magic of the cunning folk.[10] Judicial policy required concrete evidence of diabolism to convict. Magistrates were under pressure to accommodate the law to the needs of the populace: to revise the rules of evidence and make it easier to punish those accused. But the legal system, influenced by clerical concerns, seldom succumbed to popular lore and few people were indicted for witchcraft; only a small number of those were found guilty. Parris's use of the courts to punish Tituba for her countermagic created an intellectual crisis in New England that finally forced a convergence of the two disparate traditions. Popular views as articulated by his Indian woman servant and then reformulated by others in the community ultimately brought about changes in the legal definitions and theological assumptions regarding witchcraft.[11]

Parris seemed determined to prove Tituba's guilt and bring her to trial. In his worldview, dabbling in the occult signified witchcraft and Tituba's participation in the preparation of the rye meal-urine mixture was sufficient evidence of involvement in a Satanic pact. Perhaps he was concerned about his own image as a clerical leader and the imputation of

Facing page:
"Whereas m'rs Joseph Hutcheson Thomas Putnam Edward putnam, and Thomas preston Yeomen of Salem Village, in the County of Essex. personally appeared before us, And made Complaint on behalfe of theire Majesties against Sarah Osburne the wife of Alexa' Osburne of Salem Village afores'd, and titibe an Indian Woman servant, of mr. Sam'l parris of s'd place also; for Suspition of Witchcraft, by them Committed and thereby much injury don to Elizabeth Parris Abigail Williams Ann putnam, and Elizabeth Hubert all of Salem Village afores'd Sundry times with in this two months and Lately also done, at s'd Salem Village Contrary to the peace and Laws of our Sov'r Lord & Lady Wm & Mary of England &c King & Queene."

John Hathorne and Jonathan Corwin ordered Constable Joseph Herrick to "apprehend" Sarah Osborne and Tituba Indian and bring them to "the house of Lt. Nath'l Ingersalls in s'd place, and if it may be by to Morrow aboute ten of the Clock in the morning then and there to be Examined Relateing to the aboves'd premises." They were "likewise required to bring at the same tyme Eliz. parris Abig'l Williams Anna putnam and Eliz Hubert or any other person or persons that can give Evedence in the Aboves'd Case." Thus began the legal process that led to Tituba's confession and Osborne's death in prison. *(Photo courtesy Massachusetts Supreme Judicial Court, Division of Archives and Records Preservation; on deposit at Peabody Essex Museum, Salem, Mass.)*

a diabolical presence in his household. The behavior of the two girls Betty and Abigail, as well as of Tituba, was his responsibility. Tituba's improper approach to the problem of evil cast doubt on Parris's ability to maintain order in his own house. Had he somehow compromised himself by neglecting his duties to force obedience from this dependent? To control unacceptable behavior, strict discipline and punitive action were sometimes necessary and socially approved. He would not be faulted for beating either servants or children. Instead of punishing the girls, Parris elected to discipline Tituba. In so doing, by blaming Tituba for the misfortune of his family, he was able to uphold the stereotype of the Indian as Devil worshiper while distancing himself from the taint of association with the evil force she represented.

Parris's treatment of his servant woman to force an admission of complicity with the Devil was in the tradition of the European inquisitors who used torture to elicit confessions. He was rewarded with similar results. To prevent further punishment, Tituba reluctantly promised to do as he demanded and name others who were involved. Unaware of the potential consequences, he turned her over to the magistrates to answer more questions regarding the details of her devilish alliance. She would be punished as much for defying his ministerial and paternal authority as for her alleged dabbling in the occult.

The hearing was to be held at Ingersoll's Tavern on March 1. The spectacle of three women revealing the titillating details of witch activities attracted a considerable number of Salem inhabitants. By early morning, the crowd of onlookers waiting to observe the investigation had grown too large to fit into the tavern and the examinations were moved to the meeting house.[12] The curious as well as the witnesses and their families crowded into the building. The three accused women were brought into the meeting room one at a time (see Fig. 14).

Sarah Good, who in appearance fit the popular mental and physical image of a witch—an abrasive middle-aged female of low social position who was frequently involved in conflicts with others—was the first to be questioned.[13] Even though she was the mother of a five-year-old and was pregnant at the time, Good was thirty-eight years old and looked haggard. She was not helped by her reputation. She was known and feared for her sharp tongue, avoided attendance at church, and only grudgingly accepted the assistance of her apparent betters when she was destitute.[14]

Figure 14: Sketch of the reconstructed Salem Village meeting house.

Tituba's examination early in March 1692 was held at the meeting house, as were many of the other examinations. She repeated her confession in this building and was finally sent to Boston to remain in jail until April 1693. The unheated, drafty building measured 34 feet by 28 feet. Its small windows permitted very little light to enter the building. The interior, therefore, was too dark to see clearly, even during the day.

This reconstructed building is now located at the Nurse Homestead in Danvers, Massachusetts. The original site of the meeting house on Hobart Street is occupied by the John Darling house, which was moved there in the nineteenth century. *(Illustration courtesy of the Danvers Alarm List Company.)*

No images had been found in her possession, but she was assumed guilty of the charge of familiarity with evil spirits and bluntly asked about her association with the Devil. She denied any diabolical contact. Asked why she hurt the children, Sarah Good vehemently denied all allegations and explained, in defense of her absence from church, that she lacked adequate clothing.[15]

The girls, listening to her denials, began to complain of painful pinching and, crying out, accused Sarah Good of tormenting them at that moment. She denied being responsible for their distress. If not her, who then was torturing the girls? asked the magistrates. Good suggested that it was the other accused woman, Sarah Osborne. The girls, temporarily recovering their composure, agreed that it was Osborne, a reasonable assumption since she too had been arrested and was being held for questioning.[16]

Osborne, who like Good had habitually missed church services, was brought into the room after Good. Unaware that the other woman had implicated her, Osborne too denied being in league with the Devil or doing anything to hurt the children. She complained that she was more likely to be bewitched than be a witch because of her past troubles. Sarah Osborne reflected on a dream when she too had been pricked by an appearance which she described as "a thing like an indian," in an artful allusion to the Puritan stereotype of the Devil as Indian. Another time she heard voices telling her not to go to church, which she had resisted. The voices and the remembered dream were taken as evidence not of a bewitchment but of a guilty association with invisible specters.[17] Guilt would be the presumption in almost all the hearings to follow.

Tituba was brought forward last to answer her accusers in the meeting house. Parris's act in submitting his servant woman to legal action pushed Tituba to the forefront of the witchscare and set the stage for the extraordinary persecution that would follow her reluctant confession. It is possible that if the Indian woman had maintained silence during the subsequent interrogation, that witchhunt might not have occurred, or, at the least, would have followed a different course. She reluctantly and hesitatingly took the lead in implicating others beyond the boundaries of the Salem community and established the framework of a fictional conspiracy of witches linked to the Devil through a written pact. Her story would then be embellished by the fantasies, fears, and cultural biases of other witnesses, but she provided the raw material from which they could weave even more elaborate narratives.

Her earlier questioning at Parris's hands convinced her that the truth, so cherished by her Puritan mentors, would fail her as a defense in court. She had every reason to sense that her successful facade as an acculturated servant would crumble in the face of this blatantly hostile legal procedure. The truthful denial of association with the evil presence not only failed to provide protection, it was treated as an act of defiance. Her rejection of Parris's suggestion that she was in league with the Devil had challenged his authority in spiritual matters and he was determined to exact retribution. Moreover, her admission of guilt to an act of white magic in fashioning the witchcake had had grotesque results. It frightened the girls into more bizarre behavior and enraged Parris. Another means of defense had to be devised if Tituba were to escape extreme punishment.

After a preliminary and weak denial of familiarity with the Devil or of causing harm, Tituba reluctantly confessed.[18] She fulfilled her promise to Parris and began to respond positively to the accusations and charges. She confessed to consorting with the Devil, blaming Sarah Good and Sarah Osborne for forcing her to take part in a plot to hurt the children, and proceeded to elaborate on a fantastic chronicle describing a coven of witches in Boston, suggesting with telling detail how Satanic power had infiltrated their Salem community. The girls quieted as they listened with astonishment to her extraordinary story, an account of witchcraft so inspired and singular that it appeared to be plausible.[19] It was not, as some earlier historians have suggested, the "incoherent nonsense" of a confused slave woman.[20] It was a carefully crafted tale that provided satisfactory answers to the questions in the seventeenth-century mind. Tituba explained the cause of the calamities. She also created a new aura of mystery about the events in Salem. The more credulous the magistrates appeared to be, the more richly embroidered the tale became. The reluctant witch had captured her audience.

It is impossible to determine exactly what Tituba was thinking on that March 1, 1692 day when she was forced to admit to having made a Satanic pact. Her decision may have been influenced by what happened in other cases of witchcraft in Boston and how those others accused were treated by the authorities in the recent past. She may well have been aware that between 1680 and 1692, during the time she had lived in Massachusetts, only one person had been executed for witchcraft.[21] Those accused of other crimes and who demonstrated penitence by humbly confessing to their sins were treated sympathetically. In most criminal trials in Massachusetts, "magistrates from the start were lenient with penitent offenders."[22] Tituba probably thought she had only to demonstrate true repentance for her past behavior to end her trial.

Few people in New England received harsh punishment for the crime of witchcraft. Executions had virtually ended in 1663 with the hanging of Rebecca and Nathaniel Greensmith. Tituba probably knew nothing of these earlier events that predated her arrival. On the other hand, not too long after the Indian woman had landed in Boston, Mary Hale had been indicted by the provincial court for familiarity with the Devil and bewitching a man to death. There was insufficient evidence and the court found her not guilty in March of 1681. Two years later Mary Webster was also tried and found not guilty of witchcraft.[23] Tituba probably knew about Elizabeth Morse who was convicted in 1680 but managed to avoid execution. In June of 1681 Morse, after her husband's sorrowful petition, was reprieved but confined to her home and the meeting house.[24] Tituba may also have heard about Joseph Fuller of Springfield who in 1683 had at first confessed to praying to the Devil and then retracted that confession. He was, however, found not guilty of the charge but whipped for lying.[25] Thus any knowledge of the experiences of other accused persons indicated that the worst Tituba could expect for confessing even a lie might be a beating. The death penalty for witchcraft, in spite of the law, was a rare occurrence and was imposed only once in New England while Tituba was there prior to the Salem witchscare.

That recent incident of execution, however, was more ominous. The allegations against Goodwife Glover, an Irish woman who, in 1688, had received a great deal of attention in the Boston community, ran contrary to earlier experiences. The Goodwin children, like Betty Parris and Abigail Williams, had exhibited strange behaviors and Goodwife Glover was suspected of bewitching them. Glover did confess and was subsequently convicted and executed.[26] But the Glover execution was unusual and Tituba, if she knew about it, may have expected that her own earlier blameless life, unlike that of Goody Glover, would afford some leniency.

On the other hand, the Parris family had moved to Salem before the Goodwin children had been "possessed" and it is possible that Tituba was not aware of the disposition of the Glover trial and her execution. In that case Tituba's knowledge of how accused witches were treated by the authorities came from the experiences of those who were either exonerated, received minimum punishment, or were reprieved. Confession, she expected, would satisfy Parris's grim determination to find a scapegoat for his daughter's troubles and did not necessarily entail either prison or death.

Quite likely she also hoped that confessing to supernatural power would intimidate her tormentors into leaving her alone. Such a threat might at least temporarily protect her from physical punishment. Claims of occult power were not unusual ploys by servants and slaves whose repertoire of resistance tended to be more passive than active. Invoking the Devil, like the use of violence by the dispossessed, was one of those extra-legal weapons used by powerless people who would challenge law and authority.[27] Tituba devised an even more imaginative use of that kind of resistance to protect her life.

Her decision to comply with Parris's orders to confess gave new meaning to a technique that had been used successfully by other slaves to avoid punishment. Depending on the gullibility of their victims, the implied threat in the slaves' claim to magical power could provide protection against excessive abuse.[28] In Tituba's case, Parris's insistence that she had made a pact with the Devil not only forced her to claim occult power, but it also opened the possibility of deflecting attention from herself by accusing others of complicity in a witches' coven.[29] Tituba improvised a new idiom of resistance by overtly submitting to the will of her abuser while covertly feeding his fears of a conspiracy. An admission of sin, even though a lie, followed by repentance became a workable tactic of resistance that others would follow.

As is typical of witchcraft interrogation in all cultures, Tituba's questioners provided her with clues as to what her answers should be. Since those accused of witchcraft were usually innocent of the charges, such testimonies were more often an affirmation of the questioners' ideas about witchcraft than a revelation of the accused witches' particular beliefs and practices.[30] A good part of Tituba's testimony was a direct response to those questions. She certainly understood some of what they wanted her to say and did give them the evidence needed to pursue their suspicions, but she also added details and notions that were not implied in the questions and set off a broader investigation than they had intended. Tituba's testimony was not merely the frightened response of a simple slave woman to the hints put forth by the magistrates, but an effective manipulation of their deepest fears. The impact of that confession triggered the witchhunt that defied all past experience with witchhunting in New England. In the process Tituba also led an assault on gender roles, social rank, and the clergy's authority, an attack that would be pursued relentlessly by the "afflicted" girls and the other confessors.

On the surface, in this cautious exchange between Tituba and her accusers, she seemed to ally herself with the Puritan theological notions of demonic evil, collaborating to assist in the process of purifying their society.[31] But something more was at work. Hidden in that confession was not so much a Puritan concept of evil but one derived from non-Christian cultures; a set of ideas that was at once familiar and strange. The anomaly of this aberration heightened the fear of an invasive presence.

When asked if she ever saw the Devil, Tituba acknowledged that "the devil came to me and bid me serve him." Who else did she see, asked the interrogator? Because she now knew he wanted others involved, Tituba answered, there were four women and a man. And who were they? Tituba identified two likely women who fit the popular image of a witch, Sarah Osborne and Sarah Good, both quarrelsome and somewhat disreputable, but already accused by the girls and thus understood by the magistrates as potential conspirators. The other three she did not know, but one was a tall man from Boston.[32]

The man, according to Tituba's story, had visited her once before in late December or early January at the time that the children had first exhibited the bizarre symptoms. He appeared to her one night just as she was going to sleep. The Salem magistrates missed her cue. The dream was not even reported in the official record of her testimony taken by Ezekiel Cheever.[33] It does appear in a more detailed report written by Jonathan Corwin. In Corwin's version she told them that the man-like shape came to her "Just as I was goeing to sleep . . . this was when the children was first hurt."[34]

Tituba's nightmare of that evil presence may well have triggered memories of her earlier Barbados life, where dreams among both African and American Indians were thought to be the work of spirits and interpreted as omens of things to come.[35] That ominous dream of an evil presence would be confirmed, in her mind, by the continuing illness of the children in the household and her own current misfortune to be identified with witchcraft. She sensed that Parris's wrath was the cause of Betty's problems, that the minister's continuing jeremiads against the ungrateful community and his terrifying warnings of future evils were taking their toll on the mental health of his daughter. By couching her accusation in the form of a sleep reference, in line with Indian beliefs in the identification of dreams as omens, she tried to inform others of Parris's evil ways. Her subversive suggestion was ignored.

Dreams were not significant elements in Puritan theology.[36] They took her nightmare not as a visionary omen or spiritual experience but an actual occurrence that involved the specters of people they had to identify. Magistrates Hathorne and Corwin focused their questions on the activities of this odd group of creatures who inhabited the diabolical realm brought down to earth. "What is this appearance you see? . . . What did it say to you? . . . What did you say to it?" they asked.

Responding to their probing, Tituba embellished her story even more. The creatures all met in Boston at night where the five evil ones, including Sarah Good and Sarah Osborne, threatened her if she did not hurt the children. Tituba introduced a new element in witchcraft testimony, a witches' coven attended by the specters of people both known and unknown to her. The startled examiners paused to question her about this strange, distant meeting. Witchcraft accusations traditionally involved people known to each other, an aggrieved party usually could be suspected of causing harm to others. But Tituba told them that strangers were involved.

The interrogation of the other two accused women, Osborne and Good, had followed conventional tactics. In the face of continued denials, they had been asked in a prescribed sequence about the spirits they were familiar with, why they hurt the children or whom they used for that purpose, and finally about a covenant with the Devil.[37] This procedure changed with the questioning of Tituba. The examiners did not immediately pursue the issue of a satanic pact. They were distracted by her complex tale of an experience that took her from Boston back to Salem with orders to kill the children and of a specter that changed shape from that of a man to a dog and a hog. Joining this party of phantoms were a yellow bird, rats, a wolf and a cat, four women, and a hairy imp.

Additional details were elicited from Tituba on the dress and physical appearance of this group. Tituba specified that Osborne had a familiar with the head of a woman and two legs and wings similar to one previously described by Abigail.[38] The tall man wore black clothes. One of the unidentified Boston women, Tituba said, wore a black hood over a white silk hood with a top knot. The other a shorter person had a serge coat and white cap. Tituba stated that she had seen the taller woman in Boston when she had lived there, but did not know her name. The silk clothing of the tall woman would indicate that Tituba had a person of higher class in mind; the shorter woman in wool and a white cap wore the dress of the more ordinary folk.[39]

Sumptuary laws in Massachusetts prohibited men, women, and children from dressing in clothing made out of finer material. By order of October 14, 1651, the Massachusetts General Court had forbidden people of "meane condition" from wearing the "garbe of gentlemen" or women of the same rank from wearing "silke or tiffany hoodes or scarfes, which though allowable to persons of greater estates, or more liberal education, yet, we cannot but judge it intollerable in persons of such like condition."[40] The description of the woman in silk and the man in black were, therefore, veiled references to respectability and an attempt to identify maleficium with higher social status. The man's black clothing carried a connotation of dignity and formality. The silk worn by the "tall woman" denoted wealth.[41]

Tituba's extraordinary message to her examiners was to look among the elite for the evil beings. That message, delivered in a discrete and artful attack on the social class system, opened the way to the accusation of women of respectable sainthood, beginning with Martha Corey and Rebecca Nurse on March 19 and 23, respectively. The convictions of these women would be eloquent testimony to the force of Tituba's suggestion that women eligible to wear silk could be witches. Her hints regarding the dangers hidden among the obviously respectable were confirmed and reinforced by Parris's sermons later that month and by his early April warning that the Devil could lurk among the apparent saints.[42] Her testimony confirmed the predictions of reformers who had reminded their congregations of an impending catastrophe if the community continued on its worldly path.

The strange, tall, white-haired man Tituba claimed to see wearing black clothes could fit many respectable, elderly men in the community dressed in their Sunday meeting clothes.[43] In the imagination of some other confessed witches, obsessed by the rhetoric of race and in their fantasies of satanic Indians, this tall Boston mystery man would be transformed into a tawny or black man.[44] But he was clearly a white man in Tituba's recorded testimony, a devious reference to Samuel Parris, a clergyman with strong connections to Boston. In effect this part of her testimony triggered a search for an appropriate male scapegoat. The result, discussed in the next chapter, was a widening of the witchhunt to include men; the arrest, conviction, and execution of several men; and the hanging of one clergyman, George Burroughs.

Whatever her intent, the consequence of Tituba's accusation in this community where words were believed to have the force of action, was to challenge the principle of social rank and raise the possibility of clerical misconduct.[45] No one would be more likely to resent the special privilege of that class than a slave in the house of a Congregational minister. But Tituba's rudimentary anti-clericalism probably did not exist in isolation. She spoke to resentments against the special privilege and influence of the clergy harbored by other ordinary people, particularly young women.[46] They would give vent to their hostility in later testimonies and confessions as they adapted and reformulated Tituba's stories to fit their own situations. Thus others, sensing the possible subversive message of a respectable white man leading a witch's coven, transformed Tituba's suggestion of an evil stranger into a parody of their own church rites—an indirect attack on the congregational ideal.[47]

Questioned further about this strange group of people, Tituba said that they all met in Boston the night before. And how had they traveled there? Tituba described the ride through the night on "stickes," with Osborne and Good behind her. The man had appeared to her earlier that same evening while she was washing the lean-to room. This, she acknowledged, was her second encounter with the diabolical creature; he was the same one who appeared two months before in her dream.[48]

The nightmarish story continued. Sometime during the morning of February 29, she was forced to pinch Elizabeth Hubbard at Dr. Grigg's house, where "the man brought her to me and made me pinch her." She regretted causing the child pain but could not stop doing so because they, "pull mee & hall me to . . . pinch the childr, & I am very sorry for itt."[49] That night, Tituba testified, Good and Osborne had taken her spirit to Boston where they told her to "hurt the children." After returning to Salem, riding their "stickes or poale," with Good and Osborne behind her holding on to one another, Tituba was taken to the Putnams' household where they made her "hurt the Child," Ann, holding a knife to her throat, and then back to her own house to torment Abigail Williams and Betty Parris.[50] All this time Tituba reported that she had tried to resist and had struggled against the overwhelming strength of the five evil ones. They in turn were assisted by a variety of strange creatures including the wolf that had scared Elizabeth Hubbard.[51]

Suddenly, Elizabeth Hubbard, who was sitting in the Meeting House listening to the questioning, panicked at Tituba's graphic description of these evil beings and a verification of her complaint about a wolf. She fell into "an extreame fit." Pandemonium broke loose as the other girls began to cry out. Tituba was so overcome by this reaction to her story that she appeared to be "once or twice taken dumb herself."[52] As Tituba drew into a trance-like silence, the hysteria of the girls heightened. The questioning could not continue. The first examination ended abruptly.[53]

Tituba's behavior at the end of the first day of testimony was unusual for anyone steeped in English folklore. The trance, as a form of possession, was not characteristic of English witchcraft practice; only those bewitched by evil forces were as a rule possessed. Since the Reformation at least, in English and European beliefs, victims exhibited strange symptoms brought on by the power of the witches, but witches themselves did not go into a trance any more than priests did in the exercise of their duties.[54]

The case was otherwise in the African and Indian rituals in Barbados in the 1670s, where possession by the spirit resulting in a trance was a traditional part of the shaman's or obeah's function in fighting evil. In Tituba's Amerindian world, such a trance was a familiar part of magico-religious healing ceremonies. During those rites the shaman used the trance as a shield in a battle with the spirits and to establish contact with the lost souls of the sick ones.[55] Now, no doubt frightened by the hysterical response of the girls, she reverted to this technique of her earlier world that offered spiritual protection against the evil presence.

Such behavior was not part of the witch's arsenal in the Puritan seventeenth-century world. The Puritans of Tituba's time referred to a religious ceremony that involved a trance as conjuring and associated it with Devil worship.[56] Tituba's penitent tone and regret for the pain she had inflicted, however, was so convincing to her listeners that the sudden loss of vision and hearing during her examination was taken to mean that she herself was bewitched by the others. It was not necessarily her intent to claim to be a victim. It was others like Thomas Putnam who excused her behavior as bewitchment, explaining that Tituba "was her self very much afflicted."[57] That misunderstanding of her behavior, one of several such confusing encounters, added to Tituba's credibility as a witness.

The next day, March 2, in her second official examination, calm temporarily prevailed and Tituba was finally asked about a covenant with the man. The story became even more elaborate, with Tituba seemingly taking more deliberate steps to frighten her listeners. She said the man had told her he was God. He wanted her to serve him for six years and to hurt the children. In return for signing the pact with him, she would be protected from harm and would receive "many fine things."[58] Asked why she had not informed Parris of these happenings and requested his assistance, Tituba explained that she was sworn to secrecy by the two Salem women, who threatened her life if she revealed their diabolical powers. She was afraid the man "would Cutt [her] head off" if she told.[59] Fear for one's physical safety was an emotion that Puritans could sympathize with.

The officials were shocked and possibly secretly gratified by Tituba's acknowledgment of a covenant with the Devil. They took it as confirmation of their worst fears. Puritan divines had always required evidence not of maleficium—evil action—but of a Satanic influence to convict people of witchcraft.[60] Thus their questioning of suspected witches usually concentrated on their involvement with this diabolical presence and of a conspiracy resulting from it. As a result, the courts were usually unable to secure convictions of accused witches who knew nothing of such a pact. Tituba ostensibly gave them the needed evidence.

This questioning regarding a diabolical pact corresponded with a drive for moral reform that had occupied the clergy since 1675. A transcendent evil force fit what the ministers conceived as an atmosphere of "Provoking Evils" that was threatening their society.[61] Any proof of that evil gave substance to their complaints. Tituba's testimony of a diabolical conspiracy provided a new forum with which the clergy could express their dissatisfaction with the state of religious convictions in Massachusetts. A witchhunt to ferret out the malefactors could prove that the decline in religious zeal had opened the door to Satan.

On the surface, Tituba's answers regarding this pact do appear to be responses to questioning regarding the theological concepts of the covenant of grace and its inversion, the Devil's pact.[62] This notion of the covenant was a major element in Puritan theology and society and Tituba must have absorbed some of its meaning. The covenant idea was central to Puritan social and theological life—it authorized and regulated the relations between the saints and their God, between the congregation and its minister, and between the members of the community and the magistrates. A pact with Satan violated the covenant with God, parodied the very notion of the covenant, and put the community in jeopardy of punishment for those transgressions.

On the other hand, the contractual relationship was also basic to the institutional life of an English community and was an important factor in the lives of the servant class in America. Tituba's reference to a contract on a piece of paper, a contract that stipulated a limited number of years of service and with its promise of material rewards, is more reminiscent of a servant's indenture than that of a Satanic conspiracy.[63] Under such a contract, that she knew protected English servants and indentured Indians, Tituba would have a limited time of servitude—about six or fewer years—and could expect payment in goods or money as freedom dues at the end of that time. With such a contract she could benefit from some additional legal protection from abuse by a master.[64]

Tituba probably knew little about the sophisticated concept of a Devil's pact, which existed only in the minds of her more educated interrogators. Nor did she necessarily conceptualize a Devil's sabbat, that "nightmare of learned witch lore."[65] But she would have been well versed in the institution of servitude and the various levels of bondage in colonial society. Her answers to the question of what kind of "covenant" she had made with "that man that came to you?" was to voice her discontent with her present status and talk about her whimsical hopes for the future embodied in a piece of paper that she could sign. Tituba's response to their questioning was easily the reaction of a slave to the suggestion of a written agreement that could improve her life on earth.

She was not alone in this kind of reaction to her social standing. Dissatisfaction with their lot in life was a common theme in several later testimonies. William Barker expected the Devil to pay his debts so that he and his family could live comfortably.[66] Elizabeth Johnson, a widow in somewhat difficult financial circumstances, was promised money.[67] Mercy Lewis, a destitute servant in Thomas Putnam's household, in her "afflictions" was offered gold and many fine things by the Devil.[68] Abigail Hobbs struck a bargain with the Devil to serve only two years in return for "fine clothes." But she complained that when the Devil did not fulfill his part of their bargain, she refused to sign a new contract obliging her to serve him for another four years.[69] Hobbs, who had lived in the Burroughs family when they had been in Salem, was clearly disappointed in her treatment at the hands of her master. Her subsequent identification of George Burroughs as a diabolical creature was surely a metaphor for his lack of integrity to his servants. So too, Tituba's hopes for freedom from bondage to Samuel Parris were reflected in this promise of a contract with a limited term of servitude.

It took a few more leading questions before Tituba, responding to the magistrates' additional promptings regarding a Devil's book, gave her inquisitors more reason to wonder about what was happening in their community. The contract on a piece of a paper became a book with many marks. Now, mindful of the power she had to create anxiety and probably with malice in mind, Tituba had added a few more people to the supposed Satanic pact. When asked how many names she saw in the book, she said there were nine marks in the book.[70] It was sufficient evidence to arouse her questioners to the enormity of the conspiracy and further fuel their fears of a pervasive diabolical presence.

Whether Tituba understood the theological implications of her testimony is not clear. That she frightened those who heard her story is evident from the immediate hysterical reaction of the audience. Their fear was clearly demonstrated. That she fully grasped the import of a plot to ruin their Godly commonwealth and destroy Christ's church is questionable. What she told them is what she understood about the evil presence—a combination of notions from a variety of sources, some religious, some derived from an eclectic folklore, and some from the substance of her own frightening dreams about evil beings that may well have belonged to her memory of Indian beliefs.

The story told by Tituba is a blending of elements from several sets of witchcraft beliefs. The book, of course, was an artifact of literate societies only and the Devil a part of Christian theology. They would not be found in the pre-colonial Amerindian or African cultures. But the strong link to Satanism, the evil force, with its promise of power over others, was surprisingly rare in the English folk tradition or in New England. Few persons giving testimony in witchcraft cases in Massachusetts mentioned the Devil.[71] In responding to the hints regarding Satan suggested by the questioners, and tuned to the nuances of this questioning, Tituba described the Devil as she was cued, but she also added a few non-Puritan variations on the source of evil that inadvertently heightened the sense of diabolical invasion. Under the stress of questioning, Tituba began to fall back on her knowledge of Indian and Creolized folklore notions.

In tribal or folk traditions, magical power was derived from the ability to manipulate the mystical elements of the universe for one's own purposes, whether good or evil. That power did not require a separate motivating spiritual element. Among South American Indians, for instance, such evil power was believed to be inherent in individuals and required no intermediary spiritual force as in the concept of the Devil.[72] For Indians like the Arawaks, evil power could exist in different degrees of strength. The most potent evil spirit, the most feared source of evil, was a kenaima. Unlike the Christian Devil, the power of the kenaima existed in a real person of flesh and blood and not of spirit.[73] In the American Indian manner, Tituba gave the evil presence substance as a persona, identifiable in her testimony as a respectable white man living in the distant community of Boston.[74] That suggestion led to a hunt for a man as the personification of the Devil, shifting some of the investigation away from the traditional woman as witch and leaving men more vulnerable to accusation.

Her testimony, apart from the reference to the Devil and his book, is not particularly English or even European in substance, but formed part of a universal assumption about the occult. She sketched a rather generic portrait of a witch who could fly through the air, take animal or human form, and submit to oaths and ordeals involving other spirits; she hinted at the efficacy of magical techniques without going into details. These were all common characteristics of witches from Africa to Asia and throughout America.[75] Amerindians of Guyana on the coast of South America, for instance, believed that "the spirit may be passed from the body of its proper owner into that of any animal, or even into any inanimate object."[76] So Tituba described the metamorphosis of Sarah Good's spirit into a hog and a dog.

She also saw animals change into the tall man and then back again into animals, sometimes into a hog and sometimes into "a great black dogge," in a manner typical of both the European witch and the evil South American kenaima who had the power to put his spirit into the body of any animal he wished, even mythic animals.[77] But her choice of animal, a dog, as the alter ego of her respectable man, reflected a "sub-genre of insults" common in New England. To be a dog "was to lack precisely those qualities which defined ruling men: intellect, independence, and godliness."[78] Tituba's tall man was a parody of the godly. Her commitment to him was to be written in her blood—a symbol associated with many forms of witchcraft that both renewed fears of Indian cannibalism and reminded them of the blood-sucking witches of medieval legends.[79] To Tituba, however, that blood oath may have been part of her memory of her earlier life in Barbados, of Africans who sealed compacts with their blood.[80]

One almost universal quality of witch belief was the supposed ability of witches to fly through the air on a stick or pole. Both European and African traditions contained folklore of night-riding witches on sticks. The idea is so ancient that it is found in the oldest Hindu beliefs as well as in medieval Jewish lore and in Greek and Roman mythology. The object of all such nocturnal trips was to attend secret meetings and to take part in cannibalistic rituals.[81] Although the witches' meeting is a common feature of witchcraft lore, some characteristics associated with the idea were not shared.[82] Tituba's testimony contained some significant variations from the European or African model.

During her first two examinations on March 1 and 2, Tituba drew on common traditions when she told the magistrates of a ride on a "sticke" to Boston, with Osborne and Good behind her to meet the other witches she could not name. But Tituba could not give any detail of those rides, refusing to respond to the interrogator's prompting to describe the roadways. She denied seeing "trees nor path, but was presently there."[83] This description was somewhat different from the Anglo-African model of a witch on a pole sailing over the clouds to a meeting to plot harm to others. Tituba knew Boston because she had lived there with the Parrises and was also familiar with the road to Salem. During the second day of questioning, responding to some unidentified prompting, she appeared to retract part of her earlier statement about actually being in Boston at the meeting of the witches. "I was goeing & then Came back againe[.] I was never att Boston," she said. There was an echo of the folklore of American Indians in those words.

Many Indians of North and South America believed in a dream soul that could leave the body during sleep and visit faraway places without the use of a prop. Integral to this belief is the idea that all tangible objects have two parts, a body and a spirit, which separate during sleep and death. During sleep the spirit side can return to the physical object.[84] Events that occur during that dream state are considered real, tangible happenings. Thus Tituba's story of a witch meeting was shaped by the idea of a dream-like state, during which her spirit traveled to a distant city, leaving her body behind. In keeping with her artful use of Puritan notions, however, when describing these events, she carefully included an unnecessary but familiar artifact from European folklore—the witch's pole or stick, an early version of the broomstick. Nonetheless, she tried to tell her interrogators that it was not her physical presence that went to Boston—"I was never att Boston"—but that her spirit had left her temporarily.

While they could ignore the notion of a dream spirit, the Puritans could not mistake the site of the witch's meeting. Tituba placed it in Boston—outside the Salem community. By locating the evil source outside of the community, Tituba again reverted to Indian ideas. She may have been evoking the Guyanese concept of the evil persona that is rarely of the same village as his victim. Thus the evil forces feared by the Indians of the Circum-Caribbean area, including the Arawak, emanate from sources outside the immediate group and remain there.[85] Tituba saw her evil beings stationed in Boston, not Salem. Her story, at least in outline, followed the tradition of South American Indian folklore. Her hearers, however, misunderstanding her allusions, reinterpreted these unfamiliar notions.

Puritans, obsessed with the intrusion of evil power into their own community, would later transform Tituba's suggestion of a distant meeting and a plan to cause harm to the children to a meeting held within the confines of their village, led by a stranger who mocked Puritan religious rites. From the beginning of April through the trial of George Burroughs in August, all accusers described this meeting as taking place near Parris's house. Abigail Hobbs, for instance, described such a meeting in a field near the Parris household, and Abigail Williams said she saw a great number of persons at a similar mock sacramental meeting in the village.[86] The Puritans thus reshaped Tituba's vision to fit their own version of a Satanic presence. But the concept of the Indian kenaima, the evil stranger, had entered into Puritan thought. They retained the vision of an outside force that could be blamed for the evil among them, an idea that in turn would propel the witchhunt into unexpected paths.

One other Caribbean import in Tituba's testimony is the hairy imp: "a thing all over hairy, all the face hayre & a long nose . . . with two Leggs, itt goeth upright & is about two or three foot high."[87] This creature could be an Irish Leprechaun but, more likely, it too was based on the Guyanese evil kenaimas, often described as little people who lived in the depths of the forest and came out at night to attack people. The description also fits the evil spirit of the Ashanti of West Africa called Sasabonsam, a monster supposedly covered with long hair, having blood-shot eyes, and known to sit on the branches of a tree dangling his legs.[88] In Jamaica the Creole spirit came to be known as a duppy, "a malicious vindictive, imp-like spirit that haunts forests and burying grounds, a figure very likely derived from a combination of African and Amerindian beliefs."[89] Tituba relied on the prototype of an evil presence found among societies in the

Caribbean rather than the English idea. Nonetheless, the Indian and English concepts of magic and evil were close enough to allow some unfamiliar details of Tituba's story to be reinterpreted and incorporated into their English framework of belief.[90]

Tituba also added details that were not implied in the questions. She spoke of a yellow bird and later of a green and white bird and a black dog, of two rats (cats in a second version of her testimony)[91] both red and black, and of a hog. The yellow bird would appear in many other testimonies and hallucinations, as would the dog. The bird in particular probably had special significance for Tituba. Among the Arawak Indians of Guiana, birds were taken as magical messengers. The goatsucker or nightjar, the supernatural ancestor of Tituba's clan, with its weird piercing call at night, was held in particular awe by many Guiana Indians.[92] Were these birds of her fantasy a memory of her earlier existence and an attempt to draw on her guardian spirit for assistance? Whatever her intent, others found these allusions useful for their own purposes.

There was abundant material in her fantastic story for the other accused witches to draw on, and much of what she said reappeared with variations in subsequent confessions. By the end of the second day she had already given the Salem authorities many reasons to fear a Satanic presence. Over the course of the next three days she continued to confirm her story, as she repeated most of the details given at the beginning.[93]

Tituba had lived in a Barbados society among Africans and Amerindians who incorporated the trance, image-magic, divination, and similar techniques into their religious ceremonies. As an Amerindian, her world was informed by similar behavior and she proved in 1692 that she could draw on that residual knowledge when expedient. In March of 1692 Tituba found it useful to emerge from her role as a docile Puritan servant woman and demonstrate the native American side of her identity. It both fascinated and repelled her listeners. But they listened and absorbed the information needed to exorcise the Devils from their community, an evil presence that only Tituba could help them locate.

Her confession in turn was made that more easily because of cultural differences regarding the use of language. Distortion of the truth did not carry the same negative meaning among American Indians as it did in Puritan societies, where deception for personal gain or to save one's life was equated with Satanic practices. Puritans who confessed falsely endangered their souls. On the other hand, in Indian cultures a reluctance to contradict others and the use of metaphoric language were cultivated

Severall sent to Boston
Goales on acc't of witchcraft
Salem March [?]

Salem May 12th p mittimus
wch went May 13th to Boston

sent Boston
Sarah Osburne —
Sarah Good —
Titiba Indian —

1 George Jacobs sen'r —
2 Giles Cory —
3 Wm Hobs —
4 Edw'd Bushop —
5 Sarah Bushop his wife
6 Bridget Bushop — alias Oliver
7 Sarah Wild —
8 Mary Lt Nath putnams negro
9 Mary English —
10 Allice Parker —
11 Ann Pudeater —

Martha Cory
Rebecka Nurce
Dorothy Good
Sarah Cloyce
Eliz. procter
John procter

Aprill
12 send
to Boston

11

May
2d
Lydea Dastin wid. of Reding
Susannah Martin of Amesbry
Dorcas Hoar of Beverly wid
Sarah Murrell of Reding

May
9th
Bethya Carter 2 of Woburn
Ann Seirs —
Sarah Dastin —
George Burrows —

all sent to Boston

In Salem prison

Dor Eastry —
Abigail Hobs —
Hobs —
Mary Waren —

Churchwell
Jacobs Margret
Abigail Soames
Rebecca Jacobs
Sarah Buckley
mary witheridge
Sarah procter

X

Sent to Boston Wedensday the 18th May 1692

Thomas Farror of Salem
Eliz Hart of Lyn
John Willard of Salem Village
Roger Toothaker of Bilrica

Sent to salem Goale
yp 23d may 1692

Sarah pease
Sarah procter

Sent to Boston munday the 23d 1692

Mary Eastry — Mary Derich
Abigaile Soames Benjamin procter
Susannah Rootes Eliz: Cary —
Sarah Bassett

as diplomatic arts. What was to Indians a polite embellishment was understood by Puritans as a lie.[94] To protect herself in Massachusetts the Indian woman reverted to those remembered concepts and familiar practices, as she cunningly confessed to promoting an evil conspiracy that had merely been suspected.

During the five days of testimony, Tituba and the two other women were taken to jail in Ipswich, about ten miles away from the Salem village meeting house. Daily the constables, on horseback, brought the women back to the village for additional questioning. At some time during that five-day period, they were subjected to at least one minute and humiliating search of their naked bodies, including the genital area, for signs of a "witches' teat" or some mark from which, according to legend, the Devil or his familiars suckled their converts. Such marks had been used traditionally both in England and in New England as empirical evidence of a diabolical association. The examining women thought they saw some telltale sign on Tituba, but it could just as well have been the wounds from a beating shortly before the hearings. It was not there on reexamination.[95]

The two Sarahs continued to maintain their innocence. But with each session Tituba confirmed with more certainty the evil presence, as she faithfully repeated her early testimony. The Reverend Hale was convinced of her honesty because he assumed she could not have remembered all those extraordinary details if she had been lying.[96] Finally satisfied that she could offer no more information, on March 7 the magistrates sent Tituba and the other two to Boston to await trial and punishment (see Fig. 15). Sarah Osborne would die in prison on May 10, 1692;

Facing page:
"Severall sent to Boston Goale on acco' of witchcraft.
Salem March 1'd first Exam
Sent boston
Sarah Osburne . . .
Sarah Good . . . . . .
Titiba Indian . . . . ."
The first three people transported to Boston jail early in March were Sarah Osborne, Sarah Good, and Tituba Indian. In April five more women (Martha Corey, Rebecca Nurse, Dorothy Good, Sarah Cloyce, Elizabeth Proctor) were sent to the Boston jail and in May nineteen people, men and women, starting with "Lydia Dasting. Wido' of Rede" followed them, many in chains. Tituba was held in the Boston jail until April 1693. *(Photo courtesy of Massachusetts Supreme Judicial Court, Division of Archives and Records Preservation; on deposit at Peabody Essex Museum, Salem, Mass.)*

Sarah Good would be tried, found guilty, and hanged on July 19.[97] Tituba outlived them, her confession serving as a shield against any immediate drastic action.

By March 5 the magistrates had most of the pieces of their Satanic plot: evidence of the Devil's book, a cabal of night-riding witches, and incidents of maleficium. They lacked only a few elements of their diabolical fantasy. Tituba did not offer any information about sexual orgies or cannibalism, or suggest that her witches' coven had any relation to the Christian religious ceremonies. Neither concept entered into Indian lore.[98] Such ideas were too distant from Tituba's worldview to appear in her description of evil acts. She was either not asked about them or choose to ignore what was foreign to her understanding. Details on some of these notions would come in later testimonies as Tituba's story was reformulated by the beliefs of those steeped more deeply in English folklore and Christian theology.

Thomas Newton, the Attorney General preparing the first cases for trial, considered bringing her back to Salem as a witness for the June 2 court when the first trial of Bridget Bishop was conducted. There is no record that he did so, or that his recommendation to separate the witnesses from the prisoners was followed.[99] Communication and the exchange of information between the two groups continued. By the beginning of June Tituba's testimony apparently was no longer necessary; the details had entered into the folklore of New England witchcraft. Other witnesses, reformulating and embellishing her fantasy of a Satanic pact, would provide sufficient evidence to condemn the innocent to death.

If Tituba had had revenge in mind for her own enslavement, she could not have found a more effective weapon against the community than her fantastic story of a witches' meeting in Boston to plot harmful acts, a compact with an evil being, and a suspicious book with nine names. The magistrates interpreted the details of that confession as proof that the diabolical presence had invaded their community. Tituba had fueled their fantasies of a Satanic plot. As she awaited news of her fate in a Boston jail, the next stage in this witchhunt, to find those unnamed conspirators and reveal the extent of Satan's influence, was about to begin.

Creative Adaptations: Complaints and Confessions

> Many of the confessors confirmed their confessions with
> very strong circumstances: As their exact agreement
> with accusations of the afflicted; their punctual
> agreement with their fellow confessors; their relating the
> times when they covenanted with Satan, and the reasons
> that moved them thereunto; their Witch meetings, and
> that they had their mock Sacraments of Baptism and
> the Supper.
>
> —John Hale, "A Modest Inquiry into the
> Nature of Witchcraft"

O nce Tituba and the two Sarahs were committed to jail in Boston
on March 7, the witchhunt should have ended. The fate of the
trio, following previous practice in cases of witchcraft, should
then have been decided by popular will, a consensus that could be
expressed through jury trials. But in March of 1692 there was no legiti-
mate government in existence and no process for instituting court action.
Courts were suspended, awaiting the arrival of a new governor with the
authority to reestablish governmental institutions. The Salem leaders
could only investigate, not resolve, conflicts. At the same time the afflictions of the girls worsened as the month of March drew to a close. They
seemed to suffer incredible torments at invisible hands all spring.

Governor Phips, carrying a new charter, would not return to Massachusetts from England until the middle of May and by the time he
arrived many more people would stand accused of consorting with the
Devil. Twenty-six people were already under indictment on May 14, the
day of his landing, and even more were under investigation in Salem.[1]

"Many persons were grievously tormented by witches," Phips observed on his arrival, and "they cried out upon several persons by name, as the cause of their torments." He immediately issued a commission to establish a special court, Oyer and Terminer, to hear the cases of those in jail and to determine the guilt of the accused. The first trial in that court would not be heard until June 2.[2] Bridget Bishop, who was not among the earliest accused, was found guilty in the first court session and sentenced to die eight days later. More convictions and executions followed, until Phips called a halt to the use of spectral evidence as proof.

The failure to take immediate legal action against the accused and the inability of the community to fully resolve the witchscare through the usual institutional means at the beginning may well explain what happened in the weeks between March and May.[3] But at the same time Tituba's testimony had so heightened the sense of an impending doom and a diabolical presence that reverberations of her words contributed to a growing unrest in the village. The belief that there were more than three diabolical agents responsible for the girls' physical and mental anguish accentuated the urgency to identify the unknown malefactors.

Within days of Tituba's absence from Salem, the witchhunt had taken on incredible dimensions. Her confession had not only fueled the fears of her Salem audience, but gave them reasons to widen the hunt for diabolical culprits beyond the common geographic and social parameters of English witchhunts. Taking their cues from Tituba's testimony about many signatures in the Devil's book and the fact that they were the marks of strangers, the three girls began to accuse unlikely individuals of bewitching them. Their accusations acquired new definition as they borrowed details from Tituba's stories of a witches' meeting and a written contract. In their complaints, the girls confirmed the presence of Tituba's multiple evil beings; at the same time they began the transformation of Indian concepts of evil into notions more consistent with Puritan beliefs; the confessors who followed them continued to elaborate and reshape those details. The events in 1692 then offer an opportunity to follow the process of "creative adaptation," to borrow a phrase from T. H. Breen, the transformation of a set of Puritan beliefs and rituals under the influence of a Caribbean culture introduced by Tituba, the Indian woman slave.[4]

The interplay of European and Creole belief systems contributed a dynamic quality to the conflict between English elite and popular cultures.[5] Because Tituba's Caribbean beliefs reflected and distorted learned European notions of a pervasive Satanic presence, she helped to link folk ideas to learned theological concepts. Her testimony thus further blurred the lines between folklore and elite cultures. The cultural blending and the shifting of the boundary of elite notions added to the emotional tensions of the Salem events. The Puritans struggled to deal with the strangeness of the Indian woman's story and to integrate the details into their own worldview.

In outward detail, as the Reverend John Hale noted at the time, there were many similarities between Tituba's story and those of the other confessors, but the variations are significant and point up differences between the features of the Puritan mental landscape and that of the Indian woman.[6] During the course of the witchhunt, however, those uniquely Puritan qualities were gradually reshaped. The result was a modification of English Puritan notions regarding evil that demonstrate an interaction and blending of American Indian, Creolized West Indian, and English beliefs. The Salem experience was part of the ongoing process of cultural invention, a "middle ground" of cultural contact in which both Indians and Europeans, out of their need to coexist and the misunderstanding of the forms of the other, created a unique cultural mixture that was neither wholly Indian, nor wholly European, but a "realm of constant invention."[7]

Tituba herself had responded to verbal and behavioral clues that were relevant to her own experience and understanding and ignored concepts that were foreign or that did not fit comfortably with her own mental world. Accusers and accused alike did the same as they unconsciously translated the foreign elements of Tituba's story into forms more familiar to the English Puritan world. The mental promptings followed by Puritans at the beginning thus were different from those emphasized by Tituba. However, as they borrowed parts of her imagery under the powerful imaginative influence of her frightening stories, their apparent resistance to her ideas receded and they modified their own conception of the cosmic order.

This adaptive process began within days of the conclusion of Tituba's testimony. As people talked about the identity of the unnamed culprits suggested in Tituba's testimony, an answer came when Ann Putnam, the thirty-year-old wife of Thomas Putnam, complained that she was being tormented not only by Tituba, Sarah Good, and Sarah Osborne, but also by the specter of Martha Corey, another woman in the village. Corey, a covenanting member of the Village church and the wife of a prosperous landowner, could not be dismissed as easily as the two Sarahs and Tituba.[8] A lengthy investigation followed Ann Putnam's complaints as Edward Putnam and Ezekiel Cheever set up an experiment. On March 12 they went to Ann Putnam to ask her to describe what Martha Corey was wearing when her specter allegedly appeared and then they would test her memory against what they saw of Martha Corey. The experiment failed when Ann Putnam refused to go into detail and Martha Corey taunted them for their credulity.[9]

Following this attempt at empirical proof of the spectral allegations first suggested by Tituba, the younger Ann and the Putnams' servant girl, Mercy Lewis, also began to suffer from fits the two girls blamed on Corey. Two days later an angry Martha went to the Putnam household to face her accuser, the elder Ann Putnam. The results horrified the observers and also confirmed Tituba's hints: "no sonner did martha Corey Come in to the hous of thomas putnam but ann putnam fell in to grevious feets of Choking[,] blinding[,] feat and hands twisted in a most grevious maner and told martha Corey to her face that she did it, and emediately hur tonge was dran out of her mouth and her teeth fasned upon it in a most grevious maner."[10]

By the time the Reverend Deodat Lawson arrived, at Parris's invitation, on March 19, stories of meetings with Satan had acquired even more elaborate detail, somewhat in the manner of the sixteenth- and early seventeenth-century European witchhunts. There was talk of mock baptisms and the Lord's Supper, of bloodletting, of night rides on sticks, of familiars sucking witches' teats, of specters causing pain, of murdered children and wives, and spooked animals.[11] Lawson then witnessed a series of very odd behaviors at Nathaniel Ingersoll's tavern, at the homes of Samuel Parris and Thomas Putnam, and in the meeting house, behaviors that confirmed the verbal accusations of a diabolical presence.

Upon arrival in the Village he first stopped at Ingersoll's Tavern where Mary Walcott, Mary Sibley's niece, came to talk to him. Standing at the door of the tavern that afternoon, she suddenly cried out that she was being bitten on the wrist. Without apparent cause, Lawson saw the marks of teeth on both sides of Mary's wrist.[12] In the evening of that day he went to Samuel Parris's house and observed Abigail Williams in the midst of "a grievous fit":

> she was at first hurryed with Violence to and fro in the room . . . sometimes makeing as if she would fly, stretching up her arms as high as she could, and crying, "Whish, Whish, Whish!"

After Abigail complained that Rebecca Nurse's specter was in the room and trying to force her to sign the Devil's book, she cried "I wont, I wont, I wont, take it," and ran into the fireplace trying to climb up the chimney. Others told Lawson that she had attempted to go into the fire during other fits.[13]

The following day Lawson presided over a meeting at the church during which several of the girls interrupted his prayers and the singing of psalms with irrelevant and rude comments. Abigail Williams and Ann Putnam were the worst offenders, but they were joined by an increasing group of tortured females of various ages: Mrs. Bethshaa Pope, Goodwife Sarah Bibber, Mary Walcott, Mercy Lewis, and Elizabeth Hubbard. In the church that day, the "afflicted" girls and women accused Martha Corey of bewitching them. They claimed that her specter was sitting on a beam in the meeting house suckling a yellow bird between her fingers.[14] The magistrates could no longer ignore the rumors regarding Corey's involvement with the diabolical.

On Monday March 21 Martha Corey was officially questioned about her witchcraft activities, which she denied. But the accusers, now numbering about ten women and girls, said she was biting, pinching, and strangling them. They insisted that they saw her "Likeness coming to them, and bringing a Book to them." Lawson noted that whenever Corey bit her lip, her accusers cried out and produced marks of biting on the arms. During Corey's second examination, Lawson commented that whenever she moved, her motions produced similar effects on the "afflicted." They complained of pinching, bruising, tormenting at their breasts when Corey bent forward, or of pains in their backs when she leaned backwards. The older Ann Putnam collapsed and had to be carried out during the examination.[15]

A new round of accusations had begun, one marked by persecution of upper-class women and of men. Martha Corey was the first of this unusual group to be accused. As a respectable member of the community and a covenanting member of the church, she did not fit the usual description of a witch. She was, however, elderly, and in her younger years had given birth to an illegitimate mulatto son and continued to include the father of that child in the household with her present husband. This "touch of deviance" may well have made her an ideal transitional witch figure from the traditional outcast to the person of respectability.[16]

Thus Martha Corey, the first of this new group to be accused, may well have been a test of the credibility of Tituba's suggestions regarding gentility and the diabolical form. When accusations against Corey were believed, the girls were encouraged to exploit Tituba's innuendo even further. Rebecca Nurse came next. Before the furor over the examination of Martha Corey and Rebecca Nurse had died down, rumors spread in the village of more accusations of unlikely malefactors.

On Wednesday, March 23, Lawson went to Thomas Putnam's to see the older Ann and provide her with comfort. She was just recovering from one of her many fits, when she had another one in his presence. She seemed to be in a violent argument regarding scriptural texts with someone they could not see, all the time with eyes closed and stiffened body. Lawson began to read the disputed text and Ann Putnam opened her eyes and recovered from the fit, seemingly healed by the minister's action. On that day, Lawson reported also that five-year-old Dorcas Good was imprisoned.[17]

After Martha Corey was sent to jail, Ann Putnam had a miraculous recovery and continued well until April 5.[18] Her new set of symptoms occurred the day after two more women, Sarah Cloyce and Elizabeth Proctor, were accused and arrested for afflicting several of the girls. Complaints against a variety of other respectable women followed: Mary English, Mary Easty, and finally the wives of the Reverend John Hale and Governor Phips.[19] As the Attorney General assigned the task of preparing the cases against the accused remarked, "The afflicted spare no person of what quality so ever."[20]

By the beginning of April the accusations of witchcraft had extended far beyond the usual experience of seventeenth-century Massachusetts. Before these 1692 events, a typical witchcraft trial in New England involved the accused against one or two people. The accused were commonly older women of the lower classes or less productive members of the community who were disliked in some way. Like Sarah Osborne and

Sarah Good, they were often disagreeable, outspoken women, misfits who had been in trouble with their neighbors and the courts before.[21] The trials of such women usually focused on accusations of maleficium— evil magic that caused harm—but seldom involved overt Satanism, witches' pacts with the Devil, witches' sabbats, or possession by devils, all features that appeared in the Salem trials.[22] The accusations resulted from conflicts between neighbors—accusers and accused knew each other—but in Salem the girls accused people in distant communities, often strangers to them personally such as the Boston merchant John Alden. Strangely, many of the accused in 1692 were of the more "respect-able classes," including the wife of the governor, Mrs. Phips, and full members of the church such as Rebecca Nurse.

The accusers also did not spare men. Tituba had implicated a man as the leader of the conspiracy and the afflicted girls believed that at least one man was the leader. The first man to be investigated toward the end of March was the tavernkeeper, John Proctor. Early in March, Proctor, angered over his servant Mary Warren's involvement with the afflicted girls, had threatened to beat her if she did not behave. He then left town. Upon his return some weeks later on March 25, the day after Rebecca Nurse's first examination, Proctor discovered that, in his absence, Mary had again fallen into fits blamed on witchcraft and was participating in the hearings. He threatened to thrash her again. His servant, no doubt fearful of Proctor's threats and crudely reflecting Tituba's more subtle attack on Samuel Parris, accused Proctor of sending his specter to tor-ment her.[23]

The Sunday after Proctor's return, March 27, Parris added to the frightening atmosphere in Salem as he ominously warned the congrega-tion, in a bizarre echo of Tituba's testimony, that the Devil could lurk even among the saints: "There are devils as well as saints in Christ's Church," he predicted.[24] No doubt he was justifying the arrest of Rebecca Nurse, the wife of his enemy, Francis Nurse, a member of the Village Committee who had denied him his annual salary.[25] Parris had added ministerial approval to Tituba's suggestion that members of the elite were prime movers in the diabolical actions. More guilty parties would be unearthed. The following Monday Daniel Elliot overheard some of the girls accuse Elizabeth Proctor of being a witch. He thought it was in jest.[26] But the allegation was taken seriously.

The accusation against Elizabeth Proctor brought Tituba's husband within the orbit of the accusers. John's sudden appearance in these events was precipitated probably by his fear of being accused. Like his wife, he had assisted in the witchcake incident and may have felt vulnerable once he realized that the hunt for malefactors would not end with the arrest of just three women. His anxiety manifested itself in symptoms similar to those of the "afflicted" girls. He had difficulty breathing and experienced pinching and pricking sensations on his skin. No doubt mystified about the natural cause of these symptoms, he too fell back on the witchcraft explanation and accused those most recently singled out as alleged witches: Sarah Cloyce and Elizabeth Proctor.[27] Acutely aware of Tituba's testimony, he drew on her statements to elaborate his own fearful experiences. He said Sarah Cloyce bit him while he was at the meeting house on Sunday. He spoke of a "gentlewoman" who forced him to sign the book and commit himself to the Devil. His accusation against Elizabeth Proctor incensed her husband, and Proctor turned his wrath on John and threatened to "beat the Devell out of him."[28]

John's symptoms became more grotesque after this threat and the next day he fell into a fit so violent that it took four men to hold him.[29] His problems continued through May and he joined the afflicted girls several times in court during the examination of Mary Warren on April 19, John Willard on May 18, and complaints about several other women.[30] His distress may have worsened when he heard that another Indian man, Samuel Passanauton, was arrested toward the end of April.[31] At one point John pointed to some old scars on his body due, he said, to witchcraft, but which could also have been the result of earlier beatings from Parris and others who controlled his fate. He seemed determined to prove that he was a victim rather than a cause of witchcraft.

Whether these symptoms continued to be genuine physical manifestations of fearful anxiety, a pathological condition that had been there for some time, or, as Thomas Hutchinson suggested a half century later, a calculated attempt to protect himself by dissembling because he "was convinced he should stand a better chance among the afflicted then the accused," is not obvious from the record.[32] John often fell into fits and was unable to speak. The girls then spoke for him, testifying that various other accused persons were "afflicting" him.[33] He seemed unable to explain what was happening to him. Although he suffered from fits, he seldom accused particular individuals of tormenting him after he pointed to Elizabeth Proctor and Sarah Cloyce. His behavior certainly contributed to the atmosphere of diabolical invasion and may have added credibility to the alleged torture of the girls and the growing suspicion about the possibility of more men being involved.

Within a week of John's first afflictions, both Elizabeth and John Proctor were in jail. "Goodman" Proctor was followed by another twenty-five men during the course of the witchhunt. Giles Corey, Martha's husband, was arrested on April 18, accused by Ann Putnam, Mercy Lewis, Abigail Williams, Mary Walcott, and Elizabeth Hubbard.[34] Two days later William Hobbs of Topsfield was accused and questioned. Not only had the hunt for witches widened to include men, but it had begun to move beyond the boundaries of Salem Village and Town. William Hobbs's daughter Abigail had been brought from Topsfield on April 18 on suspicion of witchcraft and on the complaints of the "afflicted" girls his wife Deliverance, two other woman, and another man from Topsfield were also arrested. The list of accused outsiders included Mary Easty (sister of Rebecca Nurse), Sarah Wild, and Nehemiah Abbott, Jr.[35]

Abbott of Topsfield got off easy during this early period of accusations. He was arrested and questioned on the complaints of Mary Walcott, Mercy Lewis, and Ann Putnam on April 22. But the girls hesitated to confirm his diabolism. They did not recognize him. They scrutinized his face, but could not agree that his likeness was the one that tormented them. The lack of recognition was blamed on the dim lighting in the room. A large number of people at the windows kept out the light. Abbott was taken outside for further viewing. The girls, who obviously had never seen him before, "said he was like the man, but he had not the wen [wart or lump] they saw in his apparition." They could not agree on their identification. Ann Putnam was sure he was the man, Mary Walcott said it is like him, and Mercy Lewis denied it was the one she had seen. Because they could not agree, charges against Abbott were dismissed.[36] Others were not as fortunate as Abbott when they could not be positively identified. By the summer it was no longer necessary to recognize the accused as persons known. Absolute strangers were arrested for crimes caused by their "specters."

Tituba's testimony itself had reinforced a dichotomy between those from within and those from outside the community. She told them the witches were strangers, outsiders. She had given the Puritans of Salem reason to

look outside their community for the diabolical force, thereby trans-
forming the conventional function of witchhunts. In earlier incidents of
witchhunting in Massachusetts as in most other communities, accusations
were brought on by internal divisions and local conflicts resulting from
face-to-face contacts. Witchhunting therefore may have had some social
function in rooting out dissidents from the community and reinforcing
social cohesion.[37] The opposite happened in Massachusetts in 1692; as
the witchhunts widened their geographic and social scope, they further
divided the community with an attack on the clergy itself and on the
social class system.

Tituba's story made it possible for the magistrates to believe that a
man like George Burroughs, a minister, could be responsible for the
Satanic presence in their community when he was accused by Abigail
Hobbs and Ann Putnam. Consequently, a warrant for his arrest was
issued on April 30.[38] Burroughs was brought to Salem on May 4 and by
that time several more men were under arrest. The Indian man, Samuel
Passanauton, was in jail by April 28.[39] Philip English, a prosperous
Salem merchant, managed to escape the authorities and run away. He
was pursued and finally captured in Boston before he escaped again.[40]
On May 10 George Jacobs, Sr. and Jr., and the latter's wife, Margaret,
were arrested, as was John Willard, all of Salem. A few days later Roger
Toothaker of Billerica was also taken into custody. By the end of May
complaints were heard about both men and women in several communities—Andover, Rumney Marsh, Malden, Marblehead, Lynn, and Beverly, among other towns in Massachusetts—and began to spread to
Boston. On May 28 a warrant was issued for John Alden, a respectable
merchant in Boston and descendant of the earliest settlers in Massachusetts. He was imprisoned for a short time, but like Philip English temporarily eluded his captors.[41]

Tituba's allegation had sent the Salem magistrates all over the province
to find the co-conspirators. Neither social status nor geographic location
provided immunity from persecution, any more than gender did. Accusations against strangers were accepted as evidence of witchcraft. Unlike
the earlier case of Nehemiah Abbott, by the end of spring it was no
longer necessary to establish any link between the accused and the accusers. Face recognition was no longer required. Tituba denied knowing the
names of all those who attended her secret meeting in Boston or wrote in
the Devil's book, and others, following her lead, accused distant strangers

of tormenting them. Thus Mary Walcott testified in June that "there came to me a woman which I did not know and she did most greviously torment me by pricking and pinching me and she tould me that hir name was wilds and that she lived in Topsfiel."[42] And none of those accusing John Alden admitted that they knew him personally. They knew only of his reputation of friendly dealings with Indians.[43]

This pattern is so unlike other witchcraft cases that it has invited extensive comment from historians. Accusations of witchcraft were usually local affairs. All persons involved knew each other and had had many points of contact. They were neighbors or near neighbors. Nonetheless, Chadwick Hansen notes that 30 percent of the accused in 1692 came from Andover and only 27 percent from Salem Town and Village; the rest were from other communities.[44] This was no face-to-face acrimony. There was much less of the neighborhood bickering that characterized witchcraft episodes in other times and in other places.[45] The Salem experience was unique and reflected not only more unsettling social conditions than petty personal quarrels, but an especially sensitive response to the details of Tituba's confession.

When Tituba suggested that the evil forces in Salem were coming from the outside, she gave voice to new social impulses that were already upsetting traditional relations in Puritan New England. Salem and other eastern Massachusetts communities in late seventeenth century were part of a society in transformation. The older corporate sense of mission and the spiritual focus of the first settlers were giving way to a growing desire for individual achievement and material prosperity. Since the 1670s Puritans had stressed the responsibility of the individual for his or her own salvation. Ministers had traditionally urged their parishioners to look inward for sin and evil.[46] But the growing affluence of the expanding merchant communities, and the socioeconomic and geographic mobility of late seventeenth-century Massachusetts had shifted the focus of communal norms. Tituba gave expression to the forces repudiating the older ideal that evil came from transgressing one's obligation to God and thus sin was within the individual, to a move to shift the blame for their suffering to more impersonal forces. She did not create that need for an external malevolency, but she gave it a new form of expression.

The combination of new threats from Indians, the intrusion of royal power into Massachusetts affairs, and increasing experiences with religious dissenters also helped to lay the groundwork for a growing sentiment in favor of blaming outsiders for continuing troubles.[47] Traditionally the clergy had posited a diabolical presence within the community as an explanation for the decline of piety. In 1692 when Tituba told them that the enemy was not within but outside, she reinforced and directed what had been only an uneasy suspicion. She suggested that their misfortune was not so much their own fault as that of outsiders—impersonal forces over which they had little control. These new enemies of God that came from outside took on unusual shapes and required different forms of defense. Looking inward to their own sinfulness was no longer sufficient or even necessary to root out the evil presence. Accusers and magistrates turned to other communities and to strangers to blame for their misfortunes. They also found the Devil in unusual forms—as elite women and white men.

Tituba promoted the idea of an evil power that resided outside of the immediate community. It was a theme shortly to be echoed by Samuel Parris in his March 27 and April 3 sermons.[48] She had set the stage for the Salem worthies to project onto others what Boyer and Nissenbaum call the "unacknowledged impulses which lay within themselves."[49] In this witchhunt they could transform the internal into external threats and face them on the field of public discourse. The Puritans of Salem seized on the symbolism of distant strangers as scapegoats for their own conflicting impulses and put them on trial in open court.

Even their choice of Salem neighbors underscores this pattern of blaming outside forces. Many of the accused within the community deviated in some manner from the traditional Puritan religious and social norms. Those accused included Quakers or persons with Quaker associations such as Rebecca Nurse and Elizabeth Proctor.[50] Or they were newcomers to the community like John Willard who married into the Wilkins clan and was distrusted for his ambiguous status. He faced complaints from at least ten resentful members of that extended family during his trial, the quintessential outsider who had invaded the Salem community.[51] John Proctor also symbolized that invading outsider. His tavern was a "gathering place for wayfarers." His license stipulated that he could sell beer, cider, and liquors exclusively to strangers and thus was a conduit for outside forces to move into Salem.[52] Tituba's strangers in Boston were transformed in the Puritan mind into an unwelcome presence now resident within the community.

Puritan fears were exacerbated by the similarity between Tituba's story and the known details of the European witchhunts. In the minds of the Puritans, both lay and clerical, the parallels between her story and that of learned lore were glaringly obvious, even though the confession lacked some essential elements such as ritual murder and erotic orgies.[53] The creatures she described had odd physical qualities. They lacked the horns and cloven hoofs of familiar European legend. Nonetheless, similarities were brought out in bold relief in subsequent testimony that transformed Tituba's story with even more creative adaptations. Tituba's witches' meeting in Boston, for instance, was completely converted to a mythical Devil's' sabbat, not on the European model of a corrupt profanity, but of an inversion of the Christian holy day.[54]

This transformation from Indian lore to Puritan belief began with the announcement of a public fast in Salem to take place on March 31. Such fasts were part of the traditional Puritan cleansing ritual in the face of misfortune and were a familiar event throughout all of New England. But in Salem what had been a means of public reconciliation was transformed into a nightmare. On the day scheduled for the fast, Abigail Williams claimed to see the witches at a special ceremony. They held a "Sacrament that day at an house in the Village," she said, and at the meeting, in a parody of the Lord's Supper, "they had Red Bread and Red Drink." The next day Mercy Lewis confirmed Abigail's report that the attendants ate "Red Bread like Man's Flesh."[55] Contrary to the conventional description of the Devil as a black man, the girls described him as a white man who presided over a congregation in the process of prayer. In a possibly whimsical touch, they added the singing of psalms to the meeting. That the adults in Salem believed the girls is a testament to the power of Tituba's suggestions.

Abigail and Mercy had taken the witches' coven from Tituba's testimony and combined that fantasy with what they understood of the more learned notion of Devil worship and the practices of the Congregational church.[56] But unlike the experience of European witchhunters, the description was not extracted under torture during a legal procedure, nor was it the confession of an alleged witch. It was a freely given story by two young people who claimed to be bewitched and reported their experiences in a public tavern.[57] They were free to respond not just to the cues from the questioners but also to Tituba's notions of the evil powers. In its broad outlines, then, their witches' sabbat followed Tituba's fantasy, but in certain respects the story told by the girls represented a Puritan reformulation of that fantasy. It in turn was expanded by those accused who, for a variety of reasons, confessed to witchcraft and participation in this diabolical alliance. The result was an accommodation of the Caribbean world to the European model.

On April 11, during the examination of Sarah Cloyce and Elizabeth Proctor, Abigail was asked again about the Satanic meeting that had taken place on March 31, the day of the public fast, which she had now placed in Salem at Parris's house. The meeting, she said, was attended by about forty people but with two women, Sarah Cloyce and Sarah Good, serving as deacons.[58] Few details were added to this vision of a sabbat during the subsequent April questioning. In the early weeks of that month the magistrates concentrated on extracting evidence of the Devil's book and witnesses repeated Tituba's testimony regarding their torture at the hands of a witch to force them to sign the book to signify their commitment to Satan. They either missed the implications of Abigail Williams's allegations or preferred to ignore them temporarily. Abigail Hobbs finally brought those implications to their attention with new details.

Abigail Hobbs's sudden about-turn on April 20 is especially illuminating about the far-reaching effect of Tituba's stories. Hobbs was the first of the accused persons to confess and her testimony is significant because she patterned her story on Tituba's fantasies that had been further embellished by the complaints of Abigail Williams and Mercy Lewis. Like Tituba's confession, Hobbs gave more damaging evidence against distant persons, including men. She admitted to wickedness and described the metamorphoses of the Devil into many different animals. She told of a man-like appearance that brought her the book to sign. Possibly unaware at first that Tituba had implicated a white man, and following the tenets of English folklore, she said it was a black man. She would soon change that description to conform to Tituba's white man in black clothing. Finally, Abigail Hobbs was struck dumb much as Tituba was.[59]

The next day in her second confession, Hobbs began to implicate others, but unlike Tituba identified the evil creatures by name. One was Judah White, a servant girl she knew who had lived at Casco Bay and was now living in Boston. White was dressed inappropriately for her class in "fine Cloathes," and, in words reminiscent of Tituba's, Abigail Hobbs said that White wore a "silk Mantel, with a Top knot and an hood." The man she identified as the Reverend George Burroughs, her former master when he was the Salem minister. In 1692 he was living in Maine near Casco Bay, again confirming Tituba's allegations about the Devil in the form of a respectable white man from a distant city.[60]

Until the arrest and examination of George Burroughs that began on April 30, most testimony had focused on the alleged maleficium of the accused witches, their physical torture of the "afflicted," and some ancient neighborhood quarrels, rather than this Devil's sabbat. Ann Putnam, in a contrived attack on the church's leaders, tried to bring their attention to that meeting. She testified that on April 20 she saw an apparition of a minister. Turning to the magistrates, she coyly asked: "what are Ministers wicthes to?" The specter, she said, admitted to being a minister of both God and the Devil and his name, echoing Abigail Hobbs's allegation earlier that day, was George Burroughs. Ann also claimed that he had made others into witches, confirming the details of Abigail Hobbs's confession.[61] Several others testified to being tortured at his hands to force them to sign his book and being threatened with death if they did not do so. No additional details on Burroughs's conduct of a mock church service was immediately given. But it was evident that Ann Putnam, like Tituba, had launched a new charge against the church as she refurbished and sharpened Tituba's more indirect attack on Samuel Parris.

The significance of Tituba's confession becomes even more evident after the first trials in June. Many of those accused rushed to confess, some in hopes of a reprieve and others under pressure from friends and family who believed in their guilt. The content of those confessions incorporated fragments of Tituba's stories, now transformed into a Puritan framework of beliefs that combined various types of folklore with elite notions of witchcraft. Those features of Tituba's story that were common to English and Indian cultures reinforced English beliefs while subtly altering them. With great pain and fear, the differences were first reinterpreted and then integrated into existing beliefs.

What began early in March of 1692 as a story of a nocturnal meeting of nine witches, some of whom flew to Boston on a pole, had been transformed by the summer of that year into a new stereotype of the witch who participated in a Devil-worshiping ritual and who mocked the most sacred features of Christianity.[62] The witch, who was now like ordinary persons in their society, thus participated in a "rebellion against

God."[63] Stories were spread of an inversion of church services, complete with baptism into the Satanic cult and bread and wine transmuted into flesh and blood in a ceremony led by a white man and his female deacons. Cotton Mather curiously noted this transformation: "The Witches do say, that they form themselves much after the manner of Congregational Churches; and that they have a Baptism and a Supper, and Officers among them, abominably Resembling those of our Lord."[64]

The idea of the "black mass" or witches' sabbat was a common element in the European witch hunts of the fifteenth and sixteenth centuries, a legend created in the minds of zealous religious reformers and inquisitors who interpreted age-old popular beliefs as the worship of Satan. Their imaginings posed a witches' sabbat as a secret nocturnal assembly of wild dancing and revels, "presided over by Satan, where sexual orgies were performed and babies wasted and eaten."[65] It was as much of a fantasy as the stories that developed in Salem.

By the seventeenth century these elite notions of the Devil's pact and some elements of the witches' sabbat had begun to enter into popular lore and to converge into what David Hall calls a "new popular demonic," a somewhat tame version of the lurid European witches' sabbat.[66] Even transformed, such ideas of ritual Devil worship and of witches copulating with the Devil—the elite fantasies—continued to be relatively rare in the English experience on both sides of the Atlantic. When the Devil's pact did appear in the New England records, as it did in Salem, diabolical meetings were even more muted than in England and Scotland. They conspicuously lacked the extreme revelry, communal sexual orgies, or infanticide of the continental episodes.[67]

The absence of sexual orgies in the New England model of the Devil's sabbat is curious. Europeans linked erotic behavior to diabolism as one means of discrediting illicit sexual activity. Those continental witch trials often focused on sexual relations with the Devil in an attempt to associate unauthorized sexual behavior with disobedience to church and state and, particularly, to discredit promiscuity associated with lower-class women. The questioners could give vent to their own erotic fantasies by supplying their victims with detailed suggestions of homosexual relations, copulation with animals, and other unorthodox eroticism.[68]

New Englanders, on the other hand, only rarely associated witchcraft with sexual behavior, probably because they were not obsessed by sexuality in their ordinary world. Contrary to popular belief today, they did not experience repressive sexual lives. The courts, moreover, offered sufficient opportunities to air sexual discontent and to satisfy the prurient. When necessary they had many opportunities to discuss sexual patterns openly in blunt and explicit language. Nor did they hesitate to bring notice of the sexual misconduct of others to the attention of the authorities. Samuel Sewall made notes of court cases of sexual misdeeds in his diary when Samuel Gude was accused of "ravishing" Goodwife Nash in the pasture and Benjamin Gourd and Jonathan Gardner were punished for sexual activity with a "mare."[69] The thousands of cases relating to sex crimes in New England include some crude and lurid references to all kinds of sexuality, from sodomy and bestiality to adultery and bastardy.[70]

If Puritans needed additional reminders of their sexuality, the clergy supplied other commentaries that compared religious obligation to marital relations. In church Puritans regularly heard sermons that focused on conjugal responsibility as an analogy for grace.[71] Because of this repetition of sexual references, one historian has concluded that "Puritan theology granted sexuality a central and positive role in Christian life, although a carefully regulated one."[72] There was little need to blame sexual desire or sexuality on witchcraft; it was an accepted part of the everyday world in the seventeenth-century Puritan mind.

There were some exceptions. Increase and Cotton Mather, father and son ministers, were among the few to associate sexual activity with witchcraft. When Rebecca Greensmith confessed to Increase Mather in 1662, he commented that the Devil appeared in the form of a deer and "had frequently the carnal knowledge of her body."[73] Mary Johnson confessed to Cotton Mather that "she had been guilty of Uncleanness with Men & the Devil."[74] If similar statements had been made in the New England trials before 1692, there is no extant record of them. But there was so little mention of the Devil itself in those pre-Salem incidents, that lack of diabolical sex is not surprising.[75]

When tales of a Devil's sabbat did occur in the Salem incident, sexual references continued to be rare. During the hearings none of the accused confessed to sexual relations with Satan and there is only a single example of a man assumed guilty of an implicit sexual offense—John Willard.[76] Two other incidents vaguely reflect some of the continental ideas. Edward Bishop had claimed his wife was familiar with the Devil, that he came "bodily unto her," and Rebecca Eames accused Sarah Parker of being kissed by the Devil.[77] There was no copulation with animals or the Devil, no homosexual or autoerotic activity, no sexual fantasies in any of those testimonies.

Complainers and confessors in 1692 had instead concentrated on variations of Tituba's fantasies—reporting tales of signatures in a Devil's book, of contracting to harm others in return for favors, of participating in secrete nocturnal meetings that resembled sedate Congregational worship, of an intrusive diabolical force. They had followed Tituba's lead in this broad outline of devilish activities and, like her, neglected to add lurid tales of sexual exploits or wild revels.

For Tituba, the Indian woman, erotic factors would not enter into her concept of the witch or sorcerer. Indian witchcraft "is simply not concerned with sex."[78] As she recalled elements of occult belief from her earlier life, Tituba omitted any references to sexual activities because those specific erotic behaviors were not relevant to her mental world. She could describe monstrous imps and a distant evil being; she could integrate a written covenant with the Devil into her belief system, but sexual orgies had no role to play in her ideas about evil. The confessions that were patterned on hers were, therefore, in the absence of references to sexual exploits, markedly different from those on the continent.

One can only wonder what fantasies would have been conjured up if Tituba had included sexual orgies in her witches' meeting. What ribald imaginings would the Puritans have revealed under such a stimulus? There is no question that Puritan imagination could have supplied the missing sexual ingredients if they had wished to. The absence of allusions to erotic behavior during the Salem scare was probably a matter of choice, albeit unstated and probably unconscious. The complaining girls and the confessors expressed their hostility toward those in authority by emphasizing the similarities between Christian and anti-Christian communities, rather than the differences between the two as occurred in Europe.[79] Any inclusion of illicit sexual behavior at their witches' meetings would have associated the Devil with a flouting of the norms of human decency. This was not their intent. Their version of witchcraft denigrated the Puritan community by equating it with Satan, not by pointing out the differences between the godly and the profane. Thus, unlike the witchhunts in Europe, the Salem confessors used confessions to attack the Puritans in the very act of capitulating to them. This method of resistance was forged by Tituba when she reluctantly submitted to demands to confess.

The Puritans had transformed Tituba's witches' meeting in Boston, attended by four women and a man whose single purpose was to torture and cause harm to particular people in Salem, into an attack on the Congregational church. The attack took the form of a parody of Congregational practices, peppered with expressions of discontent about social status, gender relations, and the behavior of ministers who were now equated with the Devil. They set this subversive message in the context of a convivial social event in which all participated in eating bread and cheese and drinking wine. Food and the rituals of eating were of more concern than sex.[80] Sometimes they were very specific in their details of this social occasion, as when Mary Bridges claimed to drink "Sach drawn from a barrel" and Mary Lacey reportedly ate both bread and cheese before the meeting. In a homely touch, Deliverance Hobbs described her mother-in-law as one who served the refreshments.[81] But at no time did these feasts mimic the wild excitement and revelry of the European fantasies. These were sedate events, allusions that explored connections between the Godly and the profane, rather than separating them.

This subversive plot only gradually unfolded during the spring of 1692. Confessions in April were relatively mild in their content, with few references to the horrifying witches' sabbat. Instead, the confessing witches and their accusers focused on their physical torments at the hands of other witches to force them to sign the Devil's book. Mary Walcott's testimony against Abigail Hobbs is typical for that month: "about the 14 April 1692 I saw the Apperishtion of Abigail Hoobs the daughter of William Hoobs com and affect me by pinching and all most choaking me urging me to writ in hir book."[82] Mary Warren, another confessor, on April 19 had difficulty in speaking and was unable to give many details except that she had signed the Devil's book and named others who tormented her who were already in jail.[83] Deliverance Hobbs, Abigail's mother, confessing on April 22, said she was tormented by the shapes of Sarah Wilds and Mercy Lewis and admitted to sticking pins in dolls.[84] The next day, either under prompting from the magistrates or as a result of communication with the others in jail, she elaborated and confessed to attending a meeting with many accused witches near Samuel Parris's house, during which they drank red wine and ate red bread.[85] There were no further confessions in April or May.

The situation changed in June following the first execution. On June 10, Bridget Bishop, long reputed to be a witch and finally convicted on June 2, was the first to be hanged a week later. On July 4, Candy, Mrs. Hawkes's African-American slave, confessed shortly after her arrest. She gave evidence only of maleficium using an African form of image magic, with clothes tied into knots, a piece of cheese, and some grass. She spoke of a Devil's book brought by her mistress, but made no reference to a diabolical meeting.[86] Candy, lacking sufficient acquaintance with Puritan notions, did not respond to the pointed questioning regarding the Devil. Her knowledge of evil action was limited to practices learned in Barbados from other Africans and she could add little information to corroborate the details of Tituba's conspiracies. Like Tituba, however, Candy was sent to jail, even though she had presented non-spectral evidence of her own guilt and had provided empirical proof of her earlier occult activities. The success of Tituba's and Candy's confessions in saving their lives, even temporarily, encouraged others to follow that lead—admission of guilt became a means of worldly redemption.

On July 15, shortly before the second day of execution when five women were to die, Ann Foster of Andover broke ranks with the other innocents accused of a diabolical association and confessed to participating in that alleged witches' meeting that Abigail Williams said had taken place in Salem Village at the end of March. Foster confessed that she had traveled to that meeting on a stick. She said she saw the Reverend George Burroughs there. He, along with some 305 witches in the country, Foster said, planned to ruin the village.[87] She, like the others who had confessed, was put aside in jail and, temporarily at least, appeared to be reprieved.

The planned executions of the five unrepentant people convicted of witchcraft were carried out on July 19. Two days later, Ann Foster's daughter and granddaughter, both named Mary Lacey and also from Andover, followed the old woman's lead and confessed. They proceeded to implicate other women and men. Within a week of those confessions, three brothers, Thomas, Richard, and Andrew Carrier, also confessed after being tortured.[88] Their eight-year-old sister, Sarah, did the same on August 11.[89] The pace of confessions to a diabolical conspiracy grew faster as a new execution date of August 19 approached, when another five, four men and one woman, were to go to the gallows. Even more confessed after that day, with new and convincing particulars.

No longer was there much of a delay between the time of arrest and confession. Many of those newly accused in August were prepared in advance to tell the same story and to apologize for their transgressions. Sarah Bridges, Mary Bridges, Jr., Susannah Post, and Mary Marston, all of Andover, were arrested on August 25 and confessed immediately. Mary and William Barker, Sr., followed them a few days later.[90]

The content of the Andover confessions is an interesting contrast to those made by persons in Salem. They contain fewer elements borrowed from Tituba's story and more aspects of English belief and folklore. The geographic distance from Salem Village and some unique local problems brought new influences to bear on the testimonies of the accused in that town. Andover was torn by even more obvious social and military problems than Salem. The town suffered from Indian attacks during the winter of 1689–90, a frightening smallpox epidemic in 1690, and conflicts resulting from a land shortage.[91] A variety of internal divisions and neighborhood and family bickering finally exploded in a series of accusations that, unlike Salem, turned inward. The Andover accusers focused only on their own families and neighbors.

The Andover story begins with Roger Toothaker, a physician of Billerica, who apparently was interested in occult practices.[92] This reputation also implicated his wife's sister in Andover, Martha Carrier. When Carrier was brought to Salem by the Andover constable, Joseph Ballard, he was alerted to the possibility that the "afflicted girls might help him uncover the cause of his wife's illness."[93] Some of the girls apparently did go to Andover and Ballard subsequently accused his neighbors Mary Lacey, Sr. and Jr., of causing his wife's maladies. That also brought in Lacey Sr.'s mother, Ann Foster. The three women confessed and accused Martha Carrier and her family of forcing them into the diabolical plot. The Carrier children widened the plot by accusing another neighbor, Mrs. Bradbury.[94] Within a matter of weeks sisters were accusing their own sisters and other close friends. On July 30 Mary Bridges accused Hannah Bromage of Haverhill of tormenting John Ballard's wife.[95] Then Martha Sprague accused Mary Bridges of causing harm to Rose Foster; Bridges confessed and implicated her sisters Susannah Post and twelve-year-old Sarah Bridges.[96] Sprague also testified against William Barker, Sr.[97]

Within a short time Andover had its own coterie of afflicted persons and a rash of confessions that differed in some details from those in Salem. Several of the Andover confessions added new elements that were not part of Tituba's story, particularly references to baptism. Elizabeth Johnson, Jr., said she was baptized by the Devil as was Sarah Hawkes and her mother-in-law Sarah Wardwell.[98] They also told of meetings in Andover rather than Salem—either at Capt. Chandler's Garrison, or John Ballard's house, or Andrew Foster's pasture.[99] Somewhat distanced from Tituba's stories, the Andover confessions drew more heavily on English folklore and Christian customs than those in Salem. They too followed the Puritan tendency to situate their witches' meeting in familiar territory.

One by one these Andover confessors described a parody of their Puritan beliefs played out in mock sacraments. Other confessors would then elaborate on those themes. In most accounts George Burroughs, even after his death in July, was the minister of this diabolical congregation that varied from twenty-five to several hundred witches.[100] As Mary Bridges, Sr., testified in July, she had not only signed the Devil's book but had promised "and Covenanted, to worship him, and Several times, hath worshipped the Devil, and frequented witch meetings."[101] William Barker, with more knowledge of European legends, described his Devil as having a "cloven foot." He had attended a meeting designed to "abolish all the churches in the land."[102] Sarah Wardwell confessed to being in the "snare of the Divel 6 years." She said he carried her to a meeting in Salem on a pole where she was baptized.[103]

None of these confessors described any more lurid rites than that of being baptized and participating in a feast that mimicked the sacraments and traditions of the Congregational church.[104] Even the lectures of this diabolical figure dwelt on the same themes as the sermons of the ministers: responsibility for sin, a struggle between the kingdoms of Christ and Satan and the importance of allegiance to one's faith.[105] The message was clearly a threatening one and a challenge to the social order. For those confessing to witchcraft, the Puritan church was an enemy of God.

In spite of the subtle subversive message in the confessions, starting with Tituba most of the confessors had been spared and by July accused witches were following Tituba's lead, not just in hoping to prolong their lives, but in using more of the details of her fantasy for their own. For the examiners the repetition of these particulars was taken as confirmation of the diabolical presence.[106] The ritual of public confession, so essential to Puritan practices as evidence of a covenant with God, no longer served to confirm their divine providence. Instead of cleansing the communal taint of Satanism, the confessions heightened the fear of a Satanic plot, divided family members, and undermined the entire social fabric of the Puritan world in Massachusetts.

Tituba's unidentified evil presence, the imputations of elite responsibility, a witches' meeting, and assorted strange creatures provided a forum for the exposure of discontent with Puritan theology and ministerial intellectual demands; with the social class system and degradation of servants; with gender relations; and above all with the traditions of the late medieval world that valued communal goals above individual efforts.[107] Tituba may have omitted sexual references because Indian cultures never made the erotic side of human behavior a factor in witchcraft proceedings. Others followed her lead for different reasons—sexual exploits might have negated their intent to parody Puritan values by conflating the godly and diabolical realms. In this technique, as in others, Tituba again had supplied the outlines of a method that could be embellished and reformulated to fit the mental baggage of other cultures.

Tituba was a silent witness to the effects of her testimony. She watched the accused as they joined her in the Boston jail. Did she repeat the details of her fantasy to the newcomers? There was no reason for her to keep silent. But it probably did not matter if she did speak up. The accused and the afflicted had had many opportunities to compare their stories and share information; those in prison continued to do so.[108] The details of Tituba's confession were widely known. As others embellished her stories, the fantastic conspiracy had taken on extraordinary realism.

Devilish Indians and Womanly Conversations: Tituba's Credibility

> Sarah Good tould him that shee would not owne her selfe to be a wicth unless she is provd one[.] Shee saith that there is but one Evidence and thats and Indian and therefore she fears not.
> —Samuel Baybrook's statement at Good's hearing, in Boyer and Nissenbaum, eds., *Salem Witchcraft Papers*

W hy did the Salem worthies accept Tituba's confession as truth? There is no doubt that the devils, witches, and magic of her story were real possibilities in the Puritan mental world and Tituba offered what was to them a plausible, albeit supernatural, explanation for their troubles. The clergy in particular were prepared to believe what they had been preaching for years: that the sinful among them had let the Devil loose in the community. Tituba was providing proof of their complaints. Moreover, the constant repetition of details certainly gave the illusion of a truthful story.[1] Nonetheless, such testimony should have been rejected as unreliable because, in everyone's mind, not only was she an Indian, a category of persons that was almost by definition unworthy of trust, but she was admittedly under the influence of the Devil, the incarnation of lies and deceit.

The general prejudice against Indian testimony was shared by most sections of English society. Cotton Mather, somewhat confused by Indian rhetorical conventions and probably offended by the native American contempt for his own theological assumptions, condemned Indians as "most impudent Lyars" who "invent Reports and Stories at a strange and monstruous rate."[2] "Praying Indians," those who had been segregated into special towns for the purpose of learning English ways and receiving instruction in Christianity, were specifically forbidden to tell lies, a habit assumed to be as traditional among native Americans as wearing body grease and letting their hair grow on one part of the head, or playing ball games.[3]

Sarah Good expressed the popular prejudice against Indian testimony when she told Samuel Baybrook on March 2 of her contempt for Tituba's accusations. Good assumed that she would not be convicted on the word of an Indian. She expected to be exonerated unless that "evidence" was supported by other, more credible, witnesses.[4] The image of the deceitful Indian, born of mistaken notions about native American cultures, was a common stereotype throughout the colonial era. Indian words were usually suspect in most courts of law.[5]

Tituba's confession, with its fantastic, exotic elements, should have been discounted as the type of exaggerated speech regarded as inherent to the character of native Americans. If the common interpretation had been placed on her evidence, the witchhunt might have ended on March 1, Tituba's story rejected, as Sarah Good expected, as the uncorroborated statement of an unreliable Indian witness. But that did not happen. It is another one of the oddities of the Salem events that the testimony of an Indian against white women was accepted without question by the investigating magistrates.

In their zeal to collect evidence of a diabolical conspiracy, the Salem magistrates, clergy, and lay folk all suspended their usual reluctance to accept Indian testimony. When other witnesses against Sarah Good did, subsequently, appear, their initial evidence supported Tituba's accusations by relying on details borrowed from the Indian woman's earlier testimony. They told of Good's forcing them to sign a book and of her presence at the witches' meeting. William Allen embellished Tituba's fantasy and testified to seeing Good along with Sarah Osborne and Tituba fly off into the night sky.[6] The lay folk not only believed Tituba's story but continued to draw on her fantasies to authenticate their own illusions.

Although all confessors claimed to be under the influence of the Devil—to be sure as unwilling collaborators in his conspiracy to undermine their godly community—they too were believed. Tituba's skillful manipulation of their fears had left all in the community prey to her dire predictions and too shocked to see the contradictions in their behavior. As Thomas Brattle asked early on: "if it be thus granted, that the Devil is able to represent false ideas (to speak vulgarly) to the imagination of the confessours, what man of sense will regard the confessions, or any of the words, of these confessours?"[7] But these "men of sense" did believe those imaginings and acted on them with a vigor that continues to baffle the public today and produce seemingly endless studies of the Salem events.

The magistrates also accepted the details of a confession made under duress and that should have been suspect as defensive lying. John Hathorne and Jonathan Corwin must have known that a day or two before the questioning Tituba had been pressured by the Reverend Parris to extract a statement of involvement with the Devil. She had agreed to confess to prevent further punishment. Her passivity later became a model for others, who were either tortured or hoped to avoid other forms of psychological pressure. They too, on the surface, seemingly capitulated to the demands of the elite with the same result—confessions of a diabolical conspiracy that elevated the level of horror. As in Tituba's example, all those fantastic stories were accepted as truth.

The torturing of accused persons to elicit confessions in cases of maleficium in the English court system was a rare occurrence. Although witchhunters in Europe forced confessions for evidence, inquisitorial tactics were seldom attempted in England. There the law forbade torture or other means of duress to secure confessions of witchcraft. Nonetheless, the possibility of such tactics was kept alive in England. Both James I and the Puritan divine William Perkins had recommended torture as a technique for extracting "proof" from heretics. There was also one ready series of examples of the actual use of torture in England in a case of witchcraft. During the last great witchhunt in England of 1645–46, Matthew Hopkins had followed a European model to extract tales of sexual exploits on the part of the accused. But such means are not evident in New England trial records, or at least, there is no documented case of such pressure before 1692.[8] The Salem magistrates that year, for the first and last time, deviated from traditional local practice as well as general English legal methods.

Tituba was only the first to experience such brutal treatment. The success in extracting a confession from the Indian woman provided an incentive to repeat the tactic. A confession was the most conclusive, concrete, and empirical confirmation of a guilty act and as such an important element in proving guilt. In the months that followed Tituba's testimony, the magistrates resorted to both physical and mental torture to elicit confessions as proof of that diabolical presence. Three young sons of two accused men were physically abused. Richard and Andrew Carrier and William Proctor were all tied up into excruciatingly uncomfortable positions until they too confessed.[9] Others were forced to stand for long periods of time without sleep and finally agreed to say anything the magistrates wanted in order to be relieved.[10]

Several women were pressured to confess to witchcraft as a practical way to save their lives. They were frightened by the accusations and arrests, and demoralized by the advice of well-meaning relatives who urged them to confess to save their lives. Margaret Jacobs suffered such extreme fear during her interrogation that she finally implicated her grandfather and George Burroughs to protect herself. She was threatened with the dungeon and hanging if she did not confess to the details that would assure the guilt of the two men.[11] Sarah Churchill also reported that she was threatened with the dungeon if she did not confirm her involvement in the diabolical conspiracy. She was frightened even more when told she would be left in the dungeon with Burroughs who, she believed, was a witch.[12] Fear of worldly punishments and spectral torture temporarily overcame the horrifying spiritual consequences of telling a lie. The ultimate penalty for lying was eternal damnation.

Some confessors were convinced that if others believed they were witches, it must be so.[13] They hoped that repentance embodied in such a confession would save their souls. Fearful of damnation for their lack of repentance if they did not confess, their psychological torture was as discomforting as the physical restraints imposed on the men and boys. Told by the magistrates that they were witches, "they knew it, and we knew it . . . which made us think it was so; and our understanding, our reason, and our faculties almost gone . . . said any thing and every thing which they desired."[14]

Confession lay at the base of Puritan theology, a ritual that expressed a consciousness of sin or guilt, an awareness of the deity's omniscience, and an acknowledgment of that consciousness through the spoken or written word. In spite of the Calvinist emphasis on predestination, on God's sovereign power to choose his "saints" without regard to good works, Puritans reinterpreted that determinist doctrine to include an element of voluntarism, of individual responsibility to accept the gift of grace. Before sainthood could be assumed, the spirit went through a three-fold period of preparation and testing: a turning from sin demonstrated through a knowledge of Christian doctrines, a recognition of Christ's omnipotence in contrast to the individual's degradation and corruption, and finally an awareness of liberation that afforded a partial release from the anxiety over the fear of damnation.[15] The release was not guaranteed; no one could be absolutely sure of his or her state of grace. Nonetheless, this conversion experience, and its behavioral manifestation, confession, offered some presumptive proof of that sainthood status. The ritual was an essential test for becoming a full church member, as "Covenanted" church people (or saints) reported their conversion experience in public confessions.

Samuel Sewall's diary records a telling example of these connections between the consciousness of sin, salvation, and confession. Timothy Dwight, a goldsmith's apprentice, had fainted in church one day in 1676 and Sewall, in an attempt to comfort him, asked whether his problem was due to "some outward cause or spiritual." Spiritual was the answer. He needed help in his prayers to gain "more sight of sin, and God's healing grace." Sewall's response to this anxiety was to remind Dwight, "it is the honor of any man to see sin and be sorry for it."[16] A public renunciation of that sin, a confession, was a sign of salvation. It also provided confirmation of the Puritan creed by emphasizing the enormous gulf that separated the unworthy individual from his or her omnipotent God.

Confession as a means of redemption is not unique to the seventeenth-century Puritans. As a cleansing process it is found in many societies. Anthropologists describe confession as a means of providing proof of the effectiveness of the belief system and a procedure for reintegrating reformed deviants into the community.[17] Confession for the Puritans, as in other societies, was a part of the ritual structure necessary to reaffirm the norms of their society. That process was especially important during periods of crisis. There is no doubt that Salem in 1692 was suffering a severe social crisis brought on by newly resumed Indian warfare, political instability, increasing factional conflicts, and economic impulses that ran counter to Puritan religious and communal goals. A general public awakening might resolve the emotional conflicts; a series of confessions that demonstrated a turning away from sin was needed for the communal expiation.[18]

In seventeenth-century New England, confession by a wrongdoer denouncing an alliance with the Devil could not only uphold the value of piety but could signal a full acceptance and internalization of Puritan rituals and values.[19] Among those important values was the notion of truthful speech. Confession could rescue fallen members of the congregation from the profane life of lying and deceit, to help reintegrate them into the holy realm of truth.[20] Susannah Post confessed to having been in the "Devils snare three years." But now in her confession she was ready to renounce the Devil and could beg forgiveness.[21] Martha Corey was openly told that if she expected mercy from God she "must first look for it in Gods way by confession."[22] So too Tituba's penitent confession delivered in the accepted sorrowful mode had transformed the assumed lying Indian into a credible witness whose word, at least in this witch-hunting context, was taken as the truth. That truth, however, was what the Puritans made of it as they reformulated and reinterpreted Indian notions to fit their own cosmology. Their misunderstanding of her concept of evil and the deliberately provocative suggestion of an expanding conspiracy, saved Tituba's life.

The Salem worthies believed Tituba because she gave her story with sufficient sophisticated knowledge of Puritan practices to evoke recognizable images and emotions. Her choice of language, her metaphors, were in keeping with the ritual of Puritan confession. She admitted her sin and described the tests she had endured to resist the allures of the evil one. She testified to both her physical pain during that attempt at resistance and her sorrow at her weakness in submitting to the Devil's threats and entreaties. But with the aid of the magistrates she could expose this depraved experience, beg forgiveness for her corruption, and throw herself on their mercy much as saints did during their metamorphosis into full church members. Her self-effacement with its implied acceptance of Puritan values lent additional force to her very convincing performance of repentance.

Tituba had probably learned, as had other Indians before her, that the secret of survival in the English world was the ability to make herself inconspicuous by mimicking the behavior of others in her locale.[23] As a child in Barbados Tituba had been trained in the ways of an English household and learned to dress in the European style. She had been introduced to the religious conventions of the Puritan church early on by Elizabeth Pearsehouse and then by Samuel Parris. Her testimony in 1692 demonstrates that she had acquired the expected conversational mode of Puritan society, the acceptable attributes of female piety, and the proper deferential style and tone of an English servant. A major indication of her ability to hide her alien qualities was in language facility.

Many partly acculturated Indians living within the Puritan towns and villages continued to use a non-standard English, a Creolized version that drew on one or another native American syntax. Thus in direct contact with the English, the otherness of the Indian was revealed regularly through the hesitant use of the English tongue.[24] Tituba, on the other hand, spoke in the same idiomatic English as the Parris family and other whites in the community. Her racial type was not evident in her speech. The record of her testimony in 1692, although written down by others, provides some indication of those speech patterns.

When asked during her examination about the form of the Devil she saw, Tituba replied with the proper use of pronouns and tense: "like a man I think." She explained that "Yesterday I being in the Lentoe [lean-to] Chamber I saw a thing like a man, that tould me Searve him and I tould him noe I would nott doe Such thing."[25] This is an idiomatic use of English common in the Puritan communities of New England and of old England.

But was this really Tituba's speech pattern or was it that of the transcribers? These words were written down by the literate members of the community and it is possible that the clerks were distorting her syntax to conform to their own use. A comparison with the recorded speech of other minority ethnic peoples written down during those hearings might answer that question and throw more light on how Tituba was perceived by those in the village.

In that documentary record, Tituba's grammatical construction is quite different from that of the other Barbados woman, Candy, who spoke an obviously non-standard English omitting prepositions, articles, and most verbs. The differences in the transcription of Candy's and Tituba's testimonies are most remarkable. The two women came from the same West Indian island and they should have spoken in a similar idiom. But they did not and the difference is reflected in the transcription of their testimonies. When asked if she were a witch, Candy apparently replied, "Candy no witch in her country. Candy's mother no witch. Candy no witch, Barbados. This country mistress give Candy witch."

The transcriber, John Hathorne, heard Candy speak in this simplified pidgin English.[26] He probably recorded her words as he heard them.

Granted, these two women did not write their own confessions and their spoken words may have been reworked by the various reporters as they wrote down or summarized the answers to the questions. But the difference between the written sentence structures of the two women is so great that it is evident that the transcribers, at the least, did not perceive their characters in the same way. That perception, in some ways, may be even more important than the actual speech pattern. Ezekiel Cheever, who transcribed part of Tituba's testimony, heard her speaking what at the time was recognizable standard English and John Hathorne, transcribing Candy's evidence, heard her speaking an early Caribbean dialect. The difference in the two reports is not just because the skin colors of the two women were different, because Tituba was a "tawny" and Candy black. Not all African-Americans were assumed to be deficient in the English language. The other black woman who was questioned, Mary Black, was also perceived (in Samuel Parris's transcription) as speaking correct idiomatic English: "I cannot tell," she said, and then "I do not know," and "I hurt nobody." There is no sign of pidgin English in these curt answers given by Mary Black. Thus Mary and Tituba were perceived as acculturated women, comfortable in the linguistic patterns of their English superiors.

For reasons that can only be partially surmised from the fragmentary record, Candy was placed in a different category. She apparently was not as accustomed to English ways as the other two enslaved women and did not present the same type of testimony. What comes across very clearly in Candy's testimony is the strong influence of African and Creole practices on her understanding of the questions. Because she knew so little about Puritan religious ideas or cultural traditions, except possibly for a vague notion about books and writing, Candy could not or would not respond to the hints regarding the Devil. Instead of elaborating on the Devil's pact or following Tituba's lead in describing the witches' meeting, her testimony dealt with African occult practices unaffected by the theology or mythologies of Christianity.

Thus Candy blamed not the Devil for her knowledge but, like Tituba, her white mistress who had brought her from Barbados, Mrs. Margaret Hawkes, who she said taught her occult technique and also forced her to make a mark in a book. Then, ignoring questions about the diabolical presence and the significance of the pact, she gave a demonstration of magical techniques learned either in Africa or the Caribbean. She showed the questioners two pieces of cloth, some grass, and a piece of cheese. One of the pieces of cloth was knotted in an African fashion.[27] When Candy was forced to swallow the grass to prove its efficacy as magic, she complained of a burning sensation. The cloth was put on fire and the girls appeared to suffer burns as a result. They complained of drowning when the material was put into water.[28] Her testimony had little of the detail that the magistrates associated with diabolical pacts or witches' covens. Candy's demeanor, her knowledge, her mental images all spoke of an African-Caribbean culture. She probably did speak in a Creolized West Indian English characteristic of Barbados slaves, although the transcription may also have exaggerated that pattern.[29] Nonetheless, in the hearing and the eyes of the literate Puritans, Tituba and Candy were cultural worlds apart. These differences are clearly demonstrated in the transcriptions of their respective testimonies.

All the other verbatim versions of Tituba's testimony consistently reveal standard language use. A second and more detailed account (possibly written by Jonathan Corwin)[30] reported her as saying "the devil came to me and bid me serve him," and in response to the question of why she did not tell Parris about the activities she said, "I was a fraid. They said they would cut off my head if I told." To the question, "did you never practice witch-craft in your owne country?" she answered, "Noe Never before now." In her second day of questioning, when asked how long ago these events happened, she replied "about Six weeks & a little more fryday night before Abigall was Ill."[31] The peculiar construction of this wording is no different from those given by other seventeenth-century whites who testified.

Candy's obviously Creolized English was captured in the transcript. Tituba's more proper idiomatic use of English so similar to the testimonies of English folk marked her as an acculturated Indian whose word, in spite of her assumed weaknesses, might be trusted. Her speech, therefore, enhanced her facade as a Europeanized servant. In the past it had permitted her to be inconspicuous and unthreatening; now it transformed her into a credible witness.[32] The audience in the Salem Village meeting house heard Tituba echoing the syntax of their own colloquial English.

That dialogue contributed to a willingness to accept the testimony of an Indian in spite of their other biases.

Tituba's choice of words also reflects the proper deferential linguistic conventions expected of a servant in that socially hierarchical society. There is the occasional use of the word "sir" in response to questions. As she reported it, one conversation with the Devil was interrupted when Mrs. Parris called her from another room and Tituba showed proper deference to her mistress's demand for service. Tituba's submission to Samuel Parris's authority is evident when she admitted that she wanted to consult with him about the appearance of the strange man but did not do so only because she was forcibly restrained by the evil presence.[33] Her stated intent was to defer to the minister's will and authority. She understood that for women and servants of her time and in that place, "submissiveness to authority and careful attention to duty were the best assurance of good treatment."[34] Tituba demonstrated a deference to the minister's will and authority with the same seriousness that she, like most women, had learned was not only the proper pattern of behavior in seventeenth-century society, but the best protection against physical attacks.

Her manner in court was neither defensive nor threatening, but rather penitent and humble. Her verbal style, unlike that of condemned witches who were executed, was not impudent or defiant, but deferential. There are no strident, heated, or abusive answers in any of Tituba's testimony. Such an aggressive verbal style might have been acceptable from men but was severely condemned in women as evidence of witchcraft.[35] Her tone was repentant and pained by her admitted guilt. Even Thomas Putnam was moved by her contrite apology and sorrow for causing pain to his daughter.[36]

In contrast Bridget Bishop, the first accused to be executed, was demonstrably angry in her adamant denials and Sarah Good, who also was hanged, was heard to rail against her accusers "with base and abusive words" and mumbled some words as she passed by Parris and the children. Her husband feared that her "bad carriage" was a sign "that she either was a witch or would be one very quicly."[37] Susannah Martin, too, was known for her threats and mischievous language. Cotton Mather called Martin a "most Impudent, Scurrilous, wicked creature." She too would suffer for her abusive language when she was convicted and then hanged on July 19.

Such aggressive behaviors confirmed suspicions of diabolical association and subversive intent. They implied an attack on the authority of elite men and challenged the legitimacy of the court action.[38] To question the decisions of the magistrates or the accusers was to reject the entire legal procedure. That kind of defiant behavior tainted the testimonies of the accused and guaranteed harsher punishments. Tituba was not guilty of those crimes against Puritan society. With her deferential and pious demeanor, her willingness to supply the needed answers in standard colloquial English, she appeared to be a "compliant ally of the court."[39]

Observers found that the tone and language of Tituba's confession was sufficiently contrite, properly subservient to authority, and sufficiently humble toward the court's actions to be the acceptable Puritan response to sin.[40] Her successful verbal camouflage as a servant woman helped to convince the Puritans of the truth of her story. She neither rebuked her interrogators nor cried out nor mocked them. She was struck dumb, but silence was not as heinous a behavior as positive verbal assaults.[41] Her silence could have been taken as a sign that God was punishing her for an earlier speech offense, thus discrediting her words.[42] But the possibility of a transgression was overlooked in the wonder of her penitent confession.

Tituba humbly apologized for hurting the girls. She did not want to do so and was especially reluctant to hurt Betty, the Parris's daughter. "I loved Betty," she said. She was sorry that she caused the child pain. Hathorne made special note of her affection for the little girl.[43] As the Indian woman aroused compassion for her own misery in this test of her endurance, she became an even more persuasive witness.

Her familiarity with the norms of literate society reinforced this impression of truthfulness. Whether she could read or not, Tituba had entered the world of print through religious indoctrination under Parris's tutelage. She participated in daily prayer, heard readings from the Bible, and received instruction in Calvinist theology. Books, catechisms, and sermons were a regular part of her daily existence.[44] She knew how to respond to suggestions regarding a Devil's book, written covenants, and marks on legal documents. These were elements of literate English society she understood and had experienced while living in an English household since a child. Thus in her "conversations," a term early Americans used to define a form of social behavior that included speech as well as demeanor, she exhibited all the outward signs of "a good Christian neighbor."[45]

At the same time her deportment was so characteristic of a humble English servant that the magistrates were doubly blind to her manipulation of their fears. In her dress, behavior, and mannerisms Tituba had become, superficially at least, acculturated—when convenient in her womanly conversations she could pass as a "Red Puritan." To paraphrase Cotton Mather's description of a successful attempt to civilize an Indian, she was a Christian who, notwithstanding some of her Indian "weaknesses," was a character of "vertue and Goodness."[46] One can assume from the response to her testimony that she was one of the few Indians they thought had been successfully "reduced" to "civility."[47] In all outward manifestations, she reflected English norms. Her assumed innate deficiencies as an Indian continued to be hidden behind a modest Anglicized facade.

The credibility of Tituba's testimony was enhanced for her Salem audience, paradoxically, by her identification as an American Indian whose culture had long been associated with demonic power. Her confession thus acquired verisimilitude, not just from its fantastic detail and penitent tone, but from its assumed evil inspiration. To the Puritans, as to most Englishmen, Indian religious practices were associated with Devil worship.[48] As an Indian, then, she continued to symbolize a unique and fearful presence. For the same reason that Mary Sibley had expected Tituba to assist in the making of the witchcake, Tituba's examiners assumed that her outward appearance of civility continued to hide a Devil-worshiping Indian, but, ironically, instead of undermining her credibility, it made her story more believable.

The contradictions in the Puritan attitude toward the Indians and their place in New England society is nowhere more evident than in the disparate treatment of Tituba and Mary Sibley. Both women participated in the witchcake incident and were equally culpable; Sibley, in fact, was the acknowledged instigator. But Tituba was jailed and the other absolved of guilt for their joint action. Sibley did not suffer arrest and imprisonment. Her guilt was treated in a very different manner.

Although both women knew of the power of the cunning folk and attempted to make use of it in 1692, there is no evidence that either one had participated in such rituals previously. Both were acknowledged innocents even though they probably were familiar, as much as anyone else in the community, with the folklore of the occult. Tituba's involvement is understandable for reasons other than an imputed reputation as a conjurer. Distraught at Betty Parris's illness, plagued by nightmares, and anxious to find an effective cure, she willingly complied with Sibley's request because it fit what she understood about evil spirits and the use of magical cures, whether or not she had been a practitioner.

It is possible that it was customary for those in fearful circumstances to call on local Indians to take part in magical rites and Tituba happened to be a convenient "tawny" person. Of specific incidents of whites consulting Indian shamans, there are few reports, but those few are suggestive of the attitude toward the power of Indian practices to heal, cause pain, or foretell the future. In 1654 Mary Staples was accused of receiving Indian fetishes: "two things brighter then the light of the day." But she denied making use of them to improve her fortunes.[49] That Indian religious practices were believed to have real power is evident in the widespread belief that those who willingly joined Indian tribes had participated with shamans in their magical conjuring.[50] It was in the "wigwams of Indians," according to Cotton Mather, "where the pagan Powaws often raise their masters, in the shapes of Bears and Snakes and Fires."[51] John Gyles's story of his captivity in Maine in 1689 and his evidence of successful Indian divining practices added weight to those beliefs in the efficacy of shamanism.[52] Sibley's request, then, was in line with the common perception of Indians as the keepers of special occult powers. Tituba's physical type fit the stereotype of the Indian as conjurer, as a practitioner of the occult.

Desperation may have driven both women to resort to folk traditions. But only Tituba was arrested and questioned by the magistrates and then jailed. Sibley was questioned, counseled by Samuel Parris, permitted to repent of her transgression, and then excused for her behavior.[53] She was never arrested or accused of witchcraft and yet she was just as guilty of occult practices as Tituba.

Sibley, a full member of the church—a saint—and supposedly immune to such pagan practices on the basis of her ethnicity, could be restored to the congregation of faithful with an act of repentance. But Tituba was an outsider and never fully accepted by the Puritans. She had been born somewhere in the West Indies, came from an alien culture, and spoke of strange imps and creatures. That the Puritans could reinterpret and incorporate these foreign elements into their own cosmology did not completely erase the fact of the strangeness. The Puritans underscored the gulf that separated themselves from the Indians by accusing Tituba and not Mary Sibley of witchcraft.

Tituba's Anglicized facade could never obliterate the Puritan feelings about the devilish Indians—the outsiders in their midst. Mary Sibley's public renunciation of her guilt helped to restore her as an Englishwoman to the community of saints. Tituba's only halfway acceptance into the Puritan fold left her in a limbo, even after her confession of guilt and repentance. There was no way for her to be reunited with the community. Her penitence may have made her a credible witness, but it could not restore her to the body of God's people. Nor could she take upon herself the collective guilt of the community—a ritual that if performed by members of the community could well have permitted forgiveness and prevented the profound disruption of Puritan society.[54] Nor could her death have offered any communal expiation of guilt. The "Indian woman," as she is repeatedly identified in the records, would always be set apart, a stranger in their midst.

Tituba's physical appearance, so long associated with Satanic practices, not only predisposed her tormentors to accept her confession as truth but it also encouraged others to incorporate selective elements of her exotic fantasy into their own confessions and beliefs of an evil presence. In her fantasies of an evil power, Tituba seemed to confirm that the Devil was now among them. That story supplied the initial legal evidence to begin the process of communal exorcism—to root out the witches and purge the community of its collective sin. Her testimony, at first, was deemed essential to ferreting out the conspirators. As others, under the threat of execution, confessed and confirmed her testimony, Tituba's corroboration was no longer needed. She was left to contemplate her own misdeeds in the Boston jail, as the trials and convictions culminated in the tragedy she had inspired.

The intense impact of the demonized American Indian image permeated the legal proceedings in the Salem of 1692. Tituba's physical presence as well as her convincing words and behavior contributed to that impact. Her credibility as a witness was as much a product of her womanly "conversations" as it was her association with devilish Indians.

As a result, the Massachusetts magistrates, captives of their own cultural milieu, did not see Tituba's testimony as an artful diplomatic tactic or a manipulation of their fears. They misunderstood her notions of evil, adjusted them to match their own preconceptions, and were overwhelmed by the results—confirmation of a predicted, but terrifying, conspiracy.[55] Her confession, with its aura of repentance and renunciation of a devilish alliance, allowed the Puritans (as most historians have since) to see her as a simple slave bewitched by forces beyond her control and, therefore, unworthy of further attention. The unconscious but creative use of Tituba's testimony in 1692 propelled the witchhunt for months, prompting a profound disruption of New England society.

Altered Lives

No spectral evidence may hereafter be accounted valid,
or suffered to take away the life, or good name, of any
person or persons within this province."
—Ruling of the General Court of Massachusetts,
1703, in Boyer and Nissenbaum, eds.,
Salem Witchcraft Papers

Between March and October of 1692 over 150 people were arrested on suspicion of witchcraft. Twenty-four would die before the crisis was over—nineteen by hanging, one pressed to death, and four from other causes while in prison. Hundreds of lives would be disrupted by the jailings, the loss of property, and the absence of needed labor on the farm and in the household. Ties between children and parents, between husbands and wives, among siblings and neighbors, were frayed by accusations and counteraccusations. Some would never recover from the trauma. Five-year-old Dorcas Good, imprisoned in chains for nine months, was so terrified by the experience that she became unmanageable as she grew older. Her father reported in 1710 that "she hath ever since been very chargeable [i.e., irresponsible and a burden to him], having little or no reason to govern herself."[1] The petitions submitted to the General Court to reclaim lost property and receive restitution for the cost of imprisonment highlight some of the personal tragedies and economic costs of the witchhunt.[2] But the full impact of those events was probably much greater than those extant written sources indicate. Tituba's confession had consequences and ramifications that no one could have predicted in March of 1692 and are still being explored three hundred years later. Her own life was compellingly altered.

At the end Tituba recanted her confession, admitting that she had lied to protect herself. That action had little effect on subsequent events and was almost lost in the rush by other confessors, in fear of damnation, to admit their terrible sin. Tituba's attempt to retract her confession received scant attention at the time and was ignored in the written reports of most observers. Only Robert Calef made note of it: "The account she [Tituba] since gives of it is, that her Master did beat her and otherways abuse her, to make her confess and accuse (such as he call'd) her Sister-Witches, and that whatsoever she said by way of confession or accusing others, was the effect of such usage."[3] Hers was not the first retraction of a reluctant confession. The others had already received a great deal of attention.

The tide of accusations and confessions had started to turn during the summer. Starting with Margaret Jacobs in August, several of the confessors denied their earlier statements. Jacobs had suffered excruciating mental anguish, what she described as "the terrors of a wounded Conscience," the result of falsely implicating both her grandfather and George Burroughs. On August 18, the day before the execution of the two men, still fearful that the truth would lead to her own death, Jacobs apologized for lying, "choosing death with a quiet conscience, than to live in such horror, which I could not suffer."[4] Six Andover women retracted their confessions the following month, shortly after the September executions, complaining that they had submitted to an unbearable pressure from friends, family, and the magistrates to confess. Plagued by their consciences, they could no longer live with the anticipation of the damnation awaiting them. They too preferred death to "the great sin in belying."[5]

By the end of September the use of spectral evidence had been completely discredited. But the theological and political leadership had become suspicious of the proceedings early on. Nathaniel Saltonstall had resigned from the court after the first case in June because he disapproved of the prosecutorial methods.[6] Cotton Mather had also warned in June that spectral evidence should be received with caution because the "Demon may . . . Appear . . . in the shape of an innocent." Mather continued cautioning the governor and his Council of the dangers in using spectral evidence to convict as new complaints regarding the conduct of the court grew in volume.[7] Those recanting and describing how they were forced to confess added to the reaction against the persecutions.

The Governor was finally convinced that innocent people were being convicted on very flimsy evidence. His own wife and the very wealthy Boston widow and mother of Jonathan Corwin's wife, Margaret Thatcher, and the Reverend Samuel Willard were all accused and faced possible prosecution.[8] This brought the danger of persecution too close to his own home, threatening his personal, social, and political position. Early in October Phips dissolved the emergency court of Oyer and Terminer he had set up in May.[9] The execution of eight people on September 22 marked the end of the persecutions; after that day, the witchhunt was, to all intents and purposes, over. The Governor called for a stay of execution for those already convicted and began to empty all of the prisons. Some fifty people who had been indicted, and many others awaiting a hearing, were suffering in jails in a variety of locations. He permitted those who could afford the cost to be let out on bail.[10]

With the Governor's action in October, the possibility of execution was no longer a threat. Other confessors, succumbing to more gentle questioning in jail, described the pressures and fears that led to their false testimonies. Rebecca Eames, who had confessed on August 19, told Increase Mather and Thomas Brattle when they visited the Boston jail in October that her testimony was not true. Eames was one of the few women to confess and then be convicted and sentenced to die. She was fortunately reprieved when the Governor called a halt to the executions early in October.[11]

Sensitive, as usual, to the nuances of community trends and recognizing that she could dispense with her role as a reluctant witch, Tituba also admitted to lying about her diabolical contacts.[12] She knew by then that her life would be saved even if she admitted to lying. With the exception of Samuel Wardwell (who denied his confession at his trial), none of the others recanting their forced confessions were executed.[13] But unlike the others, in the process of recanting, Tituba also demonstrated an unusual defiance. She could not resist a final thrust at her master. Joining the pack of those who blamed Parris for the Salem tragedy, she accused him of forcing her to admit to witchcraft. As Tituba awaited the consequences of that defiance, the provincial government began to take conciliatory action.

Phips asked the legislature to establish a new Superior Court of Judicature to try the remainder of the accused, but on the recommendation of the clergy denied the use of spectral evidence in that new court. New trials of at least thirty-three of the remaining fifty-two indicted persons were held at four locations between January and May of 1693. The courts found all but three, who had confessed, innocent of the charges, but they too were reprieved. Governor Phips thought two of the three women somewhat deranged. Another seven people who awaited execution from their earlier trials by the Court of Oyer and Terminer, including Rebecca Eames, were also freed on the grounds that "the matter" had been managed badly by that court.[14]

Gradually the jails were emptied of their tortured inhabitants as the families and friends of the prisoners, including those not yet indicted, paid their jail fees.[15] Prisoners were expected to pay the cost of their own upkeep while in jail and could not be let out until that debt was taken care of. Poor people had an especially difficult time. Margaret Jacobs, acquitted in January, was unable to raise the money and remained in the filthy jail for months until someone in the town, pitying her, paid for her release.[16]

Tituba, of course, had no resources of her own. She found herself abandoned by Samuel Parris, who would not allow her back into his household, although he did not suspect her of teaching his children about witchcraft or of wanting to harm little Betty.[17] Tituba may have miscalculated the effect on Parris of retracting her March confessions, or possibly she hoped that by antagonizing him she would be sold to someone else in the community. That would free her from Parris's jurisdiction and the fear of further punishment at his hands. Tituba did not harbor kind sentiments toward her master. She had, after all, indirectly accused him of bringing evil to the community and she resented his physical abuse.

Parris may well have sensed that her confession had begun as an attack on him. Further angered by her recanting and its implied rebuke of his punitive action toward her, he refused to assist her in any way or to take her out of the Boston prison. To show compassion would have been tantamount to apologizing for unjustifiably beating her, forcing her confession, and subjecting her to thirteen months in prison. Her innocence was his guilt. And Samuel Parris in 1693 was not yet ready to apologize for his various roles in the Salem tragedy. It is also possible that Parris needed to distance himself from her and the imputations of harboring evil in his household. His parishioners were already preparing to blame him for the events of 1692 and Tituba's continuing presence, a reminder of their pain, could have been an added irritant.[18]

Tituba's punishment for her benevolent act in protecting young Betty Parris was far worse than she could have predicted. She did survive, but not only was she subjected to the psychological torture of a public interrogation and the misery of thirteen months of a meager food ration in crowded, filthy confinement—terribly cold in the winter and unbearably hot in the summer—but also endured a separation from her family.[19] She probably suffered additionally from the taunts of other inmates and visitors to the prison who feared her magical power.[20] Her confession may have saved her life, but it would not have afforded protection against the stigma of association with the Devil or of Parris's wrath.

To dispose of his reluctant witch, Parris simply refused to pay her jail fees. That meant Tituba would remain in Boston in jail until someone else volunteered to pay the cost of those months of incarceration. Some agreement must have been reached, although written evidence of those details is no longer available. Because she was a slave, she could be sold for the amount of those jail fees, which came to about seven pounds.[21] An as yet unidentified person paid those fees and took her away in April of 1693.[22] Her fate after that date is unknown. Tituba disappears from the public record at that point. But some conjecture can suggest what happened to her and her family.

Of John, her husband, we have no further information. Presumably he was sold to the person who had acquired Tituba. Puritans would have been reluctant to divide married couples, even enslaved people. The marriage bond was not just the most fundamental unit of social organization, but was also "the principal referent of Puritan experiences of God."[23] To separate the two Indian slaves would have violated too many Puritan precepts. Parris may also have been anxious to rid himself of the one man who appeared to suffer torment similar to the afflicted girls. John may well have become a burden because of his periodic episodes of fainting and falling into violent fits.[24] His presence, moreover, was another reminder of Parris's guilt in this communal horror, although John was never imprisoned nor accused of witchcraft. He too disappears from the written record after the trials.

Their daughter Violet, probably no more than three or four years of age in 1693, did not merit the same treatment. She had played no part in the tragedy and there was no social pressure to keep parents and child as a unit. Separation of children from mothers was a normal part of the life cycle for slaves as well as white people in colonial New England. Her appearance in Parris's will indicates that Violet remained in the Parris household to be trained as a domestic, eventually to take her mother's place in Elizabeth Parris's kitchen and that of Samuel's second wife, Dorothy. Violet was still alive when Samuel Parris died in 1720, an able servant and sufficiently skilled to be worth thirty pounds to the estate.[25] Dorothy Parris had died the year before her husband Samuel and the surviving members of the family probably had no need of another household slave.[26] The "Indian woman" Violet was more valuable to the family on the auction block than as a worker and she was sold off to pay some of Parris's debts.[27] Violet too would experience a sharp break with her past. She, like her parents, was sold to another unknown buyer and left no record of her ultimate fate.

In the end Tituba lost contact with both her own child and the one she had tried to protect. If she and John were kept together, she was left with only minimal contact with the people and places that afforded some stability to her life. If they were separated, Tituba may have been destitute emotionally, a repeat of her uprooting and loss of contact with kin as a child. She was still a young woman—no more than thirty years old in 1693, and capable of having more children. Whether she did we may never know. We can assume that she was probably strong enough to withstand this new trauma of separation and, as in the past, would have found the means to adjust to her newest circumstances. Her ability to survive and make the most of personal crises had been demonstrated both in Barbados and Salem. Surely she would succeed again. On the other hand, the society that had abandoned her would spend the next ten years struggling with the effects of her successful attempt to save her own life in 1692.

In an effort to conciliate those who suffered financial losses during the witchhunt, the Massachusetts General Court in 1704 reversed the bill of attainder that had deprived the families of the convicted witches of their property. Only those who had filed petitions benefited at first. Seven years later, in 1711, the legislature allowed restitution to all those who had "suffered in their Estates at that Sorrowful time."[28] Other compensation was awarded to the survivors for the cost of imprisonment. Most of those accounts were settled by 1712 but some names do not appear in those records. Tituba's account is conspicuously absent from the lists.[29] Had she been removed from the province? Was her new master too far away to claim restitution? Did he prefer that the Indian woman become invisible, ignoring the possibility of some monetary reward in favor of anonymity?

Tituba, wherever she was in 1712, if still alive, may have heard about these financial settlements, but her response if any will probably never be known. Her daughter Violet was old enough to understand but she no longer lived in Salem. Samuel Parris, widowed in 1696 when Elizabeth died, had taken his servants and his children the following year to the frontier community of Stow and then to several other Massachusetts towns. In 1712, he, his second wife Dorothy, their four children, and presumably Violet were living in Sudbury. Two of the children of his first marriage, Thomas and Susannah, had died by that time. Elizabeth (Betty) had married Benjamin Barron in January of 1710.[30] There was no recorded comment from any of the Parris household on these legislative acts.

To the members of the Salem community there was little satisfaction for the mental pain, humiliation, and physical misery Tituba's confession had fueled. It would take years of apology and repentance before the scars of that fearful experience would heal. Life could not return to normal just yet. A period of reconciliation followed. Samuel Parris, determinedly clinging to his estranged church members, was the first to acknowledge his guilt in the tragedy. In 1694 he publicly apologized to the congregation for his role as a leader in the hunt for witches. He was, he said, too zealous in his desire to protect the community from the Devil.[31] His apology did not appease those who continued to blame him for the terrible events—for stoking the fires of discontent with his own resentments and urging the young people to continue their accusations. The opposition in the village and pressure from other ministers finally convinced Parris to leave in 1697 and a new, younger, more conciliatory minister, Joseph Green, took his place.[32]

The process of healing quickened after that year. Green worked at the village level to reconcile the competing factions. He brought the dissenters back into the church and asked that excommunication of the convicted witches be rescinded.[33] At the same time, the more distant authority in

Boston took what steps it could to heal those wounds. The General Court proclaimed a fast day on January 14, 1697, in memory of those who died and as repentance for communal mistakes in "the late tragedy raised among us by Satan and his instruments." That bill, drafted by Samuel Sewall, was part of his own personal atonement for his role in the affair when he sat on the Court of Oyer and Terminer. In a public apology Sewall admitted his responsibility, contritely taking "the blame and shame of it" on himself.[34]

Other members of the community followed. Twelve men who had served on juries in Salem during the witch trials confessed their "deep sense of, and sorrow for our Errors," declaring that they "were sadly deluded and mistaken," and begged forgiveness for having "been instrumental with others, tho Ignorantly and unwittingly, to bring upon our selves . . . the Guilt of Innocent Blood."[35] Ann Putnam, Jr., twenty-seven years old in 1706, also publicly admitted her guilt. Saddened and repentant for the pain she had caused, Ann confessed in the meeting house, in what was becoming a familiar litany: "it was a great delusion of Satan that deceived me in that sad time, whereby I justly fear I have been instrumental with others, though ignorantly and unwittingly, to bring upon myself and this land the guilt of innocent blood."[36]

Deluded by Satan or under the power of suggestion fueled by an Indian's vision? To a Puritan they amounted to the same driving force: a Satanic presence, a devilish Indian, alien notions. Although unstated, Tituba's responsibility for their deluded state may well have lingered in the subconscious of those who reflected on their own roles in the tragedy. She would always be a reminder of their failure to exorcise the Devil within themselves.

Apart from the personal tragedies, what was the impact of Tituba's testimony on the larger history of New England? Did it bring about any permanent change in the values and thought processes of the Puritan community? Tituba was, of course, responsible for initiating the panic and helped to maintain the acute sense of a diabolical invasion. But after the panic had subsided, apologies were given, and attempts made at restitution, of what importance in the course of American history is the Salem incident and, by inference, Tituba's special role?

The Salem tragedy was the last time that anyone would be executed for witchcraft in Massachusetts.[37] Spectral evidence, which had never been an issue before 1692, was completely discredited. The General Court specifically outlawed the use of such non-material evidence in 1703, declaring that "no spectral evidence may hereafter be accounted valid."[38] In 1736, English and Scottish laws prescribing death for witchcraft were repealed.[39] Accusations of witchcraft, however, would continue to occur; occult practices had not lost their adherents. But the fear of witchcraft would no longer have the power to disrupt communities and destroy innocent lives. The discrediting of spectral evidence weakened the belief in occult powers, for if a witch could not be distinguished from a specter, could there truly be such a thing as a witch? As a result, the churches no longer turned to legal institutions to counter something so invisible as witchcraft.[40]

It is possible that evangelical Christianity with its revivalist techniques effectively challenged occult religion by replacing it with a new ritual for spiritual transformation and thus contributed to its decline.[41] But it certainly did not bring about its demise. Magical practices and the interest in witchcraft continue to the present.[42] Curiosity about the occult helps to fill classrooms in courses about the history of witchcraft. Salem Massachusetts is still visited by latter-day professed witches, a tourist mecca born of Tituba's testimony and indicative of an enduring interest in witchcraft. As long as there is a belief in the reality of the invisible world, beliefs in witches and the power of magical charms will continue to arouse interest or, at the very least, curiosity.

In the end, the Salem witchhunt proved to be more disruptive of the Puritan ideal of community than the expected unifying experience.[43] The new idiom of resistance articulated by Tituba uncovered a range of discontent with social, political, and religious conditions, particularly anti-clerical sentiment among young women and servants. Tituba's stories provided a forum, a focus, and a new language for that dissatisfaction. Her words encouraged the reshaping of the notion of evil to include strangers, elite men and women, and ministerial leadership. Moreover, she supplied the framework of an evil conspiracy that could be elaborated to fit both elite notions of evil and the folklore of witchcraft. The effect was a merger of the two traditions into a new elite synthesis.

Though the Puritans misunderstood and misconstrued Tituba's testimony, those very mistakes permitted them to focus on the diabolical conspiracy. But it was a conspiracy made in Salem, an imaginative combination of Indian lore and Christian fears. With the acceptance by the

Puritans of the Indian concept of an outside evil persona, Tituba had not only reshaped the popular notions of witchcraft but helped to bring those ideas into congruence with clerical fantasies of Satan.

There is general agreement that the New England mentality was somehow different after 1692: that that year was a watershed in the development of the Puritan mind and that certain aspects of belief and behavior and ritual were different afterward. Certainly the value of confession declined after 1692.[44] Tituba's confession, which became a model for resistance rather than a confirmation of Puritan values, had so distorted its meaning that, like the witch trials themselves, that ritual was discredited. Confession should have purged the sin of diabolism from the community and reaffirmed Puritan values of harmony, hierarchy, and piety—the covenant ideal. Instead, what had been a ritual of renewal became a method of resistance to authority and a subverter of those values.[45] Popular beliefs did not change; the concept of the witch among the populace—as one who did harm using magical means—remained essentially the same. It was official policy and elite notions that shifted.[46]

That process of transformation, resulting from the convergence of two traditions regarding the nature of evil—the elite and the folk—exposed the contradictions in the reforming Puritan tradition and prepared it for the eighteenth-century Enlightenment. After Salem the reformers realized that the intense personal commitment of conversion could became a "ruse" and that zealous prosecution of sin could result in "hideous enormities." The Salem witchhunt gave warning that the persistent pursuit of reform could have the opposite result—of destroying the biblical commonwealth and the holy covenants that bound the community together. The Salem experience, by discrediting some of the sacred rituals, helped to shape a more moderate Puritanism.[47]

Thus the folklore of the American Indian, embedded in Tituba's confession, interacting with English folk beliefs and elite notions of evil initiated a modifying process and lay the groundwork for the rationalism of the eighteenth-century Enlightenment. But unlike the usual trends of intellectual change, this shift to a more secular society was not brought about by the dominant class impacting on the subordinate. It was the reverse. In their great desire to make Tituba's confession believable, those hearing her stories had to accommodate her fantasy and integrate her concept of an evil persona into their own belief system. That accommodation of her Indian beliefs forced the rejection of specters and magical practices from the realm of public discourse. This was change from the bottom up, initiated by an Indian woman slave.

By focusing on Tituba's role in that tragedy, the Salem events permit us to capture a glimpse of an unusual process of exchange between high and popular cultures.[48] The lowly but acculturated slave woman, conversant with Puritan norms and protected by her subservient Anglicized demeanor, overwhelmed the dominant class and temporarily reversed the roles of the teachers and the taught. Tituba's sorcery, if it existed, was in exposing and capitalizing on a Puritan vulnerability to images drawn from popular culture. Through Tituba's agency the very practical, but deeply ingrained, mentality of the folk was able to intrude into the complex world of New England print culture. The result of this convergence of cultures in 1692 was a violent moment in early New England history, but one that ultimately redirected Puritanism into less turbulent paths. The dynamic in that process was the reluctant confession of a slave woman called Tituba who successfully brought to her own defense the multi-ethnic oral traditions of her West Indian and South American cultures.

Timetable of Accusations and Confessions, February–November 1692[1]

Name	*Confessed[2]	Residence	Date[3]	Outcome, 1692
Sarah Good		Salem V	Feb. 29	executed July 19
Tituba*	3/1	Salem V	Feb. 29	imprisoned
Sarah Osborne		Salem V	Feb. 29	died in prison
Martha Corey		Salem V	Mar. 19	executed Sept. 22
Dorcas Good		Salem V	Mar. 23	imprisoned
Rebecca Nurse		Salem V	Mar. 23	executed July 19
Rachel Clinton		Ipswich	Mar. 29	imprisoned
John Lee		not known	April 11	no record
Sarah Cloyce		Salem V	April 4	imprisoned
Elizabeth Proctor		Salem V	April 4	convicted, reprieved
John Proctor		Salem V	April 11	executed Aug. 19
Giles Corey		Salem V	April 18	pressed to death Sept. 19
Bridget Bishop		Salem V	April 18	executed June 10
Abigail Hobbs*	4/20	Topsfield	April 18	convicted, reprieved
Mary Warren*	4/21	Salem V	April 18	briefly imprisoned
Edward Bishop		Salem V	April 21	escaped
Sarah Bishop		Salem V	April 21	escaped
Mary Black		Salem V	April 21	imprisoned
Mary Easty		Topsfield	April 21	executed Sept. 22
Mary English		Salem T	April 21	escaped
Deliverance Hobbs*	4/23	Topsfield	April 21	imprisoned
William Hobbs		Topsfield	April 21	imprisoned
Sarah Wilds		Topsfield	April 21	executed July 19
Nehemiah Abbot, Jr.		Topsfield	April 21	released
Samuel Passanauton		not known	April 28	imprisoned 8 wks.
Philip English		Salem T	April 30	escaped
George Burroughs		Wells, Me	April 30	executed Aug. 19

Name	*Confessed[2]	Residence	Date[3]	Outcome, 1692
Lydia Dustin		Reading	April 30	imprisoned, died in prison
Dorcas Hoar*	9/21	Beverly	April 30	convicted, reprieved
Susannah Martin		Amesbury	April 30	executed July 19
Martha Sparks		Chelmsford	April ?	imprisoned 12 months
Sarah Morrill		Beverly	May 2	imprisoned
Sarah Dustin		Reading	May 8	imprisoned
Bethia Carter, Sr.		Woburn	May 8	imprisoned
Bethia Carter, Jr.		Woburn	May 8	no info
Ann Sears		Woburn	May 8	imprisoned
George Jacobs, Sr.		Salem T	May 10	executed Aug. 19
Margaret Jacobs*	nd	Salem V	May 10	imprisoned
John Willard		Salem V	May 10	executed Aug. 19
Alice Parker		Salem T	May 12	executed Sept. 22
Ann Pudeator		Salem T	May 12	executed Sept. 22
Abigail Somes		Salem T	May 13	imprisoned
Daniel Andrew		Salem V	May 14	escaped
Elizabeth Colson		Reading	May 14	possibly escaped
Sarah Buckley		Salem V	May 14	imprisoned
Thomas Farrer, Sr.		Lynn	May 14	imprisoned
Elizabeth Hart		Lynn	May 14	imprisoned
George Jacobs, Jr.		Salem V	May 14	escaped
Rebecca Jacobs		Salem V	May 14	imprisoned
Mary Witheridge		Salem V	May 14	imprisoned
Roger Toothaker		Billerica	May 18	died in prison June 16
Sarah Basset		Lynn	May 21	imprisoned
Sarah Proctor		Salem V	May 21	imprisoned
Susanna Roots		Beverly	May 21	imprisoned
Mary De Rich		Salem V	May 23	imprisoned
Sarah Pease		Salem T	May 23	imprisoned
Benjamin Proctor		Salem V	May 23	imprisoned
Jerson Toothaker		Billerica	May 24	no record
Mary Bradbury		Salisbury	May 26	escaped
Arthur Abbott		Ipswich	May 28	no record
Martha Carrier		Andover	May 28	executed Aug. 19
Elizabeth Cary		Charlestown	May 28	escaped
Capt. John Flood		Rumney Marsh	May 28	no record
Elizabeth How		Topsfield	May 28	executed July 19
William Proctor		Salem V	May 28	imprisoned
Wilmot Reed		Marblehead	May 28	executed Sept. 22
Sarah Rice		Reading	May 28	imprisoned
Mary Toothaker*	7/30	Billerica	May 28	no record
John Alden		Boston	May 31	escaped
Elizabeth Fosdick		Charlestown	June 2	imprisoned
Elizabeth Paine		Charlestown	June 2	no record
Mary Ireson		Lynn	June 4	imprisoned
Job Tookey		Beverly	June 4	acquitted
Ann Doliver		Gloucester	June 6	imprisoned
Margaret Hawkes*	nd	Salem T	July 1	imprisoned
Candy*	7/4	Salem T	July 1	imprisoned
Ann Foster*	7/15	Andover	July 15	convicted, died in prison
Mary Lacey, Jr.*	7/21	Andover	July 20	imprisoned
Mary Lacey, Sr.*	7/21	Andover	July 21	convicted
Andrew Carrier*	7/23	Andover	July 21	imprisoned

Name	*Confessed[2]	Residence	Date[3]	Outcome, 1692
Richard Carrier*	7/22	Andover	July 21	imprisoned
Thomas Carrier*	7/21	Andover	July 21	imprisoned
Martha Emerson*	7/23	Haverhill	July 22	case dismissed
Mary Bridges, Sr.*	nd	Andover	July 28	imprisoned
Hannah Bromage*	7/30	Haverhill	July 30	imprisoned
Sarah Carrier*	8/11	Andover	July ?	imprisoned
Mary Post		Rowley	Aug. 2	imprisoned, convicted
Mary Clarke		Haverhill	Aug. 3	no record
Margaret Scott		unknown	Aug. 5	convicted, executed 9/22
Elizabeth Johnson, Jr.*	8/10	Andover	Aug. 10	imprisoned, convicted
Abigail Faulkner, Sr.*	8/30	Andover	Aug. 11	convicted, reprieved
Francis Hutchins		Haverhill	Aug. 18	imprisoned
Ruth Wilford		Haverhill	Aug. 18	imprisoned
Rebecca Eames*	8/19	Boxford	Aug. 19	convicted, reprieved
Mary Barker*	8/29	Andover	Aug. 25	imprisoned
William Barker, Jr.*	9/1	Andover	Aug. 25	imprisoned
William Barker, Sr.*	8/29	Andover	Aug. 25	imprisoned
Mary Bridges, Jr.*	8/25	Andover	Aug. 25	imprisoned
Sarah Bridges*	8/25	Andover	Aug. 25	Imprisoned
John Howard		Rowley	Aug. 25	imprisoned
John Jackson, Jr.*	nd	Rowley	Aug. 25	imprisoned
John Jackson, Sr		Rowley	Aug. 25	imprisoned
Mary Marston*	8/29	Andover	Aug. 25	imprisoned
Hannah Post*	8/25	Boxford	Aug. 25	imprisoned
Susannah Post*	8/25	Andover	Aug. 25	imprisoned
Abigail Johnson		Andover	Aug. 29	imprisoned
Elizabeth Johnson, Sr.*	8/30	Andover	Aug. 29	imprisoned
Mary Green		Haverhill	Aug. ?	imprisoned
Stephen Johnson*	9/1	Andover	Sep. 1	imprisoned
Sarah Hawkes*	9/1	Andover	Sep. 1	imprisoned
Mary Parker		Andover	Sep. 1	convicted, executed Sept. 22
Mercy Wardwell*	9/1	Andover	Sep. 1	imprisoned
Samuel Wardwell*	9/1	Andover	Sep. 1	convicted, executed Sept. 22
Sarah Wardwell*	9/1	Andover	Sep. 1	imprisoned
Elizabeth Dicer		Gloucester	Sep. 3	imprisoned
Margaret Prince		Gloucester	Sep. 3	imprisoned
Mary Taylor*	nd	Reading	Sep. 3	imprisoned
Mary Colson		Reading	Sep. 5	case dismissed
Joseph Emons		Manchester	Sep. 5	imprisoned
Nicholas Frost		Manchester	Sep. 5	no record
Jane Lilly		Malden	Sep. 5	no record
Henry Salter		Andover	Sep. 7	no record
Abigail Barker*	nd	Andover	Sep. 8	imprisoned
Mary Osgood*	9/8	Andover	Sep. 8	imprisoned
Hannah Carrell		Salem T	Sep. 10	no record
Sarah Cole*	10/3	Salem T	Sep. 10	imprisoned
Deliverance Dane*	9/16	Andover	Sep. 16	imprisoned
Joseph Draper*	9/16	Andover	Sep. 16	imprisoned
Joannah Tyler*	9/16	Andover	Sep. 16	imprisoned
Martha Tyler*	9/16	Andover	Sep. 16	imprisoned
Dorothy Faulkner*	9/16	Andover	Sep. 16	imprisoned 1 month
Abigail Faulkner*	9/16	Andover	Sep. 16	imprisoned 1 month
Sarah Wilson, Sr.*	9/16	Andover	Sep. 16	imprisoned

Name	*Confessed[2]	Residence	Date[3]	Outcome, 1692
Edward Farrington*	9/17	Andover	Sep. 17	probably imprisoned
Joan Peney		Gloucester	Sep. 20	imprisoned
Eunice Fry*	nd	Andover	Sep. ?	imprisoned 15 wks.
Rebecca Johnson, Jr.		Andover	Sep. ?	unknown
Rebecca Johnson, Sr.*	nd	Andover	Sep. ?	imprisoned
John Sawdy*	nd	Andover	Sep. ?	imprisoned
Sarah Wilson, Jr.*	nd	Andover	Sep. ?	imprisoned
Sarah Cole		Lynn	Oct. 3	imprisoned
Rebecca Dike		Gloucester	Nov. 5	no record
Esther Elwell		Gloucester	Nov. 5	no record
Abigail Roe		Gloucester	Nov. 5	no record

DEATHS:

Died in Prison:

  Ann Foster nd

  Lydia Dustin, 3/10

  Roger Toothaker, 6/16

  Sarah Osborne 5/10

Pressed to Death:

  Giles Corey, 9/19

Executed:

June 10

    Bridget Bishop

July 19

    Sarah Good

    Elizabeth How

    Susannah Martin

    Rebecca Nurse

    Sarah Wilds

August 19

    George Burroughs

    Martha Carrier

    George Jacobs, Sr.

    John Proctor

    John Willard

September 22

    Martha Corey

    Mary Easty

    Alice Parker

    Mary Parker

    Ann Pudeator

    Wilmot Reed

    Margaret Scott

    Samuel Wardwell

Chronological List of 53 Confessions, 1692

Confessors	Date of First Confession	Confessors	Date of First Confession
Tituba	March 1	Stephen Johnson	September 1
Abigail Hobbs	April 20	Sarah Hawkes	September 1
Mary Warren	April 21	Mercy Wardwell	September 1
Deliverance Hobbs	April 23	Samuel Wardwell	September 1
Candy	July 4	Sarah Wadwell	September 1
Ann Foster	July 15	Mary Osgood	September 8
Mary Lacey, Jr.	July 21	Deliverance Dane	September 16
Mary Lacey, Sr.	July 21	Joseph Draper	September 16
Richard Carrier	July 22	Dorothy Faulkner	September 16
Thomas Carrier	July 21	Abigail Faulkner	September 16
Andrew Carrier	July 23	Joannah Tyler	September 16
Martha Emerson	July 23	Martha Tyler	September 16
Hannah Bromage	July 30	Sarah Wilson, Sr.	Septmber 16
Mary Toothaker	July 30	Edward Farrington	September 17
Elizabeth Johnson, Jr.	August 10	Dorcas Hoar	September 21
Sarah Carrier	August 11	Sarah Cole	October 3
Rebecca Eames	August 19	Abigail Barker	unknown
Mary Bridges, Jr.	August 25	Mary Bridges, Sr.	unknown
Sarah Bridges	August 25	Eunice Fry	unknown
Hannah Post	August 25	Margaret Hawkes	unknown
Susannah Post	August 25	John Jackson, Jr.	unknown
Mary Barker	August 29	Margaret Jacobs	unknown
William Barker, Sr.	August 29	Rebecca Johnson, Sr.	unknown
Mary Marston	August 29	John Sawdy	unknown
Abigail Faulkner, Sr.	August 30	Mary Taylor	unknown
Elizabeth Johnson, Sr.	August 30	Sarah Wilson, Jr.	unknown
William Barker, Jr.	September 1		

Transcripts of Tituba's Confessions

Transcripts are from SWP, III:745–55, and retain the spelling and punctuation of the original. A note on the dates. Until the late sixteenth century, Christian tradition began the year on March 25 to coincide with the spring equinox and the celebration of Easter. Reforms instituted by Pope Gregory in 1582 eliminated a ten-day error from the calendar and shifted the beginning of the year to January 1. The English Protestants refused to follow this papal injunction and continued to use the old-style or Julian calendar with the new year on March 25. Nonetheless, notations in seventeenth-century legal records usually acknowledge the difference between old-style and new-style calendars by assigning the days between January 1 and March 24 to both years, and thus February 29, 1691, became 1691/2, but should be read as 1692.

When the more accurate modern dating began in England in 1752, not only did the year start on January 1, but the English, like other Europeans almost two centuries earlier, finally "lost" the excess days (which amounted to eleven days by that time). It is usual today to ignore that discrepancy in days for the years before 1752 but to use the new-style designation for the year. I have followed that convention throughout this book.

Tituba

(Warrant vs. Tituba and Sarah Osborne)

Salem febr' the 29'th day. 1691/2

Whereas m'rs Joseph Hutcheson Thomas putnam Edward putnam and Thomas preston Yeomen of Salem Village, in the County of Essex. personally appeared before us, And made Complaint on behalfe of theire Majesties against Sarah Osburne the wife of Alexa' Osburne of Salem Village afores'd, and titibe an Indian Woman servant, of mr. Sam'l parris of s'd place also; for Suspition of Witchcraft, by them Committed and thereby much injury doñ to Elizabeth Parris Abigail Williams Anna putnam and Elizabeth Hubert all of Salem Village afores'd Sundry times with in this two moneths and Lately also done, at s'd Salem Village Contrary to the peace and Laws of our Sov'r Lord & Lady Wm & Mary of England &c King & Queene

You are there fore in theire Maj'ts names hereby required to apprehend and forthwith or as soon as may be bring before us the aboves'd Sarah Osburne, and titibe Indian, at the house of Lt. Nath'l Ingersalls in s'd place. and if it may be by to Morrow aboute ten of the Clock in the morning then and there to be Examined Relateing to the aboves'd premises—. You are likewise required to bring at the same tyme Eliz. parris Abig'l Williams Anna putnam and Eliz Hubert or any other person or persons that can give Evedence in the Aboves'd Case. and hereof you are not to faile

Dated Salem febr' 29 1691/2

> *John Hathorne
> *Jonathan. Corwin } Assis'ts

To Constable Joseph Herrick Const' in Salem

(Reverse)

(Essex County Archives, Salem—Witchcraft Vol. 1 Page 11)

(Officer's Return)

according to this warrant I have apprehended the parsons with in mentioned and have brought them accordingly and have mad diligent sarch for Images and such like but can find non

Salem village this 1. march 1691/92

p me *Joseph Herrick Constable

(Essex County Archives, Salem—Witchcraft Vol. 1 Page 11)

(Summary of Examinations of Tituba, Sarah Good, and Sarah Osborne)

Salem Village March 1'st 1691

Titiba an Indian Woman brought before us by Const' Jos Herrick of Salem upon Suspition of Witchcraft by her Commited according to the Compl't of Jos. Hutcheson & Thomas putnam &c of Salem Village as appeares p Warrant granted Salem 29 febr'y 1691/2 Titiba upon Examination and after some denyall acknowledged the matter of fact according to her Examination given in more fully will appeare and who also charged Sarah Good and Sarah Osburne with the same Salem Village March the 1'th 1691/2

Sarah Good Sarah Osborne and Titiba an Indian Woman all of Salem Village Being this day brought before us upon Suspition of Witchcraft &c by them and Every one of them Committed. titiba an Indian Woman acknowledging the matter of fact. and Sarah Osburne and Sarah Good denying the same before us: but there appeareing in all theire Examinations sufficient Ground to secure them all. And in order to further Examination they Ware all p mittimus sent to the Goales in the County of Essex.

Salem March 2'd Sarah Osburne againe Examined and also titiba as will appear in their Examinations given in

titiba againe acknowledged the fact & also accuse the other two.

Salem March 3'd Sarah Osburn and titiba Indian againe Examined the Examination now Given in

titiba againe s'd the same

Salem March 5'th Sarah Good and titiba againe Examined. & in theire Examination titiba acknowledg the same she did formerly and accused the other two-aboves'd—

   titiba againe s'd the same   p. us   *John Hathorne   }   Assis'ts
                                          *Jonathan. Corwin

(Essex County Archives, Salem—Witchcraft Vol. 1 Page 7)

(Examination of Tituba)

The Examination of Titibe

(H)   Titibe what evil spirit have you familiarity with
(T)   none
(H)   why do you hurt these children
(T)   I do not hurt them
(H)   who is it then
(T)   the devil for ought I know
(H)   did you never see the devil.
(T)   the devil came to me and bid me serve him
(H)   who have you seen
(T)   4 women sometimes hurt the children
(H)   who were they?
(T)   goode Osburn and Sarah good and I doe not know who the other were Sarah good and Osburne would have me hurt the children but I would not shee furder saith there was a tale man of Boston that shee did see
(H)   when did you see them
(T)   Last night at Boston
(H)   what did they say to you
         they said hurt the children
(H)   and did you hurt them

(T) no there is 4 women and one man they hurt the children and then lay all upon me and they tell me if I will not hurt the children they will hurt me

(H) but did you not hurt them

(T) yes, but I will hurt them no more

(H) are you not sorry you did hurt them.

(T) yes.

(H) and why then doe you hurt them

(T) they say hurt children or wee will doe worse to you

(H) what have you seen
   a man come to me and say serve me

(H) what service

(T) hurt the children and last night there was an appearance that said Kill the children and if I would no go on hurting the children they would do worse to me

(H) what is this appearance you see

(T) sometimes it is like a hog and some times like a great dog this appearance shee saith shee did see 4 times

(H) what did it say to you

(T) the black dog said serve me but I said I am a fraid he said if I did not he would doe worse to me

(H) what did you say to it

(T) I will serve you no longer then he said he would hurt me and then he lookes like a man and threatens to hurt me shee said that this man had a yellow bird that keept with him and he told me he had more pretty things that he would give me if I would serve him

(H) what were these pretty things

(T) he did not show me them

(H) what else have you seen

(T) two rats, a red rat and a black rat

(H) what did they say to you

(T) they said serve me

(H) when did you see them

(T) Last night and they said serve me but shee said I would not

(H) what service

(T) shee said hurt the children

(H) did you not pinch Elizabeth Hubbard this morning

(T) the man brought her to me and made me pinch her

(H) why did you goe to thomas putnams Last night and hurt his child

(T) they pull and hall me and make goe

(H) and what would have you doe
   Kill her with a knif
   Left. fuller and others said at this time when the child saw these persons and was tormented by them that she did complain of a knif that they would have her cut her head off with a knife

(H) how did you go

(T) we ride upon stickes and are there presently

(H) doe you goe through the trees or over them

(T) we see no thing but are there presently

(H) why did you not tell your master

(T) I was a fraid they said they would cut off my head it I told

(H) would not you have hurt others if you could

(T) they said they would hurt others but they could not

(H) what attendants hath Sarah good

(T) a yellow bird and shee would have given me one

(H) what meate did she give it

(T) it did suck her between her fingers

(H) Did not you hurt mr Currins child

(T) goode good and goode Osburn told that they did hurt mr Currens child and would have had me hurt him two but I did not

(H) what hath Sarah Osburn

(T) yesterday shee had a thing with a head like a woman with 2 leggs and wings Abigail williams that lives with her uncle mr Parris said that shee did see this same creature and it turned into the shape of goode osburn

(H) what else have you seen with g osburn

(T) an other thing hairy it goes upright like a man it hath only 2 leggs

(H) did you not see Sarah good upon elisebeth Hubbar last Saturday

(T) I did see her set a wolfe upon her to afflict her the persons with this maid did say that shee did complain of a wolf

(T) shee furder said that shee saw a cat with good at another time

(H) what cloathes doth the man go in

(T) he goes in black clouthes a tal man with white hair I thinke

(H) how doth the woman go

(T) in a white whood and a black whood with a tup knot

(H) doe you see who it is that torments these children now

(T) yes it is goode good she hurts them in her own shape

(H) & who is it that hurts them now

(T) I am blind noe I cannot see

Salem Village   written by Ezekiell Chevers

March the 1't 1691/2   Salem Village March the 1't 1691/2

(Essex County Archives, Salem—Witchcraft Vol. 1 Page 6)

(Examination of Tituba—A Second Version)

Tittuba the Ind'n Woem'ns Examn March. 1. 1691/2

Q. why doe you hurt these poor Children? whatt harme have thay done unto you? A. thay doe noe harme to me I noe hurt them att all. Q. why have you done itt? A. I have done nothing; I Can't tell when the Devill works Q. what doth the

Devill tell you that he hurts them A. noe he tells me nothing. Q. doe you never see Something appeare in Some shape? A. noe never See any thing. Q. whatt familiarity have you w'th the devill, or w't is itt if you Converse w'th all? tell the truth whoe itt is that hurts them A. the Devill for ought I know. Q. w't appearanc or how doth he appeare when he hurts them, w'th w't shape or what is he like that hurts them A. like a man I think yesterday I being in the Lentoe Chamber I saw a thing like a man, that tould me Searve him & I tould him noc I would nott doe Such thing. she charges Goody Osburne & Sarah Good as those that hurt the Children, and would have had hir done itt, she sayth she Seen foure two of w'ch she knew nott she saw them last night as she was washing the Roome, thay tould me hurt the Children & would have had me gone to Boston, ther was.5. of them w'th the man, they tould me if I would nott goe & hurt them they would doe soe to mee att first I did agree w'th them butt afterward I tould them I doe soe noe more. Q. would they have had you hurt the Children the Last Night A. yes, butt I was Sorry & I sayd, I would doe Soe noe more, but tould I would feare God. Q. butt why did nott you doe Soe before? A. why they tell mee I had done Soe before & therefore I must goe on, these were the.4.woemen & the man, butt she knew none butt Osburne & Good only, the others were of Boston. Q. att first begining w'th them, w't then appeared to you w't was itt like that Got you to doe itt A. one like a man Just as I was goeing to sleep Came to me this was when the Children was first hurt he sayd he would kill the Children & she would never be well, and he Sayd if I would nott Serve him he would do soe to mee Q. is that the Same man that appeared before to you that appeared the last night & tould you this? A. yes. Q. w't Other likenesses besides a man hath appeared to you? A. Sometimes like a hogge Sometimes like a great black dogge, foure tymes. Q. but w't did they Say unto you? A. they tould me Serve him & that was a good way; that was the black dogge I tould him I was afrayd, he tould me he would be worse then to me. Q. w't did you say to him after that? A. I answer I will Serve you noe Longer he tould me he would doe me hurt then. Q. w't other Creatures have you seene A. a bird Q. w't bird? A. a little yellow Bird. Q. where doth itt keep? A. w'th the man whoe hath pretty things there besides. Q. what other pretty things? A. he hath nott showed them [yet] unto me, butt he s'd he would show them me tomorrow, and he tould me if I would Serve him I should have the Bird. Q. w't other Creatures did you see? A. I saw 2 Catts, one Red, another black as bigge as a little dogge. Q. w't did these Catts doe? A. I dont know; I have seen them two tymes. Q. w't did they say? A. thay say serve them. Q. when did you see them? A. I saw them last night. Q. did they doe any hurt to you or threaten you? A. they did scratch me. Q. when? A. after prayer; and scratched mee, because I would not serve them and when they went away I could nott see but thay stood before the fire. Q. what Service doe thay Expect fro you? A. they Say more hurt to the Children. Q. how did you pinch them when you hurt them? A. the other pull mee & hall me to the pinch the Childr, & I am very sorry for itt, what made you hould yo'r arme when you were Searched? w't had you there? A. I had nothing Q. doe nott those Catts suck you? A. noe never yett I would nott lett them but they had almost thrust me into the fire. Q. how doe you hurt those that you pinch? doe you gett those Catts? or other thing to doe it for you? tell us, how is it done? A. the man sends the Catts to me & bids me pinch them, & I think I went over to mr Grigg's & have pinched hir this day in the morning. the man brought mr Grigg's mayd to me & made me pinch hir. Q. did you ever goe w'th these woemen? A. they are very strong & pull me & make me goe w'th them. Q. where did you goe? A. up to mr putnams & make me hurt the Child. Q. whoe did make you goe? A. man that is very strong & these two woeman, Good & Osburne but I am Sorry. Q. how did you goe? Whatt doe you Ride upon? A. I Rid upon a stick or poale & Good & Osburne behind me we Ride takeing hold of one another don't know how we goe for I Saw noe trees nor path, but was presently there. when wee were up. Q. how long Since you began to pinch mr parriss Children? A. I did nott pinch them att the first, butt he make me afterward. Q. have you Seen Good and osburne Ride upon a poule? A. yes & have held fast by mee: I was nott att mr Grigg's but once, butt it may be Send Something like mee, with or would I have gone, butt that they tell me, they will hurt me; last night they Tell me I must kill Some body w'th the knife. Q. who were they that told you Soe A. Sarah Good & Osburne & they would have had me killed Thomas putnam's Child last night. the Child alsoe affirmed that att the Same tyme thay would have had hir Cutt #[hir own throat] of hir own head for if she would nott then tould hir Tittubee would Cutt itt off & then she Complayned att the Same Time of a knife Cutting of hir when hir master hath asked hir about these things she sayth thay will nott lett hir tell, butt Tell hir if she Tells hir head shall be Cutt off. Q. whoe Tells you Soe? A. the man, Good & Osburnes Wife. Goody Goody Came to hir last night w'n hir master was att prayr & would nott lett hir hear & she Could not heare a good whyle. Good hath one of these birds the yellow bird & would have given mee itt, but I would not have itt & prayer tyme she stoped my eares & would nott lett me hear. Q. w't should you have done with itt A. give itt to the Children. w'ch yellow bird hath bin severall tymes Seen by the Children I saw Sarah Good have itt on hir hand when she Came to hir when mr parris was att prayr: I saw the bird suck Good betwene the fore finger & Long finger upon the Right hand. Q. did you never practise witch-craft in your owne Country? A. Noe Never before now. Q. did you #[ever] See them doe itt now? A. yes. to day, butt that was in the morneing. Q. butt did you see them doe itt now while you are Examining. A. noe I did nott See them butt I Saw them hurt att other tymes. I saw Good have a Catt beside the yellow bird w'ch was with hir Q. what hath Osburne gott to goe w'th hir? Some thing I dont know what itt is. I can't name itt, I don't know how itt looks she hath two of them one of them hath wings & two Leggs & a head like a woeman the Children Saw the Same butt yesterday w'ch afterward turned into a woeman. Q. What is the other Thing that Goody Osburne hath? A. a thing all over hairy, all the face hayry & a long nose & I don't know how to tell how the face looks w'th two Leggs, itt goeth upright & is about two or three foot high & goeth upright like a man & last night itt stood before the fire In mr parris's hall. Q. Whoe was that appeared like a Wolfe to Hubberd as she was goeing proctures? A. itt was Sarah Good & I saw hir Send the Wolfe to hir. Q. what Cloathes doth the man appeare unto you in? A. black Cloaths Some times, Some times Searge Coat of other Couler, a Tall man w'th white hayr, I think. Q. What apparrell doe the woeman ware? A. I don't know w't couller. Q. What Kind of Cloathes hath she? A. I don't know w't couller. Q. What kind of Cloathes hath she? A. a black Silk hood w'th a White Silk hood under itt, w'th top knotts, w'ch woeman I know not but have Seen hir in boston when I lived there. Q. what Cloathes the little woeman? A. a Searge Coat w'th a White Cap as I think. the Children having fits att this Very time she was asked whoe hurt them, she Ans'r Goody Good & the Children affirmed the same butt Hubbard being taken in an extreame fit after she was asked whoe hurt hir & she Sayd she Could nott tell, but sayd they blinded hir, & would nott lett hir see and after that was once or twice taken dumb hirself.

Second Examination. March 2. 1691/2

Q. What Covenant did you make w'th that man that Came to you? What did he tell you. A. he Tell me he god, & I must beleive him & Serve him Six yeares & he would give me many fine things. Q. how long a gone was this? A. about Six weeks & a little more fryday night before Abigall was Ill. Q w't did he Say you must doe more? did he Say you must write anything? did he offer you any paper? A. yes, the Next time he Come to me & showed me some fine things, Some thing like Creatures, a little bird something like green & white. q. did you promiss him then when he spake to you then what did you answer him A. I then sayd this I tould him I Could nott believe him God, I tould him I ask my maister & would have gone up but he stopt mee & would nott lett me Q. whatt did you promiss him? A. the first tyme I beleive him God & then he was Glad. Q. what did he Say to you then? what did he Say you must doe? A. then he tell me they must meet together. Q. w'n did he Say you must meet together. A. he tell me wednesday next att my m'rs house, & then they all meet together & thatt night I saw them all stand in the Corner, all four of them, & the man stand behind mee & take hold of mee to make mee stand still in the hall. Q. where was your master then? A. in the other Room. Q. What time of Night? A. a little before prayr time. Q. What did this man Say to you when he took hold of you? A. he Say goe & doe hurt to them and pinch them & then I went in, & would nott hurt them a good while, I would nott hurt Betty, I loved Betty, but they hall me & make me pinch Betty & the next Abigall & then quickly went away altogether & I pinched them. Q. did they pinch A. Noe, but they all lookt on & See mee pinch them. Q. did you goe into that Room in your own person & all the rest? A. yes, and my master did nott See us, for they would nott lett my Master See. Q. did you goe w'th the Company? A. Noe I stayd & the Man stayd w'th mee. Q. whatt did he then to you? A. he tell me my master goe to prayer & he read in book & he ask me what I remember, but don't you remember anything. Q. did he ask you noe more but the first time to Serve him or the secon time? A. yes, he ask me againe, & that I Serve him, Six yeares & he Come the Next time & show me a book. A. and when would he come then? A. the next fryday & showed me a book in the day time betimes in the morneing. Q. and what Booke did he Bring a great or little booke? A. he did nott show it me, nor would nott, but had itt in his pockett. Q. did nott he make you write yo'r Name? A. noe nott yett for mistris Called me into the other roome. Q. whatt did he say you must doe in that book? A. he Sayd write & sett my name to itt. Q. did you write? A. yes once I made a marke in the Booke & made itt with red Bloud. Q. did he gett itt out of your Body? A. he Said he must gett itt out the Next time he Come againe, he give me a pin tyed in a stick to doe itt w'th, butt he noe Lett me bloud w'th itt as yett butt Intended another time when he Come againe. Q. did you See any other marks in his book? A. yes a great many Some marks red, Some yellow, he opened his booke a great many marks in itt. Q. did he tell you the Names of them? A. yes of two note more Good & Osburne & he Say thay make them marks in that book & he showed them mee. Q. how many marks doe you think there was? A. Nine. Q. did they write there Names? A. thay made marks Goody Good Sayd she made hir mark, butt Goody Osburne would nott tell she was Cross to mee. Q. when did Good tell you, She Sett hir hand to the Book? A. the same day I Came hither to prison. Q. did you See the man thatt morneing? A. yes a litle in the morneing & he tell me the Magistrates Come up to Exam in mee. Q. w't did he Say you must Say? A. he tell me, tell nothing, if I did he would Cutt my head off. Q. tell us [tru] how many woemen doe use to Come when you Rid abroad? A. foure of them these two Osburne & Good & those two strangers. Q. you Say that there was Nine did he tell you whoe they were? A. noe he noe lett me See but he tell me I should See them the next tyme Q. what sights did you see A. I see a man, a dogge, a hogge, & two Catts a black and Red & the strange monster was Osburne that I mentioned before this was was the hayry Imp. the man would give itt to mee, but I would nott have itt. Q. did he show you in the Book w'ch was Osburne & w'ch was Goods mark? A. yes I see there marks. Q. butt did he tell the Names of the other? A. noe s'r Q & what did he say to you when you made your Mark? A. he sayd Serve mee & always Serve mee the man w'th the two women Came frō Boston. Q. how many times did you goe to Boston? A. I was goeing & then Came back againe I was never att Boston. Q. who Came back w'th you againe? A. the man Came back w'th mee & the woemen goe away, I was nott willing to goe? Q. how farr did you goe, to what Towne? A. I never went to any Towne I see noe trees, noe Towne. Q. did he tell you where the Nine Lived? A. yes, Some in Boston & Some herein this Towne, but he would nott tell mee wher thay were, X

(New York Public Library—Manuscripts and Archives Division)

(Indictment v. Tituba)

| Province of the Massachusetts Bay in New England Essex ss | At a Court of Asisise & Generall Goale Delivery held in Ipswich for the County of Essex aforesaid the Ninth Day of May 1962. In the fifth Yeare of their Maj'ts Reigne |

The Jurors for o'r Sov'r Lord & Lady
the King & Queen pr'sent—

That Tittapa an Indian Woman Servant to mr Samuel Parris of Salem village in the County of Essex—aforesaid—upon or about the latter end of the Yeare 1691 In the Towne of Salem Village afors'd Wickedly & felloniously A Covenant with the Devill did make & Signed the Devills Booke with a marke like A:C by which Wicked Covenanting with the Devill she the Said Tittapa is become A detestable Witch Against the peace of o'r Sov'r lord & lady the King & Queen their Crowne & Dignity & the lawes in that Case made & provided.

(On reverse side of paper)

Ignoramus
*Abraham Haseltine
foreman of the Grand Jury

(*Suffolk Court Records, Case No. 2760 Page 102*)

Abbreviations

AHR — *American Historical Review.*

BAIRB — Boston. *Abstract and Index of the Records of the Inferiour Court of Pleas Held at Boston*, 1680–1690. Boston: Historical Records Survey, 1940.

BARD — Barbados Archives. Recopied Deeds.

BAWT — Barbados Archives. Wills and Testaments.

BRRC — Boston Record's Commissioners. *Reports*, 31 vols. Boston: Rockwell and Church, Printers, 1883.

CS — *Caribbean Studies.*

CSP — *Calendar of State Papers, Colonial Series, America and the West Indies*, ed. W. Noel Sainsburg et al., 43 vols. 1860–1963 repr., London: Kraus Reprint, 1964.

EIHC — *Essex Institute Historical Collections.*

JBMHS — *Journal of the Barbados Museum and Historical Society.*

JCH — *Journal of Caribbean History.*

MCAR — *Massachusetts. Court of Assistants Records, 1630–1692.* 2 vols. Boston: Rockwell and Churchill Press, 1901–1904.

NEHGR — *New England Historical & Genealogical Record.*

NEQ — *New England Quarterly.*

NWC — George Lincoln Burr, ed., *Narratives of the Witchcraft Cases 1648–1706.* New York: Charles Scribner's Sons, 1914.

PRO — Public Record Office. London, England. C.O.1/44, No. 47.

SVW Paul Boyer and Stephen Nissenbaum, eds., *Salem-Village Witchcraft: A Documentary Record of Local Conflict in Colonial New England*. Belmont, Calif.: Wadsworth Publishing, 1972.

SWP Paul Boyer and Stephen Nissenbaum, eds., *Salem Witchcraft Papers: Verbatim Transcripts of the Legal Documents*, 3 vols. New York: DaCapo, 1977.

WMQ *William and Mary Quarterly*.

Notes

NOTES TO THE INTRODUCTION

1. The elements of that hysteria and the details of the lives of both the accused and the accusers are available in an extensive literature. See especially Paul Boyer and Stephen Nissenbaum, *Salem Possessed: The Social Origins of Witchcraft* (Cambridge: Harvard University Press, 1974); Richard Godbeer, *The Devil's Dominion: Magic and Religion in Early New England* (New York: Cambridge University Press, 1992); Larry Gragg, *The Salem Witch Crises* (New York: Praeger, 1992); Chadwick Hansen, *Witchcraft at Salem* (New York: George Braziller, 1969); Christine Leigh Heyrman, *Commerce and Culture: The Maritime Communities of Colonial Massachusetts, 1690–1750* (New York: W. W. Norton, 1984), 96–142; Carol F. Karlsen, *The Devil in the Shape of a Woman: Witchcraft in Colonial New England* (New York: W. W. Norton, 1987); George Kittredge, *Witchcraft in Old and New England* (1929 repr., New York: Russell and Russell, 1956); Lyle Koehler, *A Search for Power: The "Weaker" Sex in Seventeenth-Century New England* (Chicago: University of Illinois Press, 1980), especially 169–75; David Thomas Konig, *Law and Society in Puritan Massachusetts* (Chapel Hill: University of North Carolina Press, 1979), 158–85; Alan Krohn, *Hysteria: The Elusive Neurosis* (New York: International Universities Press, 1978), 163–66; Richard Weisman, *Witchcraft, Magic and Religion in Seventeenth-Century Massachusetts* (Amherst: University of Massachusetts Press, 1984).

For a review of the literature on Salem witchcraft see David D. Hall, "Witchcraft and the Limits of Interpretation," NEQ, 58 (June 1985), 253–81. The most complete collection of primary source material on those events is Paul Boyer and Stephen Nissenbaum, eds., *Salem Village Papers: Verbatim Transcripts of the Legal Documents*, 3 vols. (New York: Da Capo Press, 1977).

2. But see Chadwick Hansen, "The Metamorphosis of Tituba, or Why American Intellectuals Can't Tell an Indian Witch from a Negro," NEQ, 47 (March 1974), 3–12; and George Chever, "Prosecution of Philip English and His Wife for Witchcraft," *Historical Collections of the Essex Institute*, 2 (1860), 73–85.

3. See for example Samuel G. Drake, *Witchcraft Delusion in New England*, 3 vols. (Roxbury: W. E. Woodward, 1866), III:204; Charles W. Upham, *Salem Witchcraft*, 2 vols. (1867 repr., Williamstown, Mass.: Corner House Publishers, 1971), II:2–3, 27; Richard S. Dunn,

Sugar and Slaves, The Rise of the Planter Class in the English West Indies, 1624–1713 (Chapel Hill: University of North Carolina Press, 1972), 337; Herbert Leventhal, *In the Shadow of the Enlightenment: Occultism and Renaissance Science in Eighteenth-Century America* (New York: New York University Press, 1976), 68–71; and Marilynn K. Roach, " 'That Child, Betty Parris': Elizabeth (Parris) Barron and the People in Her Life," EIHC (January 1988), 124:6.

4. The more popular and fictional works that have helped to reinforce this view of Tituba's role include Marion Starkey, *Devil in Massachusetts, A Modern Inquiry into the Salem Witch Trials* (New York: Alfred A. Knopf, 1949) and *The Visionary Girls: Witchcraft in Salem Village* (Boston: Little, Brown, 1973); Arthur Miller, *The Crucible* (1952; repr., New York: Penguin Books, 1981); Shirley Jackson, *Witchcraft at Salem Village* (New York: Random House, 1963); Ann Petry, *Tituba of Salem Village* (New York: Harper & Row, 1964); Mary Ellen Kulkin, *Her Way, Biographies of Women for Young People* (Chicago: American Library Association, 1976), 284; William Carlos Williams, "Tituba's Children," in *Many Loves and Other Plays: The Collected Plays of William Carlos Williams* (New York: New Directions, 1961), 226–40. The most recent fictional depiction of Tituba, Maryse Condé, *I, Tituba, Black Witch of Barbados* (Charlottesville: University Press of Virginia, 1992) is only loosely based on the historic person. Condé uses Tituba as a metaphor for the twentieth-century African-American woman.

Bernard Rosenthal has been studying the elaboration of this myth of Tituba as an African in the literary imagination and scholarly studies. "Imagining the Puritan: Salem Story," paper presented at Millersville State University, "Puritanism in Old and New England," April 4–6, 1991, and his *Salem Story: Reading the Witch Trials of 1692* (New York: Cambridge University Press, 1993), 21–31.

5. Of particular interest are the comments by Deodat Lawson, "A Brief and True Narrative of Witchcraft at Salem Village," and John Hale, "A Modest Inquiry Into the Nature of Witchcraft," in NWC, 162 and 413. See also Robert Caleb, *More Wonders of the Invisible World. . . .* (London, 1700, 1796; repr. Boston, 1828), 225; SWP, III:745–61. For a review of the evidence supporting an American Indian background see Hansen, "Metamorphosis."

6. Upham, *Salem*, II:2.

7. Drake, *Witchcraft Delusion*, III:204.

8. NWC, 253n.

9. Irving Rouse, "The Arawak," in *Handbook of South American Indians*, ed. Julian H. Steward, 7 vols. (New York: Cooper Square Publishers, 1963), IV:507–46; E. G. Breslaw, " 'Price's His Deposition': Kidnapping Amerindian Slaves in Guyana, 1674," JBMHS, 39 (1991), 47–51.

10. BARD, RB3/10, 451. 455. See also Elaine G. Breslaw, "The Salem Witch from Barbados: In Search of Tituba's Roots," EIHC, 128 (1992), 217–38.

11. On this process of Creolization see Jerome S. Handler and Charlotte J. Frisbie, "Aspects of Slave life in Barbados: Music and Its Cultural Context," CS, 11 (1972), 5–46 and Karl Watson, *The Civilized Island of Barbados: A Social History, 1750–1816* (St. George, Barbados: Caribbean Graphic, 1979), 2, 41–42.

12. See in particular Jerome Handler "Amerindian Slave Population of Barbados in the Seventeenth and Early Eighteenth Centuries," CS, 8 (1969), 38–64; and his "Amerindians and their Contribution to Barbadian Life in the Seventeenth Century," JBMHS, 35 (1977), 189–210.

13. William P. Pierson, *Black Yankees: The Development of an Afro-American Subculture in Eighteenth-Century New England* (Amherst: University of Massachusetts Press, 1988) and Lorenzo Johnston Greene, *The Negro in Colonial New England* (New York: Atheneum, 1971)

have investigated the question of African influences but credit very little to those ethnic factors. Rather they stress the effect of English patterns on the non-white population.

14. See in particular Richard Slotkin, *Regeneration Through Violence: The Mythology of the American Frontier, 1600–1860* (Middletown, Conn.: Wesleyan University Press, 1973), 116–45; Gary B. Nash, *Red, White and Black: The Peoples of Early America*, 2d ed. (Englewood Cliffs, N.J.: Prentice-Hall, 1982), 115–40; James Axtell, *The European and the Indian: Essays in the Ethnohistory of Colonial North America* (New York: Oxford University Press, 1981), particularly 272–315, "The Indian Impact on English Colonial Culture"; Alden T. Vaughn, "English Paradigms for New World Natives," *Proceedings of the American Antiquarian Society*, 102 (1992), 33–67. One major exception to these approaches is Richard White, *Middle Ground: Indians, Empires, and Republics in the Great Lakes Region, 1650–1815* (New York: Cambridge University Press, 1991), which looks at the interactive exchange of Algonquin and French culture.

NOTES TO CHAPTER ONE

1. E. G. Breslaw, " 'Prices' His Deposition': Kidnapping Amerindian Slaves in Guyana, 1674." JBMHS, 39 (1991), 47–51 details this journey.

2. CSP, vol. 1673, No. 1132, 518–19.

3. These wars took place in 1652–54, 1655–67, 1672–74. Vere T. Daly, *A Short History of the Guyanese People* (1967 repr., London: Macmillan Education, 1975), 64.

4. CSP, vol. 1673, xx–xxiii, and No. 1132, 517–19.

5. On the Arawak swimming ability see William Henry Brett, *Indian Tribes of Guiana: Their Condition and Habits* (London: Bell and Daldy, 1868), 110.

6. Breslaw, " 'Price's,' " 51, 48.

7. Charles W. Upham, *Salem Witchcraft*, 2 vols. (1867; repr. Williamstown, Mass.: Corner House Publishers, 1971), II:2. On Indian slave-catching in Guiana see Neil L. Whitehead, *Lords of the Tiger Spirit: A History of the Caribs in Colonial Venezuela and Guyana* (Providence, R.I.: Foris Publications, 1988), 180–86.

8. Ripley P. Bullen, "Barbados and the Archeology of the Caribbean," JBMHS, 32 (1966), 16–19; Jerome S. Handler, "Amerindian Slave Population of Barbados in the Seventeenth and Early Eighteenth Centuries," CS, 8 (January 1969), 38–64.

9. Hilary Beckles, *White Servitude and Black Slavery in Barbados, 1627–1715* (Knoxville: University of Tennessee Press, 1989), 122–24.

10. Beckles, *White Servitude*, 122–24; Vincent T. Harlow, *History of Barbados* (1919 repr., New York: Negro Universities Press, 1969), 307.

11. Alfred W. Crosby, "Virgin Soil Epidemics as a Factor in the Aboriginal Depopulation in America," WMQ, 33 (1976), 292.

12. im Thurn, commenting on the inconsistency of Indian work habits, was puzzled by the fact that, "Any severe work soon tires them; though they think nothing of walking over the savannah day after day, from morning to night, yet they cannot walk any given distance even in twice the time required for the purpose by the ordinary European or negro." Everard Ferdinand im Thurn, *Among the Indians of Guiana: being sketches chiefly anthropological from the interior of British Guiana* (1883 repr., New York: Dover Publications, 1967), 189.

13. Richard Ligon, *A true and exact history of the Island of Barbados* (London: Humphrey Mosely, 1657), 54.

14. Richard Price, *The Guiana Maroons: A Historical and Bibliographical Introduction* (Baltimore: Johns Hopkins University Press, 1976), 16.

15. Hilary McD. Beckles, "A 'Riotous and Unruly Lot': Irish Indentured Servants and Freeman in the English West Indies, 1644–1413," WMQ, 47 (October 1990), 504–9.

16. Quoted by Philip D. Morgan, "British Encounters with Africans and African-Americans, circa 1600–1780," in Bernard Bailyn and Philip D. Morgan, eds., *Strangers Within the Realm: Cultural Margins of the First British Empire* (Chapel Hill: University of North Carolina Press, 1991), 196.

17. im Thurn, *Among the Indians,* 189. Note Thomas Walduck's comment regarding Barbados Indians that they "believe it is fate or destiny that their time is come; that it is folly to resist, wch makes them ye easier Submitt." "Letters from Barbados, 1710," JBMHS 15 (February 1948), 88. For a different view of the resistance of Indians to European control and enslavement see Gordon K. Lewis, *Main Currents in Caribbean Thought: The Historical Evolution of Caribbean Society in its Ideological Aspects, 1492–1900* (Baltimore: Johns Hopkins University Press, 1983), 220–22.

18. Elise M. Brenner, "To Pray or to be Prey: That Is the Question: Strategies for Cultural Autonomy of Massachusetts Praying Town Indians," *Ethnohistory,* 27 (Spring 1980), 136.

19. Handler, "Amerindian Slave Population," 52–53.

20. Hesketh Bell, "The Caribs of Dominica," JBMHS, 7 (1937), 24; C. Jesse, "Barbadians Buy St. Lucia from the Caribs," JBMHS, 32 (1967), 180–84; Robert H. Schomburgk, *The History of Barbados* (1948 repr., London: Frank Cass, 1971), 290–93.

21. On slave mortality in general see Patricia Molen, "Population and Social Patterns in Barbados in the Early Eighteenth Century," WMQ, 28 (April 1971), 289.

22. Richard S. Dunn, *Sugar and Slaves: The Rise of the Planter Class in the English West Indies, 1624–1871 3* (Chapel Hill: University of North Carolina Press, 1972), 74. This idea was considered and then rejected by Samuel Drake, *Witchcraft Delusion in New England,* 3 vols (Roxbury, Mass.: W. E. Woodward, 1866), III:204.

23. Douglas Edward Leach, *The Northern Colonial Frontier, 1607–1763* (New York: Holt, Rinehart and Winston, 1964), 56–61; Alden T. Vaughan and Edward W. Clark, eds., *Puritans Among the Indians: Accounts of Captivity and Redemption, 1676–1729* (Cambridge, Mass.: Harvard University Press, 1981), 9 and 32.

24. Almon Wheeler Lauber, *Indian Slavery in Colonial Times Within the Present Limits of the United States* (1913 repr., New York: AMS Press, 1969), 118, 169; Philip M. Brown, "Early Indian Trade in the Development of South Carolina: Politics, Economics, and Social Mobility During the Proprietary Period, 1670–1719," *South Carolina History Magazine,* 76 (April 1975), 119–25. See also Verner W. Crane, *The Southern Frontier, 1670–1732* (Ann Arbor: University of Michigan Press, 1919), 3–19.

25. Alvin M. Josephy, *Indian Heritage of America* (New York: Alfred A. Knopf, 1968), 219. On slave-capturing in South America see Whitehead, *Lords,* 180–86.

26. That area includes a part of present-day Venezuela, Guyana, Suriname (the spelling for the modern nation), and French Guiana.

27. Daly, *Short History,* 57; Alvin O. Thompson, *Colonialism and Underdevelopment in Guyana, 1580–1803* (Bridgetown, Barbados: Carib Research and Publications, 1987), 22; Arie Boomert, "The Arawak Indians of Trinidad and Coastal Guiana, ca. 1500–1650," *Journal of Caribbean History,* 19 (November 1984), 164. Handler, "Amerindian Slave Population," 52; Vincent T. Harlow, ed., *Colonising Expeditions to the West Indies and Guiana, 1623–1667* (London: Hakluyt Society, 1925), 145, 199.

28. Harlow, *History,* 318.

29. Daly, *Short History,* 64, 59.

30. See in particular CSP, vol. 1669–1674, No. 1132, Colleton to Secretary, 517–19; No. 1409, Council to the King, Dec. 17, 1674, 631; and vol. 1675–76, No. 439, Atkins to Secretary, Feb. 17, 1675, 179.

31. CSP, vol. 1675–76, No. 946, "Extract from the Journal of the Assembly of Barbados, June 13–14, 1676," 403.

32. Richard S. Dunn, "The Barbados Census of 1680: Profile of the Richest Colony in America," WMQ, 26 (January 1969), 25.

33. Lorenzo Greene, *The Negro in Colonial New England* (1942 repr., New York: Atheneum Press, 1968), 198.

34. I wish to thank John Gilmore of the Barbados National Cultural Foundation for suggesting this possible connection. The names Tituba and Tattuba may be related to the verb, titubear, although there is no indication in the records that Tituba suffered from either a stammer or had difficulty walking.

35. Boomert, "The Arawak Indians," 129; William Henry Brett, *Indian Tribes of Guiana: Their Condition and Habits* (London: Bell and Daldy, 1868), 480.

36. The name, Tetebetana, as with other subdivisions of the Arawak-speaking group, is derived from the name of an animal, in this case a nightjar bird called goatsucker in English. im Thurn, *Among the Indians*, 183. There is another similar family mentioned by im Thurn, the Tahatahabetano (or Tatabetano?), 181. Tituba could be derivative of either name or a combined form invented by her captors.

37. im Thurn, *Among the Indians*, 176–84.

38. There are a host of variant spellings used in the Salem documents from Titibe to Tattapa. See SWP, II:359 and 362; III, 745–56.

39. Roger Bastide, *African Civilisation in the New World*, trans. from the French by Peter Green (New York: Harper and Row, 1971), 8; James Axtell, *The European and the Indian: Essays in the Ethnohistory of Colonial North America* (New York: Oxford University Press, 1981), 55.

40. BARD, RB 3/10, 109; RB3/12, 172; RB3/3, 331; RB3/10, 388.

41. I suggest that the Saramaka woman, a captive from a maroon society in Guiana in the eighteenth century, called Tutúba, may have a similar Indian name origin. She is, however, identified by Richard Price as a woman of strictly African parentage. *First-Time: The Historical Vision of an Afro-American People* (Baltimore: Johns Hopkins University Press, 1983), 9. The "uba" ending of Tutúba's name, of course, is identifiably African. Price notes that Tutúba's twentieth-century descendants claim that she was "absolutely black" and not "red," alluding to light-skinned people. He argues that there is no racial connotation in the word "red" in this case. The man speaking to him was expressing an appreciation for the beauty of the "darker" rather than lighter shades of skin color in a woman. Private correspondence of December 12, 1994. It should be noted that the word "red" historically has been imposed on Indians because of the custom of applying red dyes to decorate their bodies. The expression "red slave" in South America (also poitos or macos), for instance, denoted Indians captured by Caribs and sold to the Dutch in the seventeenth and eighteenth centuries. Whitehead, *Lords*, 180–81.

It is theoretically possible that the Saramaka Tutúba had Indian kin. Indians, either as runaway slaves or cooperating tribes, were present in maroon societies at the beginning of their formation in the late seventeenth century and Indian family names did appear. A small number of local Indians were absorbed into Saramaka groups. On the background and demographic makeup of Saramaka maroon societies see Richard Price, ed., *The Guiana Maroons: A Historical and Bibliographical Introduction* (Baltimore: Johns Hopkins University Press, 1976), 16–23; and *First-Time*, 112, 115, 144–45, 162.

42. Åke Hultkranz, *The Religions of the American Indians*, trans. Monica Setterwall (Berkeley: University of California Press, 1979), 67.

43. im Thurn, *Among the Indians*, 219.

44. Harlow, *Colonising*, 132–37. The quote is on page 137.

45. The following discussion of Arawak society is based on a variety of sources, but especially the work of im Thurn, *Among the Indians*, 191–200, 324–26; James Rouse, "The Arawak," in Julian H. Steward, ed., *Handbook of South American Indians*, 7 vols. (New York: Cooper Square Publishers, 1963), IV:531–36; Boomert, "Arawak Indians," 123–88; Harlow, *Colonising*, 132–48; and Colin Henfrey, *Through Indian Eyes: A Journey Among the Indian Tribes of Guiana* (New York: Holt, Rinehart and Winston, 1964).

46. Lee Drummond, "Arawak," in Irvin Keith, ed., *Encyclopedia of Indians of the Americas* (St. Clair Shores, Mich.: Scholarly Press, 1974), II:220–22; Josephy, *Indian Heritage*, 286; Irving Rouse, "The Southeast and the West Indies," in John W. Griffin, ed., *The Florida Indian and His Neighbors* (Winter Park, Fla.: Rollins College Press, 1949), 117–19.

47. Edmund Morgan, "Labor Problem at Jamestown," *American Historical Review*, 76 (June 1971), 595–611.

48. im Thurn, *Among the Indians*, 215–16, 256.

49. On Arawak religion see especially Lewis Spence, "Brazil: The Arawaks," in James Hastings, ed., *Encyclopedia of Religion and Ethics* (New York: Charles Scribner's Sons, 1926), II:85; Andrew Landers, "American Indian or West Indian: The Case of the Coastal Indians of Guyana," CS, 16 (July 1976), 121–22; Josephy, *Indian Heritage*, 232; Rouse, "The Arawak," 535–36; im Thurn, *Among the Indians*. 341–70.

50. Hultkrantz, *Religions*, 60. On the nature of the kenaima see also Thompson, *Colonialism*, 12; im Thurn, *Among the Indians*, 328–34; Landers, "American Indian," 121–31.

51. Peter Rivière, "Factions and Exclusions in Two South American Village Systems," in Mary Douglas, ed., *Witchcraft Confessions & Accusations* (London: Tavistock Publications, 1970), 245–56; Thompson, *Colonialism*, 12.

52. Walter E. Roth, *An Inquiry into the Animism and Folk-Lore of the Guiana Indians* (Washington, D.C.: Smithsonian Institution, 1915), 174–75.

53. Hultkrantz, *Religions*, 87.

54. On the role of the piaimen see Thompson, *Colonialism*, 12–13; Hultkrantz, *Religions*, 86–101; im Thurn, *Among the Indians*, 334–40.

55. im Thurn, *Among the Indians*, 344–45.

56. On the various protective devices see im Thurn, *Among the Indians*, 368–69, 196; Roth, *Animism*, 165, 290.

NOTES TO CHAPTER TWO

1. Charles W. Upham, *Salem Witchcraft*, 2 vols. (1867 repr., Williamstown, Mass.: Corner House Publishers, 1971), II:2. The quote is from Samuel Fowler's 1866 biography of Samuel Parris in Samuel G. Drake, *Witchcraft Delusion in New England*, 3 vols. (Roxbury, Mass.: W. E. Woodward, 1866), III:204.

2. John Hale, "A Modest Inquiry Into the Nature of Witchcraft" (1702), in NWC, 414.

3. BAWT, RB6/15, 572; BARD, RB3/10, 455.

4. Tituba had been spelled variously in the Salem records as Titiba and Tatappa. Tattuba could easily be another variant of the name. SWP, III:746 and 755; and Appendix C.

5. The earliest mention of Samuel in the Barbados records is his appearance on Novem-

ber 7, 1678, collecting payment on a debt due his father from William Johnston. BARD, RB3/11, 207. On Parris's merchant activities see Larry Gragg, *A Quest for Security: The Life of Samuel Parris, 1653–1720* (New York: Greenwood Press, 1990), 13–16 and his "Barbados Connection: John Parris and the Early New England Trade with the West Indies," NEHGR, 140 (April 1986), 99–113.

6. PRO Census. Although dated 1680, most of the information was compiled between March of 1678 and December 1679. The muster rolls and lists of slaves imported include January 1680 data. For an analysis of the census and its historiograhic value see Richard S. Dunn "The Barbados Census of 1680: Profile of the Richest Colony in America," WMQ, 26 (1969), 3–30. There is a handwritten summary of this census, called the Barbados Census of 1679, with a fairly accurate index of names in the Barbados Archives. Vols. 2 and 3 of John Camden Hotten, ed., *Original List of Persons of Quality, Emigrants . . . from Great Britain to the American Plantations* (London: Chatto and Windus, 1874) reprints selected verbatim sections from that census.

The Vestry Records of St. Michaels Parish document several cases of poor white orphans apprenticed to various members of the community for care and training. JBMHS, 16 (February and May 1949), 56–59; 131–32.

7. BAWT, RB6/15, 572.

8. BARD, RB3/10, 393. As a "dower" right, the widow's third, she inherited only the use of the land during her lifetime.

9. He wrote his will on November 13, 1679 and it was probated after his death on February 10, 1680. BAWT, RB6/10, 198.

10. As the widow of Edward Thompson, Elizabeth had married Ralph Lane but was widowed again by 1667 when she married William Pearsehouse. She outlived this third husband who died in 1674. The tangled web of Elizabeth's marriages and inheritances is traced through BARD, RB3/11, 219; 3/14, 152; 3/6, 469–70; 3/7, 492–93.

11. BARD, RB3/11, 219.

12. BARD, RB3/10, 393, 485.

13. BARD, RB3/2, 799–800; RB3/5, 128. Parris also had contact with Reid, at least through Edward Elding, a leaseholder on Parris land. Elding, described as a gentleman, was called on several times to be a witness to legal and land transactions for nearby planters, including John Reid. Joanne McCree Sanders, comp. and ed., *Barbados Records: Wills and Administrations*, 3 vols. (Marceline, Mo.: Wadsworth Publishing, 1979), I:154, 163, 158, 199; BARD, RB3/4, 1–2. Reid's name is spelled variously as Read or Reade.

14. Elizabeth Reid Thompson was the Elizabeth Pearsehouse mentioned as Samuel Thompson's mother in the 1676 deed of sale. BARD, RB3/10, 393. She had remarried twice by that time—first to Ralph Lane sometime after the death of Edward Thompson ca. 1659 and then to William Pearsehouse in 1667. She was widowed again in 1674 and may have been residing in Bridgetown when Samuel Parris settled there. She died sometime before January of 1681. BARD, RB3/6, 469–70; RB3/11, 219; RB3/3, 157–58; RB3/10, 485.

15. PRO Census.

16. Ford, who had probably finished the map by 1676, thus recognized the Thompson-Prideaux partnership of the St. Thomas plantation. On the Ford map and its history see P. F. Campbell, *Some Early Barbadian History* (Barbados: Caribbean Graphics & Letchworth, 1993), 191–96.

17. BAWT, RB6/10, 198.

18. BARD, RB3/17, 160. The planters were often lax in registering deeds, waiting until it became absolutely necessary to do so. Dates of registry and of transference are sometimes many years apart.

19. Unfortunately, an identification of John cannot be established with the same degree of confidence as Tituba. We have only Upham's word that John Indian also came from Barbados. *Salem*, II:2. His name provides no clues to how and when Parris brought him into the household. There is, however, on one of the Thompson inventories a boy slave with the name of Young y John. It is possible that the middle "y" was an abbreviation for Indian but the name does not appear in the usual location for Indians on the inventories. BARD, RB3/10, 455.

20. BARD, RB3/14, 186 and 314–16.

21. "Some Early Conveyance Documents from the Lucas MS collection at the Barbados Public Library," 23 JBMHS (Feb. 1956), 116–21; BAWT, RB6/8, 519–22. For a fuller discussion of this inheritance see Gragg, *Quest*, 13.

22. BARD, RB3/10, 393; RB3/14, 538. See also James C. Brandow, comp., *Genealogies of Barbados Families* (Baltimore: Genealogical Publishing, 1983), 356.

23. Marilynn K. Roach, " 'That Child, Betty Parris': Elizabeth (Parris) Barron and the People in Her Life," EIHC, 124 (January 1988), 2; Gragg, "Barbados Connection," 112.

24. BAWT, RB6/8, 519–22; BARD, RB 6/13, 501; PRO Census; Tony Campbell, *The Printed Maps of Barbados from the Earliest Times to 1873* (London: Robert Stockwell, 1965), plate 5. See also P. F. Campbell, "The Ford Map and the 1679 Census," unpublished paper, ca. 1989. Gragg assumes that Samuel arranged for this lease, but it is obvious from Thomas Parris's will that Elding was already occupying the property before 1673. "Barbados Connection," 112, but see his *Quest*, 14–16. Elding's name appears in many legal transactions in St. James Parish as executor or as a witness during the 1660s and 1670s, a clear indication of respectable social status and his long association with the St. James leasehold. BAWT, RB/14, 405, 230; RB/13, 411.

25. BARD, RB3/14, 82–83; PRO Census. Richard Dunn estimates that a profitable working sugar plantation would have a ratio of one slave for every two acres and that a landowner with more than sixty slaves should be considered a big planter, but not among the wealthiest. "Census of 1680," 10–12. See also Alfred D. Chandler, "The Expansion of Barbados," JBMHS, 13 (May–November 1946), 106–36. Paul Boyer and Stephen Nissenbaum thought that the plantation was a relatively small tract that had been devastated by the 1675 hurricane. *Salem Possessed: The Social Origins of Witchcraft* (Cambridge: Harvard University Press, 1974), 155. The evidence in the Barbados Archives points in the opposite direction. It was a relatively large and functioning plantation in 1679. Three years later Elding did run into serious financial problems. He mortgaged part of the property to raise cash and then sold off small sections, but continued to live at Reid's Bay through the rest of the 1680s. At the end of the decade he bought 1,025 acres in Pennsylvania, which he acquired from John Edmondson of Maryland's eastern shore. BARD, RB3/14, 82, 252, 525; RB3/4, 525–26.

26. BARD, RB3/11, 564–65.

27. In 1668 the Assembly passed a law making slaves real estate for the purpose of inheritance in intestate cases to protect widows and orphans who needed the labor of the slaves. [Rawlin's Laws] *Acts of Assembly Passed in the Island of Barbados from 1648 to 1718* (London, 1721), No. 94, 63. Although the law did not apply to other conditions, it is obvious from the record of land transactions for the seventeenth century that the general practice, no doubt due to the difficulties of selling land without a resident labor force, was to treat slaves as real estate when transferring property.

28. BARD, RB3/10, 451.

29. Hilary Beckles has surmised that at about the age of four or five and until nine, children were put to work in the youngest gang of workers and afterward into the third or

children's gang until the age of fourteen. After that, they moved into the adult production teams. Tattuba was in the children's gang in 1676. *Natural Rebels: A Social History of Enslaved Black Women in Barbados* (New Brunswick, N.J.: Rutgers University Press, 1989), 107.

30. BARD, RB3/9, 72.

31. BARD, RB3/3, 276.

32. BARD, RB3/5, 124.

33. Jerome Handler, "Barbados Slave Conspiracies of 1675 and 1692," JBMHS, 36 (1982), 312–16.

34. Hilary Beckles, *Black Rebellion in Barbados, the Struggle Against Slavery, 1627–1838* (Bridgetown, Barbados: Carib Research and Publications, 1987), 38–40.

35. CSP, Atkins to Secretary, October 3, 1675, 1675–76, no. 690, 294; Robert H. Schomburgk, *History of Barbados* (1948 repr., London: Frank Cass, 1971), 45; Dunn, "Barbados Census," 14.

36. Neville Connell, "Furniture and Furnishings in Barbados During the Seventeenth Century," JBMHS (1957), 24:115; "Some Records from the Lucas MS," JBMHS, 10 (1942), 187; John Oldmixon, *British Empire in America*, 2 vols., 2d ed. (1741 repr., New York: Augustus M. Kelley, 1969), II:33–34.

37. CSP, Atkins to Secretary, Nov. 4, 1675, 1675–76, no. 707, 301; J. Frederick Fausz, "Merging and Emerging Worlds: Anglo-Indian Interest Groups and the Development of the Seventeenth Century Chesapeake," in Lois Green Carr, et al., *Colonial Chesapeake* (Chapel Hill: University of North Carolina Press, 1988), 88–89; Gary B. Nash, *Red, White and Black: The Peoples of Early America*, 2d ed. (Englewood Cliffs, N.J.: Prentice-Hall, 1982), 120.

38. Alden T. Vaughan, "Early English Paradigms for New World Natives," *Proceedings of the American Antiquarian Society*, 102 (1992), 35–44; William S. Simmons, "Cultural Bias in the New England Puritans' Perception of Indians," WMQ, 38 (January 1981), 58–60; Richard Slotkin, *Regeneration Through Violence: The Mythology of the American Frontier, 1600–1860* (Middletown, Conn.: Wesleyan University Press, 1973), 119–24.

39. CSP, 1675–76, Atkins to Secretary, April 3, 1676, no. 862, 368; and October 3, 1675, no. 690, 294.

40. CSP, Extract from the Journal of the Assembly of Barbados, June 13–14, 1676, no. 946, 403. See also Jerome S. Handler, "Amerindian Slave Population in Barbados in the Seventeenth and Early Eighteenth Centuries," CS, 8 (January 1969), 56 and his "Slave Conspiracies," 316.

41. Philip M. Brown, "Early Indian Trade in the Development of South Carolina: Politics, Economics, and Social Mobility During the Proprietary Period, 1670–1719," *South Carolina Historical Magazine*, 76 (April 1975), 119–25.

42. Handler, "Amerindian Slave," 61.

43. "An Account of His Majesty's Island of Barbados and the Government Thereof," 3, JBMHS (1935), 48.

44. The census of 1680 does not distinguish between Amerindian and African slaves. All slaves, regardless of origin, birth, or length of residency, are counted together in the one category of Negro slaves.

45. BARD, RB3/9, 72 and 494.

46. Dunn, "Barbados Census," 60; "An Account of His Majesty's Island," 48.

47. Barbados Archives, Miscellaneous Papers, RB7/2, 328.

48. Godwyn, *The Negro's and Indian's Advocate, suing for their admission into the church . . .* (London: Privately printed, 1680), 22, 70; Handler, "Amerindian Slave," 55–56.

49. BARD, RB3/9, 398; RB3/11, 36 and 341. The names Jack Surrinam and Peter

Tobago reappear in later deeds in other parishes with different spellings, but whether they are the same people who have been sold, or different people with the same names, is not clear.

50. On naming patterns see Bastide, *African Civilisation in the New World*, trans. Peter Green (New York: Harper & Row, 1971), 8. In Barbados an example of naming by geographic location in Africa can be found in BARD, RB3/11—Marie and Mingo Cormante.

51. Godwyn, "Negro's and Indians," 36.

52. See the discussion of name origins above in chapter 1, note 41.

53. Griffith Hughes, *Natural History of Barbados* (1750 repr., New York: Oxford University Press, 1972), 24–25. See also David Watts, *Man's Influence on the Vegetation of Barbados, 1627–1800* (Yorkshire, England: University of Hull, 1966), 14–16, 46.

54. Julian H. Steward, *Handbook of South American Indians*, 7 vols. (New York: Cooper Square Publishers, 1963), IV:24; W. Edwards and K. Gibson, "An Ethnohistory of Amerindians in Guyana," *Ethnohistory*, 26 (Spring 1979), 161.

55. Richard S. Dunn, *Sugar and Slaves: The Rise of the Planter Class in the English West Indies, 1624–1713* (Chapel Hill: University of North Carolina Press, 1972), 87; Robert E. Wells, *Population of the British Colonies in America Before 1776: A Survey of Census Data* (Princeton: Princeton University Press, 1975), 241.

56. Patricia Molen, "Population and Social Patterns in Barbados in the Early Eighteenth Century," WMQ, 28 (April 1971), 289.

57. V. T. Harlow, ed. *Colonising Expeditions to the West Indies and Guiana, 1623–1662* (London: Hakluyt Society, 1925), 45. I am grateful to Alden Vaughan for bringing this quote to my attention. See also Richard Ligon's comment: "As for the Indians, we have but few, and those fetcht from other Countries; some from the neighboring Islands, some from the Main, which we make slaves." *A True and exact history of the Island of Barbados* (London: Humphrey Mosely, 1657), 54.

58. Dunn, "Barbados Census," 60; "An Account of His Majesty's Island," 48.

59. Karl Watson, *Civilized Island Barbados: A Social History, 1750–1816* (Barbados: Caribbean Graphic Production, 1983), 3.

60. This description of Bridgetown is based on the following: Warren Alleyn, *Historic Bridgetown* (Barbados: Barbados National Trust, 1978), 12; Vincent T. Harlowe, *History of Barbados* (1926 repr., New York: Negro Universities Press, 1969), 333; Neville Connell, trans. "Father Labat's Visit to Barbados in 1700," JBMHS, 24 (August 1957), 166.

61. Beckles, *Natural Rebels*, 56–57.

62. Dunn, *Sugar*, 59–67.

NOTES TO CHAPTER THREE

1. Julian H. Steward, ed., *Handbook of South American Indians*, 7 vols. (New York: Cooper Square Publishers, 1963), IV:23; Everard Ferdinand im Thurn, *Among the Indians of Guiana* (1883 repr., New York: Dover Publications, 1967), 215–16; Vincent T. Harlow, ed., *Colonising Expeditions to the West Indies and Guiana, 1623–67* (London: Hakluyt Society, 1925), 132–36.

2. Richard Ligon, *A True and Exact History of the Island of Barbados* (London: Humphrey Mosely, 1657), 54. See also Jerome S. Handler, "Amerindians and their Contribution to Barbados Life in the Seventeenth Century," JBMHS, 35 (1977), 190.

3. Hilary McD. Beckles, *Natural Rebels: A Social History of Enslaved Black Women in Barbados* (New Brunswick, N.J.: Rutgers University Press, 1989), 56. The decline in the

number of white servants was widespread throughout the English colonies in America. See also Vincent T. Harlow, *A History of Barbados 1625–1685* (1926 repr., New York: Negro Universities Press, 1969), 307.

4. Ligon, *History*, 54.

5. Alden T. Vaughan, "Early English Paradigms for New World Natives," *Proceedings of the American Antiquarian Society*, 102 (1992), 45–55.

6. Handler, "Amerindians and their Contribution," 192–97 See also Jerome S. Handler and Frederick W. Lange, *Plantation Slavery in Barbados: An Archeological and Historical Investigation* (Cambridge: Harvard University Press, 1978). P. F. Campbell, "Richard Ligon," JBMHS, 37 (1985), 236 suggests that the Salymingoe of the map was related to the Syminge of the Hilliard Plantation discussed below.

7. On the treatment of Africans see Father Labat's comments in Neville Connell, trans., "Father Labat's Visit to Barbados in 1700," JBMHS, 24 (August 1957), 168–69 and Beckles, *Natural Rebels*, 29.

8. John Oldmixon's history written in the eighteenth century, the usually cited reference for a separate Indian existence, draws only on Ligon's comment about life in "Indian houses." There are no further independent observations and nothing of a later time to show that the practice of housing Amerindians separately was maintained. John Oldmixon, *British Empire in America*, 2d ed. (London, 1708, 1741 repr., New York: Augustus M. Kelley, 1969), 12.

9. Morgan Godwyn, *The Negro's and Indians Advocate* (London, 1680), 22; Ligon, *History*, 54.

10. Jerome S. Handler, "Amerindian Slave Population in Barbados in the Seventeenth and Eighteenth Centuries," CS, 8 (January 1969), 61.

11. Ligon, *History*, 22.

12. These two girls may have been the same person. BARD, RB3/2, 643 and RB3/5, 125.

13. I am grateful to Peter Campbell for pointing out the complexity of the Hilliard deeds. See also Campbell, "Ligon," 221.

14. BARD, RB3/2, 643.

15. Ligon, *History*, 54–55.

16. E. G. Breslaw, " 'Price's His Deposition': Kidnapping Amerindians in Guyana, 1674," JBMHS, 39 (1991), 47–51.

17. The literature in this area of cultural change is voluminous and interdisciplinary. Eugene D. Genovese, *Roll, Jordan, Roll: The World the Slaves Made* (New York: Random House Pantheon Books, 1974), 209–10; Roger Bastide, *African Civilisation in the New World*, trans. Peter Green from the French (New York: Harper and Row, 1971), 11; Lawrence W. Levine, *Black Culture and Black Consciousness: Afro-American Folk Thought from Slavery to Freedom* (New York: Oxford University Press, 1977), 60; Edward Brathwaite, *The Development of Creole Society in Jamaica, 1770–1820* (Oxford: Clarendon Press, 1971), 219; Sidney W. Minz and Richard Price, "An Anthropological Approach to the Afro-American Past: A Caribbean Perspective" (Philadelphia: Institute for the Study of Human Issues, Occasional papers, 1976), 18–21; and Margaret E. Crahan and Franklin W. Knight, eds., *Africa and the Caribbean, the Legacies of a Link* (Baltimore: Johns Hopkins University Press, 1979), 8–9.

18. Richard S. Dunn, *Sugar and Slaves: The Rise of the Planter Class in the English West Indies, 1624–1713* (Chapel Hill: University of North Carolina Press, 1972), 235; Larry Gragg, "Puritans in Paradise, The New England Migration to Barbados, 1640–1660, *Journal of Caribbean History*, 21 (1988), 154–67; Barbados Census of 1680, PRO.

19. Franklin W. Knight and Margaret E. Crahan, "African Migration and the Origins of an Afro-American Society and Culture," in Crahan and Knight, *Africa and the Caribbean*, 9.

20. Historians and anthropologists argue over the relative importance of these and other factors. See in particular Levine, *Black Culture*, 60; Knight and Crahan, "African," 10; Bastide, *African Civilisation*, 43; Genovese, *Roll*, 210; Allan Kulikoff, *Tobacco and Slaves: The Development of Southern Cultures in the Chesapeake, 1680–1800* (Chapel Hill: University of North Carolina, 1986), 45–46; Philip D. Morgan, "Work and Culture: The Task System and the World of Lowcountry Blacks, 1700–1880," WMQ, 39 (October 1982), 563–99.

21. This idea of psychic distance applied to a whole range of ordinary activities. See Dunn, *Sugar*, 263–99.

22. Bastide, *African Civilisation*, 103–4; Karl Watson, *The Civilised Island Barbados: A Social History, 1750–1816* (Barbados: Caribbean Graphic Production, 1983), 87; Handler and Lange, *Plantation Slavery*, 33; and Jerome S. Handler, "Slave Medicine and Obeah in Barbados," unpublished paper presented at Hamilton College, October 1992.

23. Carl and Roberta Bridenbaugh, *No Peace Beyond the Line: The English in the Caribbean, 1624–1690* (New York: Oxford University Press, 1972), 355–56; P. F. Campbell, *The Church in Barbados in the Seventeenth Century* (St. Michael, Barbados: Barbados Museum and Historical Society, 1982), 82–83; Connell, "Father Labat's Visit," 24:168.

24. Godwyn, "Negro's and Indians Advocate," 130–31. See also Edward Brathwaite, *The Development of Creole Society in Jamaica, 1770–1820* (Oxford: Clarendon Press, 1971), 219. A handful of free mulattos and possibly Amerindians did become Christians. Handler and Lange, *Plantation Slavery*, 175.

25. Dunn, *Sugar*, 249–50; "Act to Prevent Quakers from Bringing Negroes to their Meetings," April 1676, CSP 106, No. 198.

26. Handler and Lange, *Plantation Slavery*, 33; Joseph J. Williams, *Voodoos and Obeahs: Phases of West Indian Witchcraft* (New York: Dial Press, 1932), 105.

27. The population in 1655 is estimated to have been 23,000 whites and 20,000 blacks; in 1676 Africans outnumbered whites 32,475 to 21,735. Dunn, *Sugar*, 87.

28. A. Gunkel and J. Handler, "A Swiss Medical Doctor's Description of Barbados in 1661: The Account of Felix Christian Sporri," JBMHS, 33 (1969), 7.

29. On the relationship of music and dance in African rituals see Handler and Lange, *Plantation Slavery*, 5–32.

30. Harlow, *Colonising*, 46.

31. Ligon, *History*, 47.

32. "T. Walduck's Letters from Barbados, 1710," JBMHS, 15 (May 1948), 148–49. Jerome Handler has identified several types of obeah practitioners in Barbados, from approved healers and diviners to the most anti-social sorcerers. "Slave Medicine," 11–16.

33. Handler, "Slave Medicine," 9.

34. "Walduck's Letters," 148–49.

35. William D. Pierson, *Black Yankees: The Development of an Afro-American Subculture in Eighteenth-Century New England* (Amherst: University of Massachusetts Press, 1988), 81.

36. Chadwick Hansen, *Witchcraft at Salem* (New York: George Braziller, 1969), 70–71.

37. SWP, I:179–80.

38. Geoffrey Parrinder, *Witchcraft: European and African* (London: Faber and Faber, 1963), 128–40 summarizes these parallel beliefs. For other similarities see also John S. Mbiti, *African Religions and Philosophy* (New York: Doubleday, 1969), 97–118 and Williams, *Voodoos*.

39. BARD, RB3/9, 293; 3/11, 36–38.

40. John Hale, "A Modest Inquiry Into the Nature of Witchcraft," in NWC, 414; On obeah practices throughout the West Indies and their relationship to African religions, see Genovese, *Roll*, 171–72; Orlando Patterson, *Sociology of Slavery, an Analysis of the Structure of*

Negro Slave Society in Jamaica (London: Macgibbon & Kee, 1967), 188–89; Bastide, *African Civilisation*, 93; Williams, *Voodoos*, 200–214.

41. On the music and dance of African slaves in Barbados see Jerome S. Handler and Charlotte J. Frisbie, "Aspects of Slave Life in Barbados: Music and Its Cultural Context," CS, 11 (Jan. 1972), 5–46; on the Arawaks of South America, see im Thurn, *Indians*, 324–26.

42. Griffith Hughes, *The Natural History of Barbados* (1750 repr., New York: Oxford University Press, 1972), 24; im Thurn, *Among the Indians*, 191; Ligon, *History*, 28, 52. See also Dunn, *Sugar*, 284.

43. Handler, "Amerindians and their Contribution," 208.

44. Ligon, *History*, 54.

45. Handler, "Slave Medicine," 5; im Thurn, *Among the Indians*, 356; Andrew Landers, "American Indian or West Indian: The Case of the Coastal Amerindians of Guyana," CS, 16 (July 1976), 121.

46. Handler, "Slave Medicine," 4.

47. Dunn, *Sugar*, 248.

48. On kinship and adoption practices among African slaves see Barbara Bush, *Slave Women in Caribbean Society, 1650–1838* (Bloomington: Indiana University Press, 1990), 105.

49. Henry Whistler, "An Account of Barbados in 1654," JBMHS, 5 (August 1938), 185; Godwyn, "Negro's and Indians Advocate," 33.

50. Ligon, *History*, 47.

51. Beckles, *Natural Rebels*, 8–9, 94.

52. BARD, RB3/10, 393.

53. Beckles, *Natural Rebels*, 7; Dunn, *Sugar*, 314–16 suggests that females in general survived better in the tropical climate. White women also had a better survival rate than white men.

54. African-American naming patterns are complex and slaves often had several names, even though on the plantation they were forced to use assigned names. Kulikoff, *Tobacco and Slaves*, 325. On the varieties of naming customs among Africans see John Thornton, "Central African Names and African-American Naming Patterns," WMQ, 50 (October 1993), 727–42; J. L. Dillard, *Black English: Its History and Usage in the United States* (New York: Random House, 1972), 124–30.

55. Jerome S. Handler, "Father Antoine Biet's Visit to Barbados in 1654," JBMHS, 32 (May 1967), 60.

56. BARD, RB3/25, 32.

57. BARD, RB3/12, 468–87.

58. BARD, RB3/13, 132–36 and 440–42.

59. Connell, "Father Labat's Visit," 168.

60. Beckles, *Natural Rebels*, 121.

61. BARD, RB3/13, 136, March 14, 1682.

62. BARD, RB3/10, 451.

63. Philip D. Morgan, "British Encounters with Africans and African-Americans," in Bernard Bailyn and Philip D. Morgan, eds., *Strangers Within the Realm: Cultural Margins of the First British Empire* (Chapel Hill: University of North Carolina Press, 1991), 200.

64. BARD, RB3/11, 507–16.

65. BARD, RB3/12, 239–40.

66. On this practice see also Handler and Frisbie, "Aspects," 17.

67. BARD, RB3/3, 202.

68. BARD, RB3/8, 46.

69. BARD, RB3/5, 72.

70. BARD, RB3/2, 715; RB3/2, 717.

71. BARD, RB3/2, 638.

72. BARD, RB3/9, 495.

73. Sambo is a Hausa name given to a second son. Dillard, *Black English*, 130.

74. On the adoption process and the recreation of kinship links see Bush, *Slave Women*, 105–6.

75. Beckles, *Natural Rebels*, 31, 106.

76. BAWT, RB 6/15, 572, Will of Edward Thompson, April 13, 1657; BAWT, RB 6/10, 199, Will of Samuel Thompson, November 13, 1679.

77. BARD, RB 3/10, 393.

78. Indentured servants in the household (whites) were expected to participate in regular prayers; black domestics probably were excluded. Michael Craton, "Reluctant Creoles: The Planters' World in the British West Indies," in Bailyn and Morgan, *Strangers*, 338 and Dunn, *Sugar*, 249. Indians may well have been included with the white domestic servants, but this is conjecture based on the perceptions of Indians discussed above. See also Alden T. Vaughan, "Early English Paradigms for New World Natives," *Proceedings of the American Antiquarian Society*, 102 (1992), 53.

79. John Hale, "A Modest Inquiry Into the Nature of Witchcraft (1702)," in NWC, 414.

80. Elizabeth Pearsehouse's genealogy and marital history have been traced through the extant legal records in Barbados. Thompson died ca. 1659, Ralph Lane died ca. 1667 and William Pearsehouse died in 1674. See especially BARD, RB 3/10, 485; RB 3/3, 157; RB 3/6, 469; RB 3/14, 152; RB 3/11, 219.

81. On the sexual exploitation of female slaves in the West Indies see Bush, *Slave Women*, 110–18; Beckles, *Natural Rebels*, 141–43; Dunn, *Sugar*, 253.

82. BAWT, RB 6/15, 572.

83. BARD, RB 3/10, 451.

84. BARD, RB 3/11, 219; RB 3/10, 451–52, 485; and his will in BAWT, RB 6/10, 199.

85. BARD, RB 3/10, 393. Exactly how the Prideaux family was related to the Hothersalls has not been established.

86. Dunn, *Sugar*, 263–64.

87. Ligon, *History*, 44.

88. Dunn, *Sugar*, 284.

89. James H. Merrell, " 'The Customes of Our Country': Indians and Colonists in Early America," in Bailyn and Morgan, *Strangers*, 154.

90. Dunn, *Sugar*, 273. On the Atlantic trade see Harlow, *History*, 268–91; Larry D. Gragg, "The Barbados Connection: John Parris and the Early New England Trade with the West Indies," NEHGR, 140 (April 1986), 99–113.

91. Handler, "Amerindians and Their Contribution," 201.

92. On the preparation of these drinks in Barbados see Ligon, *History*, 31–32; among the Arawaks see im Thurn, *Among the Indians*, 263–64.

93. Michael Craton, "Reluctant Creoles: The Planters World in the British West Indies," in Bailyn and Morgan, *Strangers*, 354–55; Ligon, *History*, 33–36. Many of these food plants were originally introduced to Barbados by Arawak Indians from Guiana. David Watts, *Man's Influence on the Vegetation of Barbados, 1627–1800* (Yorkshire, England: University of Hull, 1966), 46.

94. Handler, "Amerindians and Their Contribution," 208.

95. Beckles, *Natural Rebels*, 29.

96. Almon Wheeler Lauber, *American Indian Slavery in Colonial Times Within the Present Limits of the U. S.* (New York: Columbia University Press, 1913), 298.

97. Samuel Thompson is not listed as a property owner in the census taken in December of that year was probably living on the Island as his name appears on the militia list for early 1680. His mother is noted on the census as the owner of nineteen slaves but with no land in her own name. Census of 1680, PRO. Samuel Thompson's will is in BAWT, RB 6/10, 198–99.

98. BARD, RB 6/10, 199.

99. Walter E. Roth, *An Inquiry into the Animism and Folk-Lore of the Guiana Indians* (Washington, D.C.: Smithsonian Institution, 1915), 201. On the treatment of Arawak women see also Irving Rouse, "The Arawak," in Steward, *Handbook*, IV: 531; im Thurn, *Among the Indians*, 221–22.

NOTES TO CHAPTER FOUR

1. Bernard Bailyn, *New England Merchants in the Seventeenth Century* (1955 repr. New York: Harper & Row, 1976), 152–57; Carl Bridenbaugh, *Cities in the Wilderness: The First Century of Urban Life in America, 1625–1742* (1938 repr., New York: Alfred A. Knopf, 1955), 17; Larry Gragg, "Barbados Connection: John Parris and the Early New England Trade with the West Indies," NEHGR, 140 (1986), 209–37; Vincent T. Harlow, *History of Barbados, 1625–1685* (1926 repr., New York: Negro Universities Press, 1964), 168–91.

2. Samuel Sewall, *Diary of Samuel Sewall, 1674–1729*, ed. M. Halsey Thomas, 2 vols. (New York: Farrar, Straus & Giroux, 1973), I:49. For a description of the seventeenth-century climatic conditions in Massachusetts, see Karen Ordall Kupperman, "Climate and Mastery of the Wilderness in Seventeenth-Century New England," in *Seventeenth-Century New England* (Boston: Colonial Society of Massachusetts, 1984), 3–37.

3. Sewall, *Diary*, I:48.

4. Walter Muir Whitehill, *Boston, A Topographical History*, 2d ed. (Cambridge: Harvard University Press, 1968), 15–18; John William Reps, *Town Planning in Frontier America* (1965 repr., Columbia: University of Missouri Press, 1980), 120–24.

5. Bridenbaugh, *Cities*, 56; Larry Gragg, *Quest for Security: The Life of Samuel Parris, 1653–1720* (New York: Greenwood Press, 1990), 24; Bailyn, *New England*, 96–97.

6. James A. Henretta, *Evolution of American Society, 1700–1811: An Interdisciplinary Analysis* (Lexington, Mass.: D. C. Heath, 1973), 96. For other estimates of this population see Evarts Boutell Greene and Virginia D. Harrington, *American Population Before the Federal Census of 1790* (New York: Columbia University Press, 1932), 19–22.

7. Lorenzo Greene, *Negro in Colonial New England* (1942 repr., New York: Atheneum Press, 1968), 117.

8. Quoted by Bridenbaugh, *Cities*, 49.

9. Almon Wheeler Lauber, *Indian Slavery in Colonial Times Within the Present Limits of the United States* (1913 repr., New York: AMS Press, 1969), 144.

10. Gary B. Nash, *Red, White, and Black: The Peoples of Early America*, 2nd ed. (Englewood Cliffs, N.J.: Prentice-Hall, 1982), 120; Roger Thompson, *Sex in Middlesex: Popular Mores in a Massachusetts County, 1649–1699* (Amherst: University of Massachusetts Press, 1986), 109.

11. Sewall, *Diary*, I:48–49.

12. Edward Randolph, "Report on the Indians in Massachusetts to the Committee for

Trade and Plantations, 1676," quoted in William Kellaway, *New England Company 1649–1776, Missionary Society to the Indians* (London: Longmans, Green, 1961), 119.

13. Nash, *Red*, 120; Alden T. Vaughan and Edward W. Clark, eds., *Puritans Among the Indians: Accounts of Captivity and Redemption, 1676–1724* (Cambridge: Harvard University Press, 1981), 9; Alden T. Vaughan, "English Paradigms for New World Natives," *Proceedings of the American Antiquarian Society*, 102 (1992), 35–45; Douglas Edward Leach, *Flintlock and Tomahawk: New England in King Philip's War* (New York: Macmillan, 1958), 225–26. On the failures of Eliot's project to turn the Indians into English-like men and women as a preliminary to their redemption, see Elise M. Brenner, "To Pray or to be Prey: That Is the Question: Strategies for Cultural Autonomy of Massachusetts Praying Town Indians" and Kenneth M. Morrison, " 'That Art of Cozning Christians': John Eliot and the Praying Indians of Massachusetts," *Ethnohistory*, 27 (Spring 1980), 135–52 and 21 (Winter 1974), 77–92; Kellaway, *New England*, 81–121; Neal Salisbury, "Red Puritans: The 'Praying Indians' of Massachusetts Bay and John Eliot," WMQ (Jan. 1974), 31:27–54.

14. Lauber, *Indian Slavery*, 146.

15. Quoted in Christine Leigh Heyrman, *Commerce and Culture The Maritime Communities of Colonial Massachusetts, 1690–1750* (New York: W. W. Norton, 1984), 225.

16. Lauber, *Indian Slavery*, 125.

17. On the successful use of such camouflage for survival see James C. Merrell, " 'The Customes of Our Country': Indians and Colonists in Early America," in Bernard Bailyn and Philip D. Morgan, eds., *Strangers Within the Realm: Cultural Margins of the First British Empire* (Chapel Hill: University of North Carolina Press, 1991), 154.

18. Yasuhide Kawashima, *Puritan Justice and the Indian: White Man's Law in Massachusetts 1630–1763* (Middletown, Conn.: Wesleyan University Press, 1968), 214.

19. On the development of slavery in seventeenth-century Massachusetts see Greene, *Negro*, 17–21, 125–28.

20. Kawashima, *Puritan*, 126–27, 130.

21. MCAR, I:295–96. Edgar J. McManus, *Law and Liberty in Early New England: Criminal Justice and Due Process, 1620–1692* (Amherst: University of Massachusetts Press, 1993), 126, assumes that wife-beating was common among Indians.

22. James P. Ronda, "Red and White at the Bench: Indians and the Law in Plymouth Colony, 1620–1691," EIHC, 110 (July 1974), 210.

23. BAIRB, 126–29.

24. Kathleen Joan Bragden, "Crime and Punishment Among the Indians of Massachusetts, 1675–1750," *Ethnohistory*, 28 (Winter 1981), 828.

25. Kawashima, *Puritan*, 133.

26. Bragden, "Crime," 828; Brenner, "To Pray," 136. On Caribbean Indian resistance see Gordon K. Lewis, *Main Currents in Caribbean Thought: The Historical Evolution of Caribbean Society in Its Ideological Aspects, 1492–1900* (Baltimore: Johns Hopkins University Press, 1983), 221.

27. McManus, *Law*, 125–27; Thompson, *Sex*, 108–9; Wilcomb E. Washburn, *The Indian in America* (New York: Harper & Row, 1975), 17–20.

28. Kawashima, *Puritan*, 108–9, 237.

29. James Axtell, *The European and the Indians: Essays in the Ethnohistory of Colonial North America* (New York: Oxford University Press, 1981), 305–8; Kellaway, *New England*, 90–91. See also Salisbury, "Red Puritans," 27–54; Brenner, "To Pray," 146.

30. Edmund S. Morgan, *Puritan Family: Religion and Domestic Relations in Seventeenth-Century New England*, rev. ed. (New York: Harper & Row, 1966), 119.

31. Laura Thatcher Ulrich, *Good Wives: Image and Reality in the Lives of Women in Northern New England, 1650–1750* (1980 repr., New York: Random House, 1991), 26; Richard S.

Dunn, *Sugar and Slaves: The Rise of the Planter Class in the English West Indies, 1624–1713* (Chapel Hill: University of North Carolina Press, 1972), 270; William Wood, *New England's Prospect*, ed. Alden T. Vaughan (Amherst: University of Massachusetts Press, 1977) 30.

32. Morgan, *Puritan Family*, 118; Greene, *Negro*, 139.

33. Jerome S. Handler and Charlotte J. Frisbie, "Aspects of Slave Life in Barbados: Music and Its Cultural Context," CS, 11 (Jan. 1972), 10.

34. Richard P. Gildrie, *The Profane, the Civil, and the Godly: The Reformation of Manners in Orthodox New England, 1679–1749* (University Park: Pennsylvania State University Press, 1994), 112.

35. On servant dress and behavior see Patricia Trautman, "Dress in Seventeenth-Century Cambridge, Massachusetts: An Inventory-Based Reconstruction," in Peter Benes, ed., *Early American Probate Inventories* (Boston: Boston University Scholarly Publications, 1989), 51–62; Morgan, *Puritan Family, 123*; Gildrie, *Profane*, 24–35; James Axtell, *School Upon a Hill: Education and Society in Colonial New England* (1974 repr., New York: W. W. Norton, 1976), 61.

36. Morgan, *Puritan Family*, 112–13.

37. Alden Vaughan, "Puritan Statutory Law and the Indians: A Comparative Analysis," unpublished paper presented at a conference at Millersville University, April 4–6, 1991, 4.

38. Morgan, *Puritan Family*, 136; Gragg, *Quest*, 70.

39. During her testimony in 1692, Tituba indicated an ability to recognize names. SWP, II:362.

40. P. F. Campbell, *The Church in Barbados in the Seventeenth Century* (Barbados: Barbados Museum and Historical Society, 1982), 147–48.

41. Marilynn K. Roach, " 'That Child, Betty Parris': Elizabeth (Parris) Barron and the People in Her Life." EIHC, 124 (January 1988), 3; G. Andrews Moriarty, "More Notes on New England and Barbados," JBMHS, 15 (May 1948), 124–26; Bailyn, *New England Merchants*, 87–88.

42. Gragg, *Quest*, 30, 13.

43. Gragg, *Quest*, 33–49, describes this transformation in Parris's public life.

44. BRRC, vol. 9, *Boston Births, Baptisms, Marriages, 1630–1699*, (microfiche), 155, 158.

45. Gragg, *Quest*, 33.

46. BRRC, *Boston Births*, 175.

47. Roach, " 'That Child,' " 5.

48. Kenneth Silverman, *The Life and Times of Cotton Mather* (New York: Harper & Row, 1984), 62.

49. Silverman, *Mather*, 63.

50. Gildrie, *Profane*, 112; 189.

51. Silverman, *Mather*, 64.

52. Christine Leigh Heyrman, "Specters of Subversion, Societies of Friends: Dissent and the Devil in Provincial Essex County, Massachusetts," in David Hall et al., eds., *Saints and Revolutionaries: Essays on Early American History* (New York: W. W. Norton, 1984), 59.

53. "Parris' Record of Deaths," NEHGR, 36 (April 1882), 187

54. Gragg, *Quest*, 49.

55. "Parris' Record of Deaths," 188.

56. The description of this household arrangement is drawn mainly from that described by Ulrich, *Good Wives*, 18–26, based on a Newbury, Massachusetts, inventory of 1672. The Newbury house was approximately the same size as the Parris's parsonage.

57. SWP, III:750.

58. Lauber, *Indian Slavery*, 243.

59. This description of the New England diet is based on conclusions of Sarah F. McMahon, "A Comfortable Subsistence: The Changing Composition of Diet in Rural New England, 1620–1840," WMQ, 42 (January 1985), 26–65.

60. Dunn, *Sugar and Slaves*, 273.

61. Wood, *New England*, 36; Darrett B. Rutman, *Winthrop's Boston: Portrait of a Puritan Town, 1630–1649* (Chapel Hill: University of North Carolina Press, 1965), 178.

62. McMahon, "Comfortable," 35.

63. Ann Leighton, *Early American Gardens: 'For Meate or Medicine'* (Amherst: University of Massachusetts Press, 1970), 92, 96; McMahon, "Comfortable," 32, 42–43.

64. Dunn, *Sugar and Slaves*, 278.

65. Josselyn, *New England Rarities Discovered* (London, 1672), 8; McMahon, "Comfortable," 39–41; 58.

66. McMahon, "Comfortable," 35.

67. Greene, *Negro*, 200–205; Lauber, *Indian Slavery*, 127.

68. Morgan, *Puritan Family*, 128.

69. BRRC, vol. 9, *Births, Baptisms, Marriages, 1630–1699* did not register any Indian marriages for those years.

70. Greene, *Negro*, 216.

71. Kawashima, *Puritan Justice*, 166.

72. Greene, *Negro*, 213.

73. John Demos, *A Little Commonwealth: Family Life in Plymouth Colony* (New York: Oxford University Press, 1970) 73, 120–23; Morgan, *Puritan Family*, 66.

74. The most significant demographic studies of these marital patterns are Philip J. Greven, "Family Structure in Seventeenth-Century Andover, Massachusetts," WMQ, 23 (1966) 234–56; and idem, *Four Generations: Population, Land, and Family in Colonial Andover, Massachusetts* (Ithaca, N.Y.: Cornell University Press, 1970), 33–36; Kenneth A. Lockridge, *A New England Town The First Hundred Years: Dedham, Massachusetts, 1636–1736* (New York: W. W. Norton, 1970), 66–67; Daniel Scott Smith, "Demographic History of Colonial New England," *Journal of Economic History*, 32 (1972), 165–83. See also Carol F. Karlsen, *The Devil in the Shape of a Woman: Witchcraft in Colonial New England* (New York: W. W. Norton, 1987), 203.

75. He was working in Ingersoll's tavern in the spring of 1692. Robert Calef, *More Wonders of the Invisible World* (1700 repr., Boston, 1828) 238.

76. BRRC, vol. 9, *Births, Baptisms, Marriages, 1630–1699*.

77. Morgan, *Puritan Family*, 31–32.

78. Demos, *Little Commonwealth*, 132. See also Henretta, *Evolution*, 112–13.

79. Ernest E. Caulfield, "Early Measles Epidemics in America," *Yale Journal of Biology and Medicine*, 15 (1942), 531.

80. John Duffy, *Epidemics in Colonial America* (Baton Rouge: Louisiana State University Press, 1953), 48, 116, 207.

81. Jim Potter, "Demographic Development and Family Structure," in Jack P. Greene and J. R. Pole, eds., *Colonial British America: Essays in the New History of the Modern Era* (Baltimore: Johns Hopkins University Press, 1984), 141.

82. "Parris' Record of Deaths," 188.

83. SVW, I:196.

84. Roach, " 'That Child,' " 21.

85. Roach, " 'That Child,' " 23–24.

86. On slave prices in Massachusetts see Greene, *Negro*, 44. He gives an average price of slaves in the eighteenth century as between twenty and thirty pounds, but fluctuations

make it difficult to pin down a more precise range over the course of the late seventeenth and early eighteenth centuries. A price under twenty pounds would be the value of only a "second-rate" Negro. On the other hand, thirty pounds would have been a substantial price for any slave in 1720. Children were valued at lesser amounts. For instance, in 1710 an Indian girl was mortgaged for fifteen pounds. See "Relics of a 'Peculiar Institution' in Salem," *Historical Collections of the Essex Institute*, 1 (1859), 14.

87. Larry Gragg, *The Salem Witch Crisis* (New York: Praeger, 1992), 37–38.

88. See "Parris' Record of Deaths," 187–89 for war-related deaths.

89. Gragg, *Salem*, 39; Paul Boyer and Stephen Nissenbaum, *Salem Possessed: The Social Origins of Witchcraft* (Cambridge: Harvard University Press, 1974), 170.

90. SWP, III:750.

NOTES TO CHAPTER FIVE

1. John Hale, "A Modest Inquiry, Into the Nature of Witchcraft" (1702) in NWC, 413.

2. On the background of the girls, see especially Charles Upham, *Salem Witchcraft*, 2 vols. (1867 repr., Williamstown, Mass.: Corner House Publishers, 1971), II:277.

3. Richard Godbeer, *The Devil's Dominion: Magic and Religion in Early New England* (New York: Cambridge University Press, 1992), 53. On the variety of occult practices in both the Old and New World, see Chadwick Hansen, *Witchcraft in Salem* (New York: George Braziller, 1969); Norman Cohn, *Europe's Inner Demons: An Enquiry Inspired by the Great Witch-Hunt* (New York: Basic Books, 1975); Joseph Klaits, *Servants of Satan: The Age of the Witch Hunts* (Bloomington: Indiana University Press, 1985); Geoffrey Parrinder, *Witchcraft: European and African* (London: Faber and Faber, 1963); Keith Thomas, *Religion and the Decline of Magic* (New York: Charles Scribner's Sons, 1971); George Kittredge, *Witchcraft in Old and New England* (1919 repr., New York: Russell & Russell, 1956).

4. SWP, I:228.

5. Quoted in SWP, I:4.

6. Richard Weisman, *Witchcraft, Magic and Religion in Seventeenth-Century Massachusetts* (Amherst: University of Massachusetts Press, 1984), 231n; Marc Simmons, *Witchcraft in the Southwest: Spanish and Indian Supernaturalism on the Rio Grande* (Lincoln: University of Nebraska Press, 1974), 164.

7. Thomas, *Religion*, 177.

8. Thomas, *Religion*, 512–13; 543. See also Chadwick Hansen, "Andover Witchcraft and the Causes of the Salem Witchcraft Trials," in Howard Kerr and Charles L. Crow, eds., *The Occult in America: New Historical Perspectives* (Urbana: University of Illinois Press, 1983), 42–43.

9. Weisman, *Witchcraft*, 39–40.

10. Weisman, *Witchcraft*, 55.

11. Parrinder, *Witchcraft*, 44; Cohn, *Inner Demons*, 220–23.

12. Cohn, *Inner Demons*, 17, 101–9; Christina Larner, *Enemies of God: The Witchhunt in Scotland* (Baltimore: Johns Hopkins University Press, 1981), 10.

13. As an example and the source of much misunderstanding about Tituba, see especially Marion Starkey, *Devil in Massachusetts, A Modern Inquiry into the Salem Witch Trials* (New York: Alfred A. Knopf, 1949). The recent novel by Maryse Condé, *I, Tituba* (Charlottesville: University Press of Virginia, 1992) will, no doubt, reinforce these misconceptions regarding Tituba's actions.

14. Hansen, *Witchcraft*, 30.

15. Samuel Parris, Records of Salem Village Church, March 27, 1692 in SVW, 297–98.

16. Robert Calef, *More Wonders of the Invisible World . . . in Five Parts* (1700 repr., Boston, 1828), 225. On the reliability of Calef's account see below chapter 6, note 5.

17. Chadwick Hansen, "The Metamorphosis of Tituba, or Why American Intellectuals Can't Tell an Indian Witch from a Negro," NEQ, 47 (March 1974), 3–5.

18. SWP, III:752. See the comment during the Nurse questioning, SWP, II:587, "When this witchcraft came upon the stage there was no suspicion of Tituba."

19. *Hansen, Witchcraft*, 31.

20. Godbeer, *Devil's Dominion*, 31, 37.

21. Godbeer, *Devil's Dominion*, 47–54; Kittredge, *Witchcraft*, 7–23; David D. Hall, *Worlds of Wonder, Days of Judgment: Popular Religious Beliefs in Early New England* (New York: Alfred A. Knopf, 1989), 71–114.

22. SWP, II:362.

23. SWP, III:756.

24. See the examinations of Martha Corey on March 21 and of Rebecca Nurse on March 24. SWP, I:256–57; II:588–89.

25. For discussions on the connection between witchcraft and the somatic symptoms of hysteria see Lyle Koehler, *A Search for Power: The "Weaker Sex" in Seventeenth-Century New England* (Chicago: University of Illinois Press, 1980), 169–75; Alan Krohn, *Hysteria: The Elusive Neurosis* (New York: International Universities Press, 1978), 163–66; Ilza Veith, *Hysteria, The History of a Disease* (Chicago: University of Chicago Press, 1965), 70–72; Hansen, *Witchcraft*, 1–20.

26. Paul Boyer and Stephen Nissenbaum, *Salem Possessed: The Social Origins of Witchcraft* (Cambridge: Harvard University Press, 1974), 170; Larry Gragg, *Quest for Security: The Life of Samuel Parris, 1653–1720* (New York: Greenwood Press, 1990), 100.

27. Godbeer, *Devil's Dominion*, 59. For example, see Hale, "Modest Inquiry"; and Cotton Mather, "Memorable Providences, Relating to Witchcraft and Possessions" (1689), in NWC, 406–8, 135.

28. Marilynn K. Roach, " 'That Child, Betty Parris': Elizabeth (Parris) Barron and the People in Her Life," EIHC 124 (January 1988), 8; Upham, *Salem*, II:3. On the role of the jeremiad in Puritan life see especially Sacvan Bercovitz, *American Jeremiad* (Madison: University of Wisconsin Press, 1978), chapters 1 and 2.

29. Godbeer, *Devil's Dominion*, 16.

30. Weisman, *Witchcraft*, 9, 43; Thomas, *Religion*, 531; Larner, *Enemies*, 8–10.

31. Hale, "Modest Inquiry," 413.

32. Lutherans retained some element of the Catholic rites of exorcism, but the followers of Calvin, Puritans, rejected all such practices. See Thomas, *Religion*, 253–79.

33. Calef, *More Wonders*, 224; Lawson, "A Brief and True Narrative of Witchcraft at Salem Village," in NWC, 163.

34. SWP, III:745.

35. On the lack of privacy see especially Robert Thompson, *Sex in Middlesex: Popular Mores in a Massachusetts County, 1649–1699* (Amherst: University of Massachusetts Press, 1986), chapter 11, "Community Control."

36. SVW, 395 map for location.

37. "Samuel Parris's Statement on the Witchcraft Outbreak," in SVW, 278; Calef, *More Wonders*, 225.

38. Herbert Leventhal, *In the Shadow of the Enlightenment: Occultism and Renaissance Science*

in Eighteenth-Century America (New York: New York University Press, 1976), 82; Upham, *Salem*, I:405.

39. This practice of sympathetic magic postulated a connection between all parts of the physical world, a belief in a cosmos as "an organic unity in which every part bore a sympathetic relationship to the rest." Because the nail parings or urine were thought to retain a connection to the person, manipulating those substances would have an effect on the source. Thomas, *Religion*, 437–38.

40. On the use of technical aids in English witchcraft see especially Thomas, *Religion*, 437, 453; Weisman, *Witchcraft*, 40; Hansen, "Andover," 42. Kittredge, *Witchcraft*, 73–103 gives some examples of image magic in English history up to the nineteenth century. On Caribbean developments see Jerome Handler, "Slave Medicine and Obeah in Barbados," unpublished paper presented at Hamilton College, October 1992, 13.

41. William S. Simmons, "Cultural Bias in the New England Puritans' Perception of Indians," WMQ, 38 (January 1981), 56; William Kellaway, *New England Company, 1648–1776, Missionary Society to the Indians* (London: Longmans, Green, 1961), 82. This distorted image of the Indians is discussed in more detail in chapter 8.

42. See for example the complaint by Elizabeth Goodman of New Haven in 1653 that her neighbor was a witch because she was married to an Indian spirit and of Mary Staples of Fairfield in 1654 when she claimed to be visited by Indians who gave her fetishes that would bring her good luck. David D. Hall, ed., *Witch-Hunting in Seventeenth-Century New England: A Documentary History, 1638–1692* (Boston: Northeastern University Press, 1991), 62, 78.

43. Hale, "Modest Inquiry," 414; SWP, III:752, II:587.

44. SWP, III:612; 756.

45. SWP, II:368–69; 375.

46. SWP, I:92–94.

47. SWP, I:124–25.

48. SWP, III:708.

49. Hale, "Modest Inquiry" in NWC. 414.

50. Robert Galbreath, "Explaining Modern Occultism," in Kerr and Crow, *Occult*, 16; Everard F. im Thurn, *Among the Indians of Guiana* (London: Kegan Paul, Trench, 1883), 349; Alvin O. Thompson, *Colonialism and Underdevelopment in Guyana, 1580–1803* (Bridgetown, Barbados: Carib Research and Publications, 1987), 12. See also Godbeer, *Devil's Dominion*, 35–46; Kittredge, *Witchcraft*, 7–22; and Joseph Klaits, *Servants of Satan: The Age of the Witch Hunts* (Bloomington: Indiana University Press, 1985), 173.

51. John Mbiti, *African Religions and Philosophy* (New York: Doubleday, 1969), 97; Eugene D. Genovese, *Roll, Jordan, Roll: The World the Slaves Made* (New York: Random House Pantheon Books, 1974), 224; Orlando Patterson, *The Sociology of Slavery, An Analysis of the Origins, Development and Structure of Negro Slave Society in Jamaica* (London: Macgibbon & Kee, 1967), 183.

52. Hall, *Worlds*, 71.

53. On this idea see Hall, *Worlds*, 71–114, and Weisman, *Witchcraft*, 125–31.

54. Kenneth Silverman, *The Life and Times of Cotton Mather* (New York: Harper and Row, 1984), chapter 4, "Letters of Thanks from Hell," 83–137; John Putnam Demos, *Entertaining Satan: Witchcraft and the Culture of Early New England* (New York: Oxford University Press, 1982), 97–220.

55. Åke Hultkrantz, *Religions of the American Indians*, trans. Monica Setterwall (Berkeley: University of California Press, 1979), 29; Orlando Patterson, *Sociology of Slavery: An Analysis*

of the Origins, Development and Structure of Negro Slave Society in Jamaica (London: Macgibbon & Kee, 1967), 183; John S. Mbiti, *African Religions and Philosophy* (New York: Doubleday, 1969), 97–102.

56. Harry Hoetink, "The Cultural Links," in Margaret E. Crahan and Franklin W. Knight, eds., *Africa and the Caribbean, the Legacies of a Link* (Baltimore: Johns Hopkins University Press, 1979), 28; Lawrence W. Levine, *Black Culture and Black Consciousness: Afro-American Folk Thought from Slavery to Freedom* (New York: Oxford University Press, 1977), 60.

57. Roger Bastide, *African Civilization in the New World*, trans. Peter Green (New York: Harper & Row, 1971), 30. See also Genovese, *Roll, Jordan*, 181; and Levine, *Black Culture*, 60.

58. On the hysterical fit see Krohn, *Hysteria*, 163–66; 169–72; Veith, *Hysteria*, 72, 151; Hansen, *Witchcraft*, 1–2, 15–19.

59. Calef, *More Wonders*, 180–283.

60. Hale, "Modest Inquiry," 413.

61. Calef, *More Wonders*, 224; Lawson, "True Narrative," 163.

62. Cotton Mather, "Memorable Provinces," 106.

63. Parris' Record of Deaths," NEHGR, 36 (April 1882), 189.

64. Quoted in Samuel Drake, *Witchcraft Delusion in New England*, 3 vols. (Roxbury, Mass.: W. E. Woodward, 1866), I:xi.

65. Godbeer, *Devil's Dominion*, 18. See also Thomas, *Religion*, 255; Kittredge, *Witchcraft*, 4; and William Simmons, "Conversion from Indian to Puritan," NEQ, 52 (June 1979), 200.

66. SVW, 142; 155–56.

67. Thomas Hutchinson, writing in the 1760s, suggests that Tituba was accused first because of this witchcake experiment and the accusations of the two Sarahs followed. His notes are transcribed in "Witchcraft Delusion of 1692," *New England Historical and Genealogical Register and Antiquarian Journal*, 34 (1870), 394. The sequence of accusations at the end of February is not clarified in the written record, although internal evidence would indicate that Good and Osborne were questioned first and Tituba last. No reference is made to Tituba's accusations during the examinations of the other two. It is clear, however, that all three women were arrested and questioned on the same day. SWP, II:355, III:745.

68. Robert Calef, *More Wonders*, 225.

69. John Putnam Demos, *Entertaining Satan: Witchcraft and the Culture of Early New England* (New York: Oxford University Press, 1982), 275–312; Thomas, *Religion*, 552–54.

70. Thomas, *Religion*, 531.

71. For example see Mary K. Matossian, "Ergot and the Salem Witchcraft Affair," *American Scientist* (1982), 70:355–57; John Demos, "Underlying Themes in the Witchcraft of Seventeenth-Century New England," AHR, 75 (June 1970), 1311–26; David Thomas Konig, *Law and Society in Puritan Massachusetts* (Chapel Hill: University of North Carolina Press, 1979), esp. chapters 6 and 7; Boyer and Nissenbaum, *Salem*, esp. 133–51; Gragg, *Quest*, chapters 6 and 7; Klaits, *Servants*, 119–21; Leventhal, *Shadow*, 122; Godbeer, *Devil's Dominion*, chapter 6.

72. Calef, *More Wonders*, 224.

73. SWP, III:745–57, II:361–62. Calef, writing shortly after these events, mistakenly assumes that the witchcake incident was just a few days previous to the arrival of the ministers on March 11, *More Wonders*, 342. The chronological order of these early arrests and testimonies can be best followed in W. Elliot Woodward's compilation, *Records of Salem Witchcraft Copied from the Original Documents*, 2 vols. in 1 (Roxbury, Mass.: Privately Printed, 1864). A recent attempt to re-create the chronology of those events is Bernard Rosenthal,

Salem Story: Reading the Witch Trials of 1692 (New York: Cambridge University Press, 1993).

74. The terms "Mrs." and "Goodwife" or "Goody" reflect social standing. Mrs. and Mr. were reserved for the gentry; the other terms could signify any married woman. Boyer and Nissenbaum, *Salem*, 5.

75. Upham, *Salem*, I:272–305; Boyer and Nissenbaum, *Salem*, see especially 80–109.

76. Hansen, "Andover," 40.

NOTES TO CHAPTER SIX

1. Carol F. Karlsen, *Devil in the Shape of a Woman: Witchcraft in Colonial New England* (New York: W. W. Norton, 1987), 40–41. For a list of those deaths, see Appendix A in this volume.

2. Keith Thomas, *Religion and the Decline of Magic* (New York: Charles Scribner's Sons, 1971), 443; Christine Larner, *Enemies of God: The Witchhunt in Scotland* (Baltimore: Johns Hopkins University Press, 1981), 20; Herbert Leventhal, *In the Shadow of the Enlightenment: Occultism and Renaissance Science in Eighteenth-Century America* (New York: New York University Press, 1976), 78–79.

3. Richard Weisman, *Witchcraft, Magic and Religion in Seventeenth-Century Massachusetts* (Amherst: University of Massachusetts Press, 1984), 15. As an example of this process, see the "Warrant for Jurors" in SWP, III:869–70.

4. SWP, II:355, 609; III:745–46.

5. Robert Calef, *More Wonders of the Invisible World . . . in Five Parts* (1700 repr., Boston, 1828), 225. We have only Calef's word that Parris beat Tituba to extract a confession. His account is not always reliable because Calef wrote to discredit Increase and Cotton Mather (father and son) for encouraging the populace to believe in witchcraft. Thus Calef could have exaggerated Tituba's penitence and Parris's violence out of a distaste for the role of the Mathers and the superstitious beliefs that they represented. Burr, "Introduction," NWC, 293–94. But John Hale confirms that Parris and the visiting ministers did question Tituba before the hearing was held. "A Modest Inquiry Into the Nature of Witchcraft (1702)," NWC, 414. Therefore some pressure was put on Tituba to confess; moreover, the use of violence against accused witches was not unusual in 1692. See below chapter 7 for other incidents of abusive treatment during the hearings.

6. SVW, 278–79.

7. SWP, III:752.

8. Hale, "Modest Inquiry," 414.

9. On these distinctions see Max Gluckman, *Custom and Conflict in Africa* (1956 repr., Oxford: Basil Blackwell, 1970), 87–89; John S. Mbiti, *African Religions and Philosophy* (New York: Doubleday, 1969), 258–61; Larner, *Enemies*, 7–9. On English folklore see in particular George Kittredge, *Witchcraft in Old and New England* (1929 repr., New York: Russell and Russell, 1956), 7–23; Thomas, *Religion*, 438–42; Weisman, *Witchcraft*, 56–57.

10. Richard Godbeer, *Devil's Dominion: Magic and Religion in Early New England* (New York: Cambridge University Press, 1992), 158. He argues that this clash of cultures and the difficulty in resolving the conflict between judicial policy and popular beliefs before 1692 resulted in an increase in popular fears about witchcraft and a concomitant rise in occult practice, 153–78.

11. David D. Hall, "Witchcraft and the Limits of Interpretation," NEQ, 58 (June 1985), 276.

12. Charles W. Upham, *Salem Witchcraft*, 2 vols. (1867 repr , Williamstown, Mass.; Corner House Publishers, 1971), II:12.

13. John Putnam Demos, *Entertaining Satan: Witchcraft and the Culture of Early New England* (New York: Oxford University Press, 1982), in a "Collective Portrait" describes and summarizes the characteristics of accused witches in New England, 57–94. The image of the witch as a poor, old, abrasive, and sexually threatening woman was a post fifteenth-century development in Europe. Witchhunting became decidedly gender specific during the worst of the Protestant-inspired witchcraze of the sixteenth century, a stereotype inherited by the Puritans of Massachusetts. Allison P. Coudert, "The Myth of the Improved Status of Protestant Women: The Case of the Witchcraze," in Jean R. Brink, Allison P. Coudert, and Maryanne C. Horowitz, eds., *The Politics of Gender in Early Modern Europe* (Kirksville, Mo.: Sixteenth Century Journal Publishers, 1989), 62–65. I am grateful to Ellen Macek for bringing this work to my attention.

14. Paul Boyer and Stephen Nissenbaum, *Salem Possessed: The Social Origins of Witchcraft* (Cambridge: Harvard University Press, 1974), 203–4; Karlsen, *Devil*, 110–12.

15. SWP, II:356–58.

16. SWP, II:358–60.

17. SWP, II:360, 609–10.

18. The various reports of her two testimonies in the hearings are in SWP, II:361–62, III:745–57.

19. W. Elliot Woodward, *Records of Salem Witchcraft copied from the original Documents*, 2 vols. (Roxbury, Mass.: Woodward, 1864), I:49; Upham, *Salem*, II:31.

20. The phrase is taken from Samuel G. Drake, *Witchcraft Delusion in New England*, 3 vols. (Roxbury, Mass.: W. E. Woodward, 1866), III:187.

21. Weisman, *Witchcraft*, 113.

22. John M. Murrin, "Magistrates, Sinners, and a Precarious Liberty: Trial by Jury in Seventeenth-Century New England," in David Hall et al., *Saints and Revolutionaries: Essays on Early American History* (New York: W. W. Norton, 1984), 173.

23. MCAR, I:188–89, 229–33. Mary Webster was eventually murdered by a mob that dragged her out of the jail. Karlsen, *Devil*, 25–26, 30.

24. MCAR, I:159, 189. For a fuller description of this case see Karlsen, *Devil*, 68 and Demos, *Entertaining*, 132–38.

25. MCAR, I:228–29. Karlsen, *Devil*, 51–52, notes that men confessing to witchcraft were rebuked as liars. Confessing women, on the other hand, were convicted and hanged. Those executions, however, all happened before Tituba arrived in Massachusetts.

26. Demos, *Entertaining*, 7–9.

27. David Thomas Konig, *Law and Society in Puritan Massachusetts* (Chapel Hill: University of North Carolina Press, 1979), 144–48. See also Weisman, *Witchcraft*, 86–90.

28. Konig, *Law*, 144–51. On disowning responsibility for misfortune see Eugene D. Genovese, *Roll, Jordan, Roll: The World the Slaves Made* (New York: Random House, 1974), 219; and Weisman, *Witchcraft*, 58.

29. Leventhal, *Enlightenment*, 71.

30. Geoffrey Parrinder, *Witchcraft: European and African* (London: Faber and Faber, 1963), 165; Thomas, *Religion*, 216–17.

31. On repentance see Elizabeth Reis, "Witches, Sinners, and the Underside of Covenant Theology," EIHC, 129 (January 1993), 108–18; Konig, *Law*, 173–80.

32. SWP, III:747.

33. SWP, III:748.

34. SWP, III:750.

35. T. Walduck, "Letters from Barbados, 1710," JBMHS, 15 (February 1948), 88. On the meaning of dreams see James Axtell, *European and the Indian: Essays in the Ethnohistory of Colonial North America* (New York: Oxford University Press, 1981), 73–75; Julian Pitt-Rivers, "Spiritual Power in Central America," 190; Irving Rouse, "The Arawak," in Julian H. Steward, *Handbook of South American Indians*, 7 vols. (New York: Cooper Square Publishers, 1963), IV:535; Everard Ferdinand im Thurn, *Among the Indians of Guiana* (1883 repr., New York: Dover Publications, 1967), 344.

36. For other examples of European misinterpretation of Indian dream revelations see Richard White, *The Middle Ground: Indians, Empires, and Republics in the Great Lakes Region, 1650–1815* (New York: Cambridge University Press, 1991), 328–30.

37. See the early examination of Sarah Good, SWP, II:356–57.

38. SWP, III:752.

39. The silk clothing denoted a woman of substance, but the serge cloth of her coat could have been of any class. *Oxford English Dictionary*, s. v. "serge."

40. Quoted in James Axtell, *School Upon a Hill: Education and Society in Colonial New England* (1974 repr., New York: W. W. Norton, 1976), 159–60.

41. On the social construct of clothing styles see Patricia Trautman, "Dress in Seventeenth-Century Cambridge, Massachusetts: An Inventory-Based Reconstruction," in Peter Benes, ed., *Early American Probate Inventories* (Boston: Boston University Scholarly Publications, 1989), 51–73; John Demos, *Little Commonwealth: Family Life in Plymouth Colony* (New York: Oxford University Press, 1970), chapter 3, "Clothing," 52–58.

42. Samuel Parris, "Christ Knows How Many Devils There Are," A sermon delivered March 27, 1692, in SVW, 129–31. Richard P. Gildrie, *The Profane, the Civil, and the Godly: The Reformation of Manners in Orthodox New England, 1679–1749* (University Park: Pennsylvania State University Press, 1994), 170 suggests that Tituba had "assimilated" the notions associated with a clerical crusade for reformation of religious norms and that she was merely reflecting Parris's ideas as expressed in his sermons. See also Larry Gragg, *Quest for Security: The Life of Samuel Parris, 1653–1720* (New York: Greenwood Press, 1990), 123–26; Weisman, *Witchcraft*, 144. Nonetheless, Tituba's hints about elite involvement with the Devil were made prior to Parris's sermon and could not have been ignored when he was preparing to make those accusations. They may well have been his inspiration.

43. SWP, III:749.

44. See especially Deodat Lawson, "A Brief and True Narrative . . ." in NWC, 156, 159–61; Calef, *More Wonders*, 246, 254, 284.

45. On the significance of speech see Jane Kamensky, " 'A Mouthful of Wrong': John Porter, Jr., and His Father(s)," unpublished paper delivered at Millersville University (Pa.) Conference on Puritanism in Old and New England, April 1991, 118.

46. On this anticlericalism see Hall, "Religion and Society," in Jack P. Greene and J. R. Pole, eds., *Colonial British America: Essays in the New History of the Modern Era* (Baltimore: Johns Hopkins University Press, 1984), 331–32; and Gildrie, *Profane*, 119–20.

47. Richard Godbeer, "Chaste and Unchaste Covenants: Witchcraft and Sex in Early Modern Culture," in Peter Benes, ed., *Wonders of the Invisible World, 1600–1900* (forthcoming, Boston: Boston University Press), 62–67. For similar views see Chadwick Hansen, *Witchcraft at Salem* (New York: George Braziller, 1969), 55–56; and George Chever, "Prosecution of Philip English and His Wife for Witchcraft," *Historical Collections of the Essex Institute*, 2 (1860), 21–27.

48. SWP, III:750.

49. SWP, III:751.

50. The Corwin and Cheevers transcripts differ in the details they report of these incidents, but they are not contradictory. Compare SWP, III:749 and 751.

51. All the summaries of Tituba's testimony include a reference to this wolf, even when other details are omitted. SWP, II:361, 362; III:749, 752.

52. SWP, III:753.

53. SWP, III:757.

54. Weisman, *Witchcraft*, 63–64.

55. On the role of the trance in African religions see Geoffrey Parrinder, *Witchcraft: European and African* (New York: Barnes & Noble, 1963), 128–30; and Roger Bastide, *African Civilisations in the New World*, trans. Peter Green (New York: Harper & Row, 1971), 120–22. On the Indians see Åke Hultkrantz, *Religions of the American Indians* (Berkeley: University of California Press, 1979, trans. of 1967 ed.), 87–90.

56. Cotton Mather, "Memorable Provinces Relating to Witchcraft and Possessions (1689)," in NWC, 115.

57. SWP, III:757.

58. SWP, III:753.

59. SWP, III:754.

60. Godbeer, *Devil's*, especially 162–74.

61. Gildrie, *Profane*, 160–70.

62. It is usually assumed that this Devil's pact was a parody of the church covenant, but it could also connote hopes on the part of a bondsperson. For examples of this attitude see below and Boyer and Nissenbaum, *Salem*, 210.

63. SWP, III:743–44.

64. Abbot Emerson Smith, *Colonists in Bondage: White Servitude and Convict Labor in America, 1607–1776* (1947 repr., New York: W. W. Norton, 1971), 226–52; Richard B. Morris, *Government and Labor in Early America* (1946 repr., New York: Harper & Row, 1965), 390–97.

65. Norman Cohn, "Myths of Satan," in Mary Douglas, ed., *Witchcraft Confessions & Accusations* (London: Tavistock Publications, 1970), 11; Thomas, *Religion*, 443–45; Gildrie, *Profane*, 169.

66. SWP, I:65–66.

67. SWP, I:503. See also Karlsen, *Devil*, 219.

68. Boyer and Nissenbaum, *Salem*, 210; Karlsen, *Devil*, 228.

69. SWP, II:405–7.

70. SWP, III:754.

71. Larner, *Enemies*, 10; Parrinder, *Witchcraft*, 128; Leventhal, *Enlightenment*, 122.

72. On the South American Indian concept of evil see Marc Simmons, *Witchcraft in the Southwest: Spanish and Indian Supernaturalism on the Rio Grande* (Lincoln, Neb.: University of Nebraska Press, 1974), 14; William Curtis Farabee, *The Central Caribs* (Philadelphia: University of Pennsylvania Museum, 1924), 75; Hultkrantz, *Religions*, 32–33.

73. Alvin O. Thompson, *Colonialism and Underdevelopment in Guyana, 1580–1803* (Bridgetown, Barbados: Carib Research & Publications, 1987), 12; im Thurn, *Among the Indians*, 328–33; Andrew Landers, "American Indian or West Indian: The Case of the Coastal Amerindians of Guyana," CS, 16 (July 1976) 121–22.

74. SWP, III:746.

75. Jerome Handler and Frederick W. Lange, *Plantation Slavery in Barbados: An Archeological and Historical Investigation* (Cambridge: Harvard University Press, 1978) 213; Mbiti, *African Religions*, 102; Lawrence W. Levine, *Black Culture and Black Consciousness: Afro-*

American Folk Thought from Slavery to Freedom (New York: Oxford University Press, 1977), 60; Joseph J. Williams, *Voodoo and Obeahs, Phases of West Indian Witchcraft* (New York: Dial Press, 1932), 53.

76. im Thurn, *Among the Indians*, 349; Mather, "Memorable Provinces," 99.

77. im Thurn, *Among the Indians*, 332. See also Lawrence E. Sullivan, *Icanchu's Drum; An Orientation to Meaning in South American Religions* (New York: Macmillan, 1988), 445–47.

78. Kamensky, "Mouthful," 16.

79. Parrinder, *Witchcraft*, 132–36; Norman Cohn, *Europe's Inner Demons: An Enquiry Inspired by the Great Witch-Hunt* (New York: Basic Books, 1975), 222; Richard Slotkin, *Regeneration Through Violence: The Mythology of the American Frontier, 1600–1860* (Middletown: Conn.: Wesleyan University Press, 1973), 124.

80. Such a practice is noted among maroon societies of runaway African slaves in Guiana in the eighteenth century and may well have been found earlier in Barbados. Richard Price, *Maroon Societies: Rebel Slave Communities in the Americas* (Baltimore: Johns Hopkins University Press, 1979), 301–2.

81. Axtell, *European*, 73; Parrinder, *Witchcraft*, 38, 128–40; Cohn, *Europe's Inner Demons*, 106–223 and 206–20; Williams, *Voodoo*, 129; Wallace Notestein, *History of Witchcraft in England From 1558 to 1718* (New York: Russell & Russell, 1911), 237; Larner, *Enemies*, 10.

82. Parrinder, *Witchcraft*, 39.

83. SWP, III:751; Axtell, *European*, 73.

84. Hultkrantz, *Religions*, 131; Sullivan, *Icanchu's Drum*, 241–43; im Thurn, *Among the Indians*, 329.

85. im Thurn, *Among the Indians*, 33; Thompson, *Guyana*, 12.

86. SWP, II:423; SVW, 99. Ann Foster testifying later confirmed Hobbs's story, SWP, II:343. See also SVW, 103–5; SWP, I:164, 172; 409–11.

87. SWP, III:752. There is some evidence that Puritans were predisposed to blame these disturbances on an external cause, to see evil not as a personal failing but as an alien, intrusive force. On this point see especially Godbeer, *Devil's*, 181–203. The fact that Tituba's Boston meeting was transmuted by her listeners into a Salem event, however, testifies to the tenacity of the belief that evil came from within. This idea is explored further below in chapter 7.

88. SWP, III:752; Landers, "American Indian," 131; Williams, *Voodoo*, 130.

89. Orlando Patterson, *The Sociology of Slavery: An Analysis of the Origins, Development and Structure of Negro Slave Society in Jamaica* (London: Macgibbon & Kee, 1967), 204.

90. Salem was not unusual in this kind of cultural integration. Other examples of the process of reinterpretation and incorporation of alien culture traits were found by Julian Pitt-Rivers among the Indians and Spaniards in Central America, "Spiritual Power in Central America," in Douglas, *Witchcraft Accusations*, 197–99. For a similar creative interaction between Algonquian Indians and the French in Canada see White, *Middle Ground*, 50–93.

91. SWP, III:752.

92. im Thurn, *Among the Indians*, 119, 183; Walter E. Roth, *An Inquiry into the Animism and Folk-Lore of the Guiana Indians* (Washington, D.C.: Smithsonian Institution, 1915), 274–75.

93. Hale, "Modest Inquiry," 415.

94. Karlsen, *Devil*, 147; Axtell, *European*, 79. See also Gerald Sider, "When Parrots Learn to Talk and Why They Can't: Domination, Deception and Self-Deception in Indian-White Relations," *Comparative Studies in Society and History* (1987), 29:3–23.

95. Hale, "Modest Inquiry," 415; Weisman, *Witchcraft*, 101–3.

96. Hale, "Modest Inquiry," 415.
97. SWP, II:609, 355.
98. Pitt-Rivers, "Spiritual," 198.
99. Upham, *Salem*, II:255; SWP, III:867.

NOTES TO CHAPTER SEVEN

1. Larry Gragg, *Salem Witch Crisis* (New York: Praeger, 1992), 84.
2. Governor William Phips to the Earl of Nottingham (February 21, 1693), in SVW, 120. According to the new charter only the legislature, which had not yet met, could set up a court system. Phips, anxious to resolve the legal issues, used his authority to create an ad hoc court to hear cases of witchcraft only. This was the court of Oyer and Terminer. The words mean to hear and to determine. On the limited powers of this court see David Thomas Konig, *Law and Society in Puritan Massachusetts* (Chapel Hill: University of North Carolina Press, 1979), 170–73.
3. The legal ramifications are explored by Konig, *Law*, 158–85; and Richard Weisman, *Witchcraft, Magic and Religion in Seventeenth Century Massachusetts* (Amherst: University of Massachusetts Press, 1984), 117–31.
4. I have borrowed this phrase from T. H. Breen, "Creative Adaptations: Peoples and Cultures," in Jack P. Greene and J. R. Pole, eds., *Colonial British America: Essays in the New History of the Early Modern Era* (Baltimore: Johns Hopkins University Press, 1984), 195–232. Although Breen emphasizes the influence of African peoples on developing American societies, Indian cultures were part of the same process of adjustment and incorporation that often generated tensions and hostilities. On this adaptive process, see also Marc Simmons, *Witchcraft in the Southwest: Spanish and Indian Supernaturalism on the Rio Grande* (Lincoln: University of Nebraska Press, 1974), 39–54; Roger Bastide, *African Civilisation in the New World*, trans. Peter Green (New York: Harper & Row, 1971), 30; Lawrence W. Levine, *Black Culture and Black Consciousness: Afro-American Folk Thought from Slavery to Freedom* (New York: Oxford University Press, 1977), 60; and Richard White, *The Middle Ground: Indians, Empires, and Republics in the Great Lakes Region, 1650–1815* (New York: Cambridge University Press, 1991), 50–93.
5. David Hall, "Witchcraft and the Limits of Interpretation," NEQ, 58 (June 1985), 276–77; Richard Godbeer, *Devil's Dominion: Magic and Religion in Early New England* (New York: Cambridge University Press, 1992), 18–28; Weisman, *Witchcraft*, 53–72; Herbert Leventhal, *In the Shadow of the Enlightenment: Occultism and Renaissance Science in Eighteenth-Century America* (New York: New York University Press, 1976), 266.
6. Although not published until after his death in 1702, John Hale had finished "A Modest Inquiry Into the Nature of Witchcraft" early in 1698. NWC, 398.
7. White, *Middle Ground*, 52.
8. Paul Boyer and Stephen Nissenbaum, *Salem Possessed: The Social Origins of Witchcraft* (Cambridge: Harvard University Press, 1974), 146.
9. SWP, I:260–61.
10. SWP, I:264.
11. Hale, "Modest Inquiry," 416–17.
12. Deodat Lawson, "A Brief and True Narrative of some Remarkable Passages . . . , April 1692," NWC, 153.

13. Lawson, "Brief and True," 153–54.

14. Lawson, "Brief and True," 154.

15. Lawson, "Brief and True," 155.

16. Boyer and Nissenbaum, *Salem*, 146–47. There is some evidence that the association of the disadvantaged with witchcraft was already undergoing transformation as early as the 1650s in New England with an increasing proportion of accusations against women of property and men. But it was not until Salem that a new definition of the witch irrelevant to social status emerged. Carol F. Karlsen, *Devil in the Shape of a Woman: Witchcraft in Colonial New England* (New York: W. W. Norton, 1987), 27–28, 50.

17. Lawson, "Brief and True," 157–58.

18. Lawson, "Brief and True," 159–60.

19. Boyer and Nissenbaum, *Salem*, 32.

20. SWP, III:867.

21. On the typical witch see Keith Thomas, *Religion and the Decline of Magic* (New York: Charles Scribner's Sons, 1971), especially chapter 17, "Witchcraft in the Social Environment," 535–69; Lyle Koehler, *A Search for Power: The "Weaker" Sex in Seventeenth-Century New England* (Chicago: University of Illinois Press, 1980), 278–85; John Demos, *Entertaining Satan: Witchcraft and the Culture of Early New England* (New York: Oxford University Press, 1982), 72–94; Wallace Notestein, *History of Witchcraft in England from 1558–1718* (New York: Russell & Russell, 1911), 66.

22. Leventhal, *Enlightenment*, 122–24.

23. SWP, II:680.

24. SVW, 129.

25. Boyer and Nissenbaum, *Salem*, 149.

26. SWP, II:665.

27. SWP, II:658–59.

28. SWP, II:670.

29. SWP, II:678.

30. SWP, III:793, 840; Robert Calef, *More Wonders of the Invisible World . . . in Five Parts* (1700 repr., Boston, 1828), 238–39.

31. SWP, III:954.

32. Thomas Hutchinson, "Witchcraft Delusion of 1692," NEHGR, 34 (1870), 397.

33. See especially the accusations during John Willard's questioning, SWP, III:840.

34. SWP, I:239. Some men had been accused before 1692 but they were seldom convicted. It was not until the Salem outbreak that the "secular authorities relinquished to any significant degree their assumption that witches were women." Karlsen, *Devil*, 50.

35. SWP, II:429. Deliverance Hobbs is mistakenly called Deborah in this arrest warrant.

36. SWP, I:49–50.

37. Godbeer, *Devil's Dominion*, 201–4.

38. SWP, I:151.

39. SWP, III:954.

40. SWP, I:313–15.

41. SWP, I:54.

42. SWP, III:811.

43. He was accused of selling "Powder and Shot to Indians and French, and lies with the Indian Squaes, and has Indian papooses." SWP, I:52.

44. Chadwick Hansen, "Andover Witchcraft and the Causes of the Salem Witchcraft Trials," in Howard Kerr and Charles L. Crow, eds., *The Occult in America: New Historical*

Perspectives (Urbana, Ill.: University of Illinois Press, 1983), 40. See also Gragg, *Salem*, 141; Richard P. Gildrie, "Salem Witchcraft Trials as a Crisis of Popular Imagination," EIHC, 128 (October 1992), 284; Boyer and Nissenbaum, *Salem*, 190.

45. Thomas, *Religion*, 535–56; Alan Macfarlane, "Witchcraft in Tudor and Stuart Essex," in Mary Douglas, ed., *Witchcraft Confessions & Accusations* (London: Tavistock Publications, 1970), 87–89; Christine Larner, *Enemies of God: The Witchhunt in Scotland* (Baltimore: Johns Hopkins University Press, 1981), 82–83; Demos, *Entertaining*, 275–312.

46. Godbeer, *Devil's Dominion*, 203.

47. Godbeer, *Devil's Dominion*, 203–4, emphasizes the importance of these external threats for the witchhunt of 1692 but does not recognize Tituba's role in reinforcing and directing those fears.

48. Parris's responsibility in this regard is explored by Larry Gragg, *Quest for Security: The Life of Samuel Parris* (New York: Greenwood Press, 1990), 130–47; and Boyer and Nissenbaum, *Salem*, 153–78.

49. Boyer and Nissenbaum, *Salem*, 215.

50. Christine Leigh Heyrman, *Commerce and Culture: The Maritime Communities of Colonial Massachusetts, 1690–1750* (New York: W. W. Norton, 1984), 107–12.

51. Konig, *Law*, 184; Boyer and Nissenbaum, *Salem*, 195–96.

52. Boyer and Nissenbaum, *Salem*, 201.

53. Norman Cohn, *Europe's Inner Demons: An Enquiry Inspired by the Great Witch-Hunt* (New York: Basic Books, 1975), 7; Richard P. Gildrie, "Salem Witchcraft Trials as a Crisis of Popular Imagination," EIHC, 128 (October 1992), 284.

54. On the similarities between Congregational practice and these supposed Satanic rites see Richard Godbeer's "Chaste and Unchaste Covenants: Witchcraft and Sex in Early Modern Culture," in Peter Benes, ed., *Wonders of the Invisible World, 1600–1900* (Boston: Boston University Press, forthcoming), 62–67. Dr. Godbeer very graciously permitted me to read this essay before it was published.

55. The report on these events is in Lawson, "Brief and True," in NWC, 160–61.

56. Thomas, *Religion*, 455.

57. Godbeer, "Chaste," 67–68.

58. SWP, II:659.

59. SWP, II:405–8.

60. SWP, II:409–10. Abigail Hobbs's initial testimony does not implicate Burroughs directly—only referring to his servant girl Judah White. The first reference to him by name is in a statement by Ann Putnam (SWP, I:164), but Ann was only two years old when Burroughs was in Salem and she could not have remembered him. Abigail Hobbs, on the other hand, had lived near Burroughs in Casco Bay in Maine and probably did know him by sight. Charles W. Upham, *Salem Witchcraft*, 2 vols. (1867 repr., Williamstown, Mass.: Corner House Publishers, 1971), II:130. Abigail was acquainted with Judah White and she did confirm Burroughs's guilt when she was in prison. It is possible that she named him earlier in a part of the record that is lost. She had most likely suggested Burroughs's name to Ann Putnam. SWP, I:154.

61. SWP, I:164.

62. Richard P. Gildrie, *The Profane, the Civil, and the Godly: The Reformation of Manners in Orthodox New England, 1679–1749* (University Park, Pa.: Pennsylvania State University Press, 1994), 177.

63. Upham, *Salem*, I:402.

64. Cotton Mather, "Wonders of the Invisible World (1693)," NWC, 246. See also

George Chever, "Prosecution of Philip English & His Wife for Witchcraft," 2d part, *Historical Collections of the Essex Institute*, 2 (1860), 73–78.

65. Norman Cohn, "Myths of Satan and His Human Servants," in Douglas, *Witchcraft*, 11. On the creation of this legend see especially Cohn, *Inner Demons*, 225–57 and Joseph Klaits, *Servants of Satan: The Age of the Witch Hunts* (Bloomington:Indiana University Press, 1985), 173.

66. Hall, "Witchcraft," 276–77.

67. Thomas, *Religion*, 438–44; Larner, *Enemies*, 152–54.

68. Koehler, *Search*, 270; Klaits, *Servants*, 76–85.

69. Samuel Sewall, *Diary*, 2 vols. (New York: Farrar, Straus & Giroux, 1973), I:9, 4, 64.

70. Godbeer, "Chaste," 69–71; Louis J. Kern, "Eros, the Devil, and the Cunning Woman: Sexuality and the Supernatural in European Antecedents and in the Seventeenth-Century Salem Witchcraft Cases," EIHC, 129 (October 1993), 32.

71. Amanda Porterfield, *Female Piety in Puritan New England: The Emergence of Religious Humanism* (New York: Oxford University Press, 1992), 14–18.

72. Porterfield, *Female*, 35.

73. Cotton Mather, "Remarkable Providences Relating to Witchcraft and Possessions (1689)," in NWC, 20. See also Koehler, *Search*, 200–201.

74. "Memorable Provinces," NWC, 136. Kenneth Silverman, *The Life and Times of Cotton Mather* (New York; Harper & Row, 1984), describes him as "a highly sexual man." 188.

75. Godbeer, "Chaste," 54.

76. Kern, "Eros," 26–32. This absence is also explained by Elizabeth Reis, "The Devil, the Body, and the Feminine Soul in Puritan New England," 18, paper delivered at conference "Puritanism in Old and New England," Millersville, Pa., April 1991. See also John Demos, "Underlying Themes in the Witchcraft of Seventeenth Century New England," *American Historical Review*, 75 (June 1970), 1321.

77. These incidents are reported by Godbeer, "Chaste," 56.

78. Julian Pitt-Rivers, "Spiritual Power in Central America," in Douglas, *Witchcraft*, 198.

79. This statement and the following analysis regarding the nature of the attack on the Congregational church are based on the research and conclusions of Godbeer, "Chaste," 54–60.

80. Porterfield, *Female*, 151.

81. SWP, I:135; II:423; John Hale, "Modest Inquiry," 418–19.

82. SWP, II:416.

83. SWP, III:793–801.

84. SWP II:421–22.

85. SWP II:423.

86. SWP, I:179–81. On the African sources of her puppet images see William D. Pierson, *Black Yankees: The Development of an Afro-American Subculture in Eighteenth-Century New England* (Amherst: University of Massachusetts Press, 1988), 81.

87. SWP, II:341–43.

88. SWP, II:526; I:203; 197–99.

89. SWP, I:201–2.

90. See the tables of arrests and confessions in the Appendix.

91. Gildrie, *The Profane*, 177.

92. SWP, III:772–73.

93. Calef, "More Wonders," 260. On the Andover events see Hansen, "Andover."

94. SWP, I:198.

95. SWP, I:143–44.

96. SWP, I:133–37.

97. SWP, I:67.

98. SWP, II:503, 920, 212. See Karlsen, *Devil*, 105, for the relationship of these women.

99. SWP, I:328 (Abigail Faulkner, Sr.), 135, 140 (Mary Bridges), 144 (Hannah Bromage).

100. See the testimony of Elizabeth Johnson, Jr., SWP, II:503–5.

101. SWP, III:924.

102. SWP, I:67.

103. SWP, III:791–92.

104. See especially SWP III:917–20 testimonies of Mary Tyler, Sarah Wardwell, and Sarah Hawkes.

105. Godbeer, "Chaste," 66.

106. Hale, "Modest Inquiry," 416–19.

107. Boyer and Nissenbaum, *Salem*, 209–13; Porterfield, *Female*, 8–9; Jon Butler, *Awash in a Sea of Faith: Christianizing the American People* (Cambridge: Harvard University Press, 1990), 55.

108. Petition of Mary Easty, SWP, II:304.

NOTES TO CHAPTER EIGHT

1. John Hale, "A Modest Inquiry Into the Nature of Witchcraft," in NWC, 415.

2. Quoted in James Axtell, *European and the Indian, Essays in the Ethnohistory of Colonial North America* (New York: Oxford University Press, 1981), 160.

3. Neal Salisbury, "Red Puritans: The 'Praying Indians' of Massachusetts Bay and John Eliot," WMQ, 31 (January 1974), 33.

4. Elliot Woodward, *Records of Salem Witchcraft copied from the Original Documents*, 2 volumes in one (Roxbury, Mass.: W. Elliot Woodward, 1864), I:30; SWP, II:363.

5. Yasuhide Kawashima, *Puritan Justice and the Indian: White Man's Law in Massachusetts, 1636–1763* (Middletown, Conn.: Wesleyan University Press, 1986), 130–33.

6. SWP II:371.

7. Thomas Brattle, Letter of October 8, 1692, in NWC, 174.

8. On the methods used in Europe and England see Joseph Klaits, *Servants of Satan: The Age of the Witch Hunts* (Bloomington: Indiana University Press, 1985), 132–45; for New England see Richard Godbeer, *The Devil's Dominion: Magic and Religion in Early New England* (New York: Cambridge University Press, 1992), 158; David Thomas Konig, *Law and Society in Puritan Massachusetts* (Chapel Hill: University of North Carolina Press, 1979), 172.

9. Godbeer, *Devil's Dominion*, 206–10; Konig, *Law*, 172.

10. Robert Calef, "More Wonders of the Invisible World," in NWC, 376.

11. SWP, II:490–91.

12. SWP, I:211–12.

13. John M. Murrin, "Magistrates, Sinners, and a Precarious Liberty: Trial by Jury in Seventeenth-Century New England," in David Hall et al., eds., *Saints and Revolutionaries:*

Essays on Early American History (New York: W. W. Norton, 1984), 173–96; David Hall, *Worlds of Wonder, Days of Judgment: Popular Religious Beliefs in Early New York* (New York: Alfred A. Knopf, 1989), 174–75.

14. Calef, "More Wonders," 375.

15. Perry Miller, *New England Mind in the Seventeenth Century* (1939 repr., Cambridge, Harvard University Press, 1954), 378–400. See also Charles Lloyd Cohen, *God's Caress: The Psychology of Puritan Religious Experience* (New York: Oxford University Press, 1986), especially chapters 3 and 4.

16. Samuel Sewall, *Diary, 1674–1729*, 2 vols. (New York: Farrar, Straus and Giroux, 1973), I:19.

17. See for instance R. G. Willis, "Instant Millennium: The Sociology of African Witch-cleansing Cults," and Robert Brain, "Child Witches," in Mary Douglas, ed., *Witchcraft Confessions & Accusations* (London: Tavistock Publications, 1970), 130–33; and 176–77.

18. On the significance of confessions in Puritan theology see Hall, *Worlds*, 175–94; Elizabeth Reis, "Satan's Familiars: Sinners, Witches, and Conflicting Covenants in Early New England," (Ph.D. diss., University of California, Berkeley, 1991), 108–10; Klaits, *Servants*, 151.

19. Richard Weisman, *Witchcraft, Magic, and Religion in Seventeenth-Century Massachusetts* (Amherst: University of Massachusetts Press, 1984), 97.

20. Klaits, *Servants*, 151.

21. SWP, I:647–49.

22. SWP, I:250.

23. On these techniques of survival used by Indians see James H. Merrell, " 'Customes of Our Country': Indians and Colonists in Early America," in Bernard Bailyn and Philip D. Morgan, eds., *Strangers Within the Realm: Cultural Margins of the First British Empire* (Chapel Hill: University of North Carolina Press, 1991), 154. On other strategies used by Indians see Elise M. Brenner, "To Pray or to Be Prey: That Is the Question: Strategies for Cultural Autonomy of Massachusetts Praying Town Indians," *Ethnohistory*, 27 (Spring 1980), 135–52.

24. On the inability of many Indians to speak acceptable idiomatic English and its consequences, see Merrell, " 'Customes'," 127–30.

25. SWP, III:750. The use of uninflected verbs (lacking tense, number, or other variations), especially in irregular verbs such as "to be," is a major characteristic of pidgin languages and was often found in the Creole developing of the West Indies. Ives Goddard, "Some Early Examples of American Indian Pidgin English from New England," *International Journal of American Linguistics*, 43 (January 1977), 39; J. L. Dillard, *Black English: Its History and Usage in the United States* (New York: Random House, 1972), 41–42. It is also a quality of seventeenth-century English usage, a time when standards of verb use were still in flux. Note in the questioning of Mary Black, she was asked: "Tell me be you a witch?" SWP, I:113. On regional and social variations of English usage in England, particularly in East Anglia, see the studies in James and Lesley Milroy, eds., *Real English: The Grammar of English Dialects in the British Isles* (New York: Longmans Publishers, 1993), especially 5–12; 221–30.

26. SWP, I:179. Both Dillard, *Black English*, 79 and Frederic G. Cassidy, "Barbadian Creole—Possibility and Probability," *American Speech*, 61 (Fall 1986), 199, assume that Tituba's speech reflects Creole influences. For reasons given in the above note I disagree. On the other hand Candy's English is obviously an early use of pidgin English. On the development of pidgin languages see also James M. Crawford, *Mobilien Trade Language* (Knoxville: University of Tennessee Press, 1978); and Lois M. Feister, "Linguistic Commu-

nication Between the Dutch and Indians in New Netherlands, 1609–1664," *Ethnohistory*, 20 (Winter 1973), 25–38.

27. William D. Pierson, *Black Yankees: The Development of an Afro-American Subculture in Eighteenth-Century New England* (Amherst: University of Massachusetts Press, 1988), 81.

28. SWP, I:179–80. This scene is graphically described by Chadwick Hansen, *Witchcraft at Salem* (New York: George Braziller, 1969), 70–71.

29. Audrey Burroughs, "Barbadian Creole: A Note on Its Social History and Structure," in Lawrence D. Carrington et al., eds., *Studies in Caribbean Language* (St. Augustine, Trinidad: Society for Caribbean Linguistics, 1983), 38–45, describes the development of that distinctive Creole speech pattern.

30. Charles W. Upham, *Salem Witchcraft*, 2 vols. (1867 repr., Williamstown, Mass.: Corner House Publishers, 1971), II:26.

31. SWP, III:752, 747–49, 753.

32. Merrell, "Indians," 127–30.

33. SWP, III:744–45.

34. Laurel Thatcher Ulrich, *Good Wives: Image and Reality in the Lives of Women in Northern New England, 1650–1750* (New York: Alfred A. Knopf, 1980), 188–89.

35. Jane Kamensky describes the cursing and vituperative language of the witch as "verbal aggression" in "Words, Witches, and Women Trouble: Witchcraft, Disorderly Speech and Gender Boundaries in Puritan New England," EIHC, 128 (October 1992), 291. See also Robert St. George, " 'Heated' Speech and Literacy in Seventeenth-Century New England," in David D. Hall and David Grayson Allen, eds., *Seventeenth-Century New England* (Boston: Colonial Society of Massachusetts, 1984), 278–85.

36. SWP, I:361.

37. SWP, I:85, II:357, 362.

38. Konig, *Law*, 173–75.

39. Weisman, *Witchcraft*, 144.

40. Hale, "A Modest Inquiry," 415.

41. Kamensky, "Words," 294.

42. St. George, " 'Heated Speech,' " 286.

43. SWP, III:747, 753, II:587.

44. Hall, *Worlds*, points out that literacy had less to do with formal schooling and more with learning scripture and the catechism, 34–38. On the Puritan method of catechizing see C. John Sommerville, *The Discovery of Childhood in Puritan England* (Athens: University of Georgia Press, 1992), 136–37.

45. Kamensky, "Words," 303; Richard P. Gildrie, *The Profane, the Civil, and the Godly: The Reformation of Manners in Orthodox New England, 1679–1749* (University Park: Pennsylvania State University Press, 1994), 2–5.

46. Cotton Mather, "Another Brand Pluck'd Out of the Burning," NWC, 308.

47. Axtell, *European*, 45–46.

48. Richard Slotkin, *Regeneration Through Violence: The Mythology of the American Frontier, 1600–1860* (Middletown, Conn.: Wesleyan University Press, 1973), 128–45; 199; William S. Simmons, "Cultural Bias in the New England Puritan Perception of Indians," WMQ, 38 (January 1981), 56–64; James E. Kenses, "Some Unexplored Relationships of Essex County Witchcraft to the Indian Wars of 1675 and 1689," EIHC, 120 (July 1984), 186–91; Upham, *Salem*, I:8. On the association of Indian practices with Devil worship see in particular the testimony of Mary Toothaker in SWP, III:767–69.

49. Richard Godbeer "Chaste and Unchaste Covenants: Witchcraft and Sex in Early Modern Culture," in Peter Benes, ed., *Wonders of the Invisible World, 1600–1900* (forthcoming, Boston: Boston University Press), 54–60.

50. Simmons, "Cultural," 64–68.

51. "Memorable Providences, Relating to Witchcraft and Possessions," in NWC, 99.

52. Alden T. Vaughan and Edward W. Clark, eds., *Puritans Among the Indians: Accounts of Captivity and Redemption, 1675–1724* (Cambridge: Harvard University Press, 1981), 114–15. See also John Demos, *The Unredeemed Captive: A Family Story from Early America* (New York: Alfred A. Knopf, 1994), 153–54, for similar credulous reactions to Indian religious practices in Canada; and John Brickell, *The Natural History of North Carolina* (Dublin, 1737), 374, for contemporary comments about the effectiveness of Indian conjuring in the Carolinas.

53. SVW, 278.

54. Paul Boyer and Stephen Nissenbaum, *Salem Possessed: The Social Origins of Witchcraft* (Cambridge: Harvard University Press, 1974), 215.

55. Richard White, in his analysis of Indian-French contacts in Canada, comes to a similar conclusion and argues that in their accommodation to each other "diverse peoples adjust their differences through what amounts to a process of creative, and often expedient, misunderstandings" into a middle ground of congruences. *The Middle Ground: Indians, Empires, and Republics in the Great Lakes Region, 1650–1815* (New York: Cambridge University Press, 1991), x, 52–53.

NOTES TO THE EPILOGUE

1. William Good's Petition of 1710 in SVW, 16.

2. The petitions are in W. Elliot Woodward, *Records of Salem Witchcraft Copied from the Original Documents*, 2 vols. (repr. 1969, Roxbury, Mass., 1864), 218–47. See also SWP, III:875ff.

3. "More Wonders of the Invisible World," NWC, 343.

4. SWP, II:490–92.

5. Calef, "More Wonders," and Thomas Brattle's Letter of October 8, 1692, NWC, 374–75, 189, 377n.

6. SVW, 117–18.

7. Calef, "More Wonders," 369–73.

8. Charles W. Upham, *Salem Witchcraft*, 2 vols. (repr. 1867, Williamstown, Mass., Corner House Publishers, 1971), II:344–45.

9. Brattle's Letter, NWC, 189.

10. Upham, *Salem*, II:349; Phips, Letter, SVW, 121.

11. Upham, *Salem*, II:406; SWP, I:284; NWC, 366.

12. Calef, "More Wonders," 343.

13. Brattle's Letter, NWC, 189.

14. SWP, III: 903; Phips, Letter, SVW, 122.

15. Calef, "More Wonders," 384; SWP, III:903–44.

16. Upham, *Salem*, II:353–54.

17. NWC, 343n. See also Parris's report on Rebecca Nurse's examination and the statement: "When this witchcraft came upon the stage there was no suspicion of Tituba." SWP, II:587.

18. "Petition to the Governor (July 7, 1693)," SVW, 258–59.

19. SWP, III:881. On prison conditions see Edgar J. McManus, *Law and Liberty in Early New England: Criminal Justice and Due Process, 1620–1692* (Amherst: University of Massachusetts Press, 1993) 178–79.

20. See the reaction of Mercy Short to Sarah Good described by Cotton Mather, "Brand Pluck'd Out of the Burning," NWC, 259.

21. At the usual cost of 2s 6d a week in the Boston jail, the expense of thirteen months would have amounted to about seven pounds. I have computed this sum from the information available about the actual costs of others in the Boston jail. SWP, III:953–54.

22. Calef, "More Wonders," 343.

23. Amanda Porterfield, *Female Piety in Puritan New England: The Emergence of Religious Humanism* (New York: Oxford University Press, 1992), 11.

24. SWP, III:657, I:209; Calef, "More Wonders," NWC, 348.

25. Will of Samuel Parris, SVW, 197.

26. Samuel Drake, *Witchcraft Delusion in New England: Its rise, progress, and termination . . .* , 3 vols. (Roxbury, Mass.: W. E. Woodward, 1866), II:211.

27. Marilynn K. Roach, " 'That Child, Betty Parris': Elizabeth (Parris) Barron and the People in Her Life," EIHC, 124 (January 1988), 21–24, mistakenly concludes that she was really an African-American bought by Elizabeth (Parris) Barron and lived into her eighties. But that Violet in the Barron household would have been only eleven years old in 1720 and unlikely to be identified as an "Indian Woman" or worth thirty pounds as a child. These are two different women called Violet, one African-American and the other Indian.

28. Woodward, *Records*, II:221.

29. SWP, III:977–1012.

30. Larry Gragg, *Quest for Security: The Life of Samuel Parris, 1653–1720* (New York: Greenwood Press, 1990), 177–80, 36n40.

31. Larry Gragg, *Salem Witch Crisis* (New York: Praeger, 1992), 184.

32. Upham, *Salem*, II:493–95, 506.

33. Paul Boyer and Stephen Nissenbaum, *Salem Possessed: The Social Origins of Witchcraft* (Cambridge: Harvard University Press, 1974), 218–20.

34. Quoted in Chadwick Hansen, *Witchcraft at Salem* (New York: New American Library, 1969), 208–9.

35. Calef, "More Wonders," 387–88.

36. Hansen, *Salem*, 209.

37. There would be one more person executed for witchcraft in the British American colonies and that would be in Bermuda when Sarah Bassett, a Negro slave, was burned at the stake in 1730 for murdering her master with magical charms. Hansen, *Salem*, 220.

38. SWP, III:970.

39. Hansen, *Salem*, 221.

40. David Hall, *Worlds of Wonder, Days of Judgment: Popular Religious Beliefs in Early New England* (New York: Alfred A. Knopf, 1989), 196; Carol F. Karlsen, *Devil in the Shape of a Woman; Witchcraft in Colonial New England* (New York: W. W. Norton, 1987), 42.

41. Jon Butler, "Magic, Astrology and the Early American Religious Heritage, 1600–1760," *American Historical Review*, 84 (April 1979), 341.

42. For a description of the continuing interest in the occult see Herbert Leventhal, *In the Shadow of the Enlightenment: Occultism and Renaissance Science in Eighteenth-Century America* (New York: New York University Press, 1976), chapter 3, "Witchcraft," 84–107.

43. Richard Weisman, *Witchcraft, Magic and Religion in Seventeenth-Century Massachusetts* (Amherst: University of Massachusetts Press, 1984), 185.

44. Hall, *Worlds*, 196.

45. Richard Godbeer, "Chaste and Unchaste Covenants: Witchcraft and Sex in Early Modern Culture," in Peter Benes, ed., *Wonders of the Invisible World, 1600–1900* (forthcoming, Boston: Boston University Press, 1995), 68–70.

46. Weisman, *Witchcraft*, 183.

47. Perry Miller, *New England Mind: From Colony to Province* (Cambridge: Harvard University Press, 1953), 207. On the changes in Puritan thinking see also Hall, *Worlds*, 174–96; Jon Butler, *Awash in a Sea of Faith: Christianizing the American People* (Cambridge: Harvard University Press, 1990), 55–63; Richard P. Gildrie, *The Profane, the Civil, and the Godly: The Reformation of Manners in Orthodox New England, 1679–1749* (University Park: Pennsylvania State University Press, 1994), 178–81.

48. For a parallel analysis of the popular roots of high culture in sixteenth-century Europe see Carlo Ginzburg, *The Cheese and the Worms: The Cosmos of a Sixteenth-Century Miller* (Baltimore: Johns Hopkins University Press, 1980).

NOTES TO APPENDIX A

1. Compiled from SWP; and Appendices C and D in Richard Weisman, *Witchcraft, Magic and Religion in Seventeenth-Century Massachusetts* (Amherst: University of Massachusetts press, 1984).

2. The date of the initial confession. Many of the confessors repeated and elaborated their stories afterwards.

3. The date is either that of the arrest warrant, or when that date is not known, the date of the public examination, or the best estimate of the date of arrest based on what is known about the case.

Index

Abbot, Nehemiah, 142, 183; accused, 141
Abbey, Samuel (accuser), 98
African slaves in Boston, 67, 68. *See also*
 Slaves in Barbados; Slavery in New En-
 gland; Slave trade
Alden, John, 184; accused, 139, 142, 143
Amacura River, 3, 6, 10, 11, 13, 14, 33
American Indian slaves: in Barbados, 10–
 12, 26, 27, 29, 30–34, 40; contact with
 African cultures, 41, 43, 44, 49; in New
 England, 68, 70; outlawed in Barbados,
 9, 11, 32; resistance to slavery, 7–8,
 204 n. 17. *See also* Slaves in Barbados;
 Slave trade
American Indians: concept of evil, 126–29;
 metaphoric language, 129–30; in New
 England, xxiii–iv, 68–73; sexuality, 150;
 swimming ability, 5, 6, 15; uprisings of,
 31, 34, 70, 78, 88, 142. *See also* Arawak
 Indians; Carib Indians; King Philips's
 War
American Indians, perception of: in Barba-
 dos, 31, 34, 41, 42; in New England,
 xxiii, 72, 99, 100, 112, 120, 156–57,
 167–69
Andover, Massachusetts, 142, 143; confessed witches in, 153–54; witches' meet-
 ing in, 154
Andros, Sir Edmund, 77, 78
Arawak Indians, xxii, 5, 10–12, 14, 15,

35; in Barbados, 6–8, 12, 30; as domestic servants, 8, 58; significance of dreams
 for, 19, 20, 118, 127; religious beliefs of,
 17–19, 129; women, 15, 17, 62. *See also*
 Kenaima; American Indians

Barbados, 28, 35–37; hurricane of 1675,
 31, 34; population, 35–37, 212 n. 27;
 sugar economy, 37, 38, 42. *See also*
 Slaves in Barbados; American Indians;
 Cultural exchange
Barker, Mary, 153, 185
Barker, William, 124, 153, 154, 185
Barron, Betty. *See* Parris, Elizabeth (Betty)
Best, John (accuser), 98
Birds, 18, 19, 119, 129, 137, 205 n. 36
Bishop, Bridget, 183, 186; accused, 98,
 149; tried, 132; executed, 152, 165
Black, Mary, 163, 183
Blood rituals, xx, 19, 126
Boston, 65, 66; Africans in, 67, 68; Indi-
 ans in, 68; in Tituba's testimony, 121,
 127, 128, 132, 144, 145, 147, 151;
 witches of, 142
Bradbury, Mary, 184; accused, 98, 153
Bradstreet, Simon, 77
Brattle, Thomas, 158, 173
Bridges, Mary, 151, 153, 154, 185
Bridges, Sarah, 153, 185
Bridgetown, Barbados, 36, 37